Jeff Stelling is a lifelong supporter of his hometown side, Hartlepool United. He was a presenter on LBC's *Sportswatch* programme in the early 1980s before moving to BBC Radio 2's *Sport on 2*. He spent time as a sports newsreader then moved to Sky Sports in 1992 to present coverage of horse racing, snooker and darts. Three years later, Jeff became presenter of what is now called *Gillette Soccer Saturday*, and the rest is broadcasting history. From 2009 until 2011 Jeff presented Channel 4's *Countdown*, and in 2010 he was voted Sports Broadcast Journalist of the Year for the fifth year running. Jeff's first book, *Jelleyman's Thrown a Wobbly*, was a *Sunday Times* bestseller in 2009. In 2011, he started hosting Sky Sports' coverage of the Champions League.

Co-author Matt Allen is an award-winning football and music journalist whose work appears in Q and *FourFourTwo*. His books credits include *Jelleyman's Thrown a Wobbly*, *Jimmy Greaves: The Biography*, Paul Merson's *How Not to Be a Professional Footballer* and *The Crazy Gang: The Inside Story of Vinnie, Harry, Fash and Wimbledon FC*.

JEFFANORY

Stories from Beyond
Soccer Saturday

Jeff Stelling

with Matt Allen

headline

First published in 2012 by
HEADLINE PUBLISHING GROUP

First published in paperback in 2013 by
HEADLINE PUBLISHING GROUP

2

Cataloguing in Publication Data is available from the British Library

Paperback ISBN 978 0 7553 6347 6

Typeset in Minion Pro by Avon DataSet Ltd,
Bidford-on-Avon, Warwickshire

Printed and bound in Great Britain by Clays Ltd, St Ives plc

HEADLINE PUBLISHING GROUP
An Hachette UK Company
338 Euston Road
London NW1 3BH

www.headline.co.uk
www.hachette.co.uk

To the fans, players, managers, chairmen and referees –
good, bad and indifferent – who made this book possible.
But especially the bad.

ACKNOWLEDGEMENTS

Thanks to:

Mrs Jeff, for her patience and for permitting the Stelling Towers décor;
Robbie, Matt and all the Winchester Youth FC players, for making Sundays such fun;
Olivia, for putting up with wall-to-wall football;
All the gang at *Gillette Soccer Saturday*, for their suggestions!;
The *Countdown* crew, for largebaps and leotards;
To Jonathan Taylor at Headline, for allowing me a second crack;
And to Matt Allen, for his enthusiasm, hard work and friendship.

CONTENTS

Introduction: 'Let Me Tell You a Story . . .'   1

1. 'Who's the Anchorman in the Black?!'   11

2. Spotting the Cheats   23

3. Harry Redknapp's TV Burp   37

4. Clarke Carlisle's a Football Genius!   49

5. Farewell *Countdown*, Hello Alesha Dixon   61

6. We Need to Talk About Paul   69

7. Off the Wall: The Weird World of the Football
    Club Chairman   81

8. The Good, the Bad and the Vegan   93

9. Away Days   105

10. 'Here, Jeff, Do You Think it's a Good Idea to
    Streak in Here?'   119

11. 'We're All Going On an Alcoholiday'   133

12. The Unsung Heroes of *Soccer Saturday*   143

13. Big Sam's Health Farm (and How I Nearly Got
    the Sack from Sky)   157

14. Money, Money, Money . . .   169

15. Fan Aid   181

16. Sunday, Bloody Sunday   193

17. A History of Violence and Football Fisticuffs   207

18. Watch Out, Gazza's About   221

19. Win or Lose, We're on the Booze   235

20. Twitter Ye Not
    (#ijustdontunderstandtheinternetsometimes)   247

21. What a Load of *Jeffanory*!   265

    Credits   281

    Index   291

'LET ME TELL YOU A STORY ...'

A long time ago, while relaxing in the drawing room of Stelling Towers, I was struck with the idea for this book. Now, before we go any further, dear reader, I know what you're thinking. You're thinking, 'I bet that Jeff lives in a right fancy pad with tellies in every room, each one playing a different non-league match from around the country and everything.' And you would be right. My home is a veritable football Pentagon. A safe house for the Beautiful Game's waifs and strays, not to mention a statistical superhighway for anchormen the length and breadth of the country. It's also a nice little semi-detached property on a leafy country lane near the M3, which could make for an interesting addition to ITV's DIY show *60 Minute Makeover* if ever Mrs Jeff and I tire of the Hartlepool United wallpaper. Which we won't, despite what she might say to her friends.

Anyhow, deep in the bowels of my expansive, hi-tech football research facility (the basement) I run a really rather salubrious working space (the aforementioned drawing room), complete with a comprehensive library of books and newspapers. Among the tomes dating back to football's year zero is my pristine collection of the *Sky Sports Football Yearbook* from 1888 through to 2012, and the autobiography of former Liverpool skipper and *Soccer Saturday* pundit Phil Thompson – a literary work entitled *Stand Up Pinocchio*, which is a reference to his prominent hooter, one of the few genuine monstrosities on 3D telly.

I must confess, it's a really rather cosy 'man cave', what with the framed portrait of *Soccer Saturday*'s charismatic panel hanging from the wall in one corner and a life-sized statue of my TV hero Des Lynam in the other. You won't be surprised to know that at times of stress, I often come here to play a football DVD on my Cineplex telly, just to cheer myself up. A Greatest Goals compilation solely featuring the work of *Soccer Saturday*'s roving reporter Chris 'Kammy' Kamara does wonders after a heavy day at the football coalface, though at 2 minutes 47 seconds in length, the thrills and laughs are all too brief.

On the rare occasions that I'm not preparing for my role as the suave anchorman on *Soccer Saturday* – the six-hour football TV marathon that most of you would have watched during breaks from decorating the dining room at the weekend – I like to come here in a smoking jacket and slippers, to kick back in my big chair with nothing more than a local newspaper to read. It helps to clear the mind. More importantly, it keeps me in touch with some of the weird and wonderful stories that make up the intricate fabric of our Beautiful Game, from the grassroots to the top flight; the kind of tales not picked up by the national press where 'Back me or sack me pleas' and 'Transfer war chests' are king. Instead,

I like to indulge myself in a world where tea ladies double up as club mascots on match days and Sunday football teams become embroiled in mass brawls because somebody has noisily broken wind during a particularly tense penalty shootout.

And so it was while flicking through the *Bradford Telegraph & Argus*, a glass of Gavi di Gavi in hand, that my latest literary muse began to blossom. Somewhere at the back of the paper, among the ads for window cleaners and a local panto starring former QPR motormouth Rodney Marsh (as Widow Twankey, I believe), was the rather odd tale of a goalkeeper called Mike Clark who played for non-league AFC Emley. During a game with Eccleshill United – in which Emley were winning 1–0 after 88 minutes – Clark made a bit of a clanger when he carried the ball over his own goal line. In his defence, he had been under pressure from an opponent in the penalty area, but what followed was sheer farce.

As the ref awarded a goal which brought the two teams level, Clark was convinced that the ball had been handled by one of Eccleshill's players and began to complain – he was so angry he wouldn't hand the ball back. In fact, he protested so hard that the ref had no option but to book him. That act alone was like a red rag to a bull and Clark stormed off to the dressing room in a huff, taking the match ball with him and leaving his team mates and opponents looking at one another in disbelief. There was much toing and froing with the match officials and managers; several attempts were made to coax Clark back on to the pitch. When he finally returned, the keeper refused to hand the ball back, which resulted in a second yellow and a subsequent red.

At that point, Clark lost the plot completely and declined to leave the pitch, which would have been a very unpopular move because I'm sure Emley's players would have felt that closing out a draw in the remaining minutes was within their reach, even with ten men; Eccleshill might have snatched a winner, so they would have been equally unhappy. But the goalkeeper was having none of it. Neither was the referee who abandoned the game, presumably fed up with all the fuss and commotion.

'I have been in football many years but I have never seen anything like that,' said Eccleshill's shocked chairman, Adrian Benson. 'The referee had no option but to abandon the game. If there had been anything untoward in the match, it might have been easier to explain. But the game had been played in a very good spirit. I was stunned. In fact, I'm still in shock, to be honest. It puts Carlos Tevez's little strop in the shade.'

As I sat there chortling to myself, I was struck by two things: the first being, 'Why didn't they just boot him off the pitch and play on without him?' My second thought was, 'It's such a shame that I don't have a place for that story on *Soccer Saturday*. What a waste of a good yarn.'

Of course, some of you might not know what *Soccer Saturday* is. You might have bought this book hoping for an old *Countdown* annual, in which case I'd like to apologise in advance for the distinct lack of puzzle pages and tricky conundrums as seen on Britain's favourite quiz show. However, I think it's best that I give everyone a brief rundown of what my weekend job involves, just so we're all on the same page from the start.

Now, I don't want to shortchange anyone at this point, so if you're feeling a sense of déjà vu having read my locally acclaimed, 'Pie-litzer Prize' winning book, *Jelleyman's Thrown a Wobbly – Saturday Afternoons in Front of the Telly*, then I apologise, but the sensation will have abated by the start of the next chapter. In fact, skip forward a page or two if you like. But be warned: you will miss at least one pun and maybe a laboured gag or three.

For those of you who have stayed with me, *Soccer Saturday* takes a bit of explaining because it is a strange concept. Basically it's a football programme that doesn't show any live football. Instead, on a Saturday afternoon (that explains one half of the title) the show covers all the football topics of the week (the other half of the title) and at 3 p.m. when the matches have kicked off, we relay the action to our viewers via a number of match reporters who have been strategically placed at football grounds around the country, because we're not allowed to show any live football on a Saturday afternoon due to broadcasting regulations. Meanwhile, our four studio panellists, a gang of ex-professional footballers, each watch one of four designated games on a telly positioned on the desk in front of them. Every now and then, they deliver updates and surreal, often garbled match reports to a captivated audience of millions, which momentarily shrinks to hundreds whenever match reporter and former Crystal Palace player John Salako pops up on the screen, which sadly he does at least three or four times a show (only kidding, John).

Of course, to the untrained eye, *Soccer Saturday* must look like a madhouse, and it is. The panellists, for starters, are a motley crew of former hellraisers and troublemakers. Among them is 'Champagne' Charlie Nicholas, an Arsenal legend and former playboy, while professional eater and Southampton maverick Matt 'Le Tiss' Le Tissier has become a studio regular. Alongside him sits Paul 'Merse' Merson, another Arsenal hero and a former cocaine addict, alcoholic, compulsive gambler and one-time Walsall manager (I still haven't decided what experience would have been the most traumatic), while some semblance of calm is provided by Philip Bernard 'Thommo' Thompson, Liverpool's European Cup-winning captain from a dim and distant past and a myopic Kopite. Elsewhere, one of our matchday reporters is the aforementioned Stoke, Leeds, Pompey, Middlesbrough, Luton Town, Brentford and Swindon Town journeyman, Chris 'Kammy' Kamara – a Lionel Richie lookalike who has somehow forged a cultish career for himself by shouting 'Unbelievable, Jeff!' whenever possible, usually while staring at the camera in a rather odd manner. Often his expression seems so pained that Kammy resembles a man with a wasp trapped in his trousers.

Somewhere in the middle of this chaos, I have to remain cool; an ocean of calm, delivering the results and goalscorers with cold, clinical aplomb. Of course, that rarely happens and what you usually get is 90 minutes of shouting, mild panic and the occasional technical glitch where the sound disappears, or Paul Merson eats his crisps too close to the microphone. But who cares? It's great fun. And if you want cardboard cut-out presenters and the cold, hard facts, then I guess you can always watch The Other Lot on The Other Side.

One of the real joys of working on *Soccer Saturday* is that we try to give as much PR oxygen to the likes of Plymouth Argyle and Bradford on the lower rungs of the football ladder as we do the top, top drawer boys (© Harry Redknapp). I'm a huge Hartlepool fan, as you would have guessed if you knew anything about the show, so teams in and around the Football League's bottom, bottom drawer (© Jeff Stelling) are always going to get a pretty loud crack of the whip. There is a hitch to that, though. During the build-up to the games we focus solely on the Premier League. That means when the matches have kicked off and goals are flying in all over the country, it becomes very difficult to discuss the issues surrounding clubs such as Burton Albion or Accrington Stanley in detail. I simply haven't got the time. The videprinter – the rolling, flashing panel at the bottom of your screen, which lists the latest scores, scorers, half-time and full-time results, not to mention all the bookings and red cards – can change at a hell of a pace. If I were to dwell too long while retelling an interesting story about a particular club, then it would take me for ever to catch up with the other scores and updates, at which point I would probably get the sack.

That means that I always have to be on the ball. Whenever a goal or a result comes in, I need to recall all the relevant stats about the scorer, not to mention any information on the fixture in question. If Torquay United have failed to score in five away matches, I need to be able to rattle off that particular fact in a heartbeat; if keeper Paul Robinson is about to face a penalty, I have to know that he's saved three spot kicks already that season. All of the data has come from my own laboured research, and for over a decade I have spent all my working weeks hoovering up the latest happenings like a football Dyson.

To digest all this vital information (stuff that non-football fans would dismiss as 'nonsense', but I can tell you it isn't), I usually take a bag of local and national newspapers to the drawing room of Stelling Towers and read. Then I'll read some more. If the house is too busy, what with the kids running around (mine – I'm not referring to the pundits from *Soccer Saturday* here, though it wouldn't be an inaccurate description), I often retreat to the Winchester motorway services facility – North or South-bound depending on my mood – where I pore over the latest editions of the *Cat Up Tree Echo* and the *Man Falls Off Roof &*

Survives Despite Landing On His Head Observer for snippets of lower-league tittle-tattle. It's quite a therapeutic experience. The Northbound services is blessed with the branch of a well-known coffee chain plus a fast-food restaurant that specialises in deep-fried chicken and gloopy sauces, should my brain need further stimuli.

Sadly a lot of the football knowledge that I've amassed over the years has gone to waste because there's been very little room for it on the show, which has been very frustrating for me. Imagine a comedian, maybe Ronnie Corbett, sitting on his best jokes. He would feel incredibly annoyed at not being able to share them with the public. I suffer from a similar dilemma: for over a decade now, I've been unable to open up my collection of football anecdotes to the general public, and it's for this very reason that I have gathered together the veritable football potpourri that makes up much of *Jeffanory*.

In these very pages I will retell yarns involving murdered club mascots, unsung heroes in the lower leagues and scandals involving semi-professional players. I have gathered together stories that include crackpot managers, drunk referees and boozy health-farm breaks with Sam Allardyce. In the upcoming chapters you will read about the world's fastest sending off, the most violent football match ever and my brief stint as a referee. I have even uncovered lost fables from pub teams and faraway clubs in football backwaters that would sound remote and unfamiliar to the average fan, such as Cape Verde and Scotland.

Along the way, I've had to become a media explorer; a younger, more spritely, football version of Sir David Attenborough. A shortish man with towering tales. After all there's much more to my job than simply maintaining an aura of composure as a witty and sophisticated anchorman. While the other members of the *Soccer Saturday* team have crashed their cars into Ministry of Defence lorries on the M40 (Merse) or embroiled themselves in spats with Southampton chairmen (Le Tiss), I have spent my spare time collating the strangest and most shocking stories in football, ranting and raving into my typewriter as I've gone along. The results of this somewhat crazy, cathartic process have been: a) a lot of strange looks from Mrs Jeff and the family, and b) *Jeffanory*, a football treasure trove of tall tales and bedtime stories to while away the hours between matches on the telly.

So, if you're sitting comfortably, cup of tea and pork pie in hand, let me begin . . .

Jeff

Stelling Towers, February 2012

CHAPTER ONE

'WHO'S THE ANCHORMAN IN THE BLACK?!'

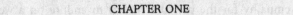

At a time when rivers were made of real ale and wishes could come true, there was a referee called Mike Dean, and one of the Premiership's leading refs he was too. Mike's only problem was that he looked so bloody grumpy whenever he stomped out of the players' tunnel at the weekend, ball tucked under his arm, bulldog-eating-a-nettle scowl spread across his chops. Want to know why? Well, I can tell you, dear *Jeffanory* reader: Mike knew that every time he stepped on to a pitch he would have to experience a life under the football microscope, his every decision judged by an audience of millions, usually on a football programme such as the one that I happen to present every Saturday lunchtime in HD, 3D and 'Wobblevision' (Charlie Nicholas's idea of a joke). And while I'm unable to defend Mike's Scrooge-like demeanour, I can share empathy for the pressure he has to endure on a weekly basis. You see, I've also spent time as a top, top drawer ref when I recently officiated three under-14 games for a *Soccer Saturday* Christmas Special, but unlike Mr Dean I at least managed a smile or three for the cameras.

My stint in charge came after eight of our studio panellists – Kammy and Paul Jewell, Merse and Matt Le Tissier, Thommo and Charlie, Alan McInally and Iain Dowie – were paired up to manage the Hampshire schoolboy teams of St Francis Rangers, Eastleigh Juniors, Baddesley Park and Earls. The idea was that these four sides would play one another in a knockout tournament and the ensuing chaos would be screened on the telly. On paper, it provided some of our panellists with the opportunity to show off their managerial prowess once more. Kammy had previously managed at Bradford City and Stoke, Paul Jewell had been in charge at a number of clubs including Sheffield Wednesday, Wigan, Derby and Ipswich. Meanwhile the other lads had various levels of coaching experience: Merse (Walsall), Thommo (Liverpool) and Iain Dowie (Crystal Palace, Charlton and Hull among others). They were all eager to experience the buzz of a stint in the dugout again, the only difference being that they could make their decisions without the omnipresent fear of boardroom discontent – a feeling familiar to most of them, I'd imagine.

While this was an exciting challenge for the boys, I was initially left feeling like a spare wand at a wizard's wedding. In the weeks before the recording was due to take place I could tell that nobody was going to offer me a coaching role and I had the nagging suspicion that somebody might notice my unemployed status for the day and instead present me with the thankless role of kitman, or worse, something incredibly undignified like a job as an on-the-road matchday reporter. Mercifully, it was suggested that I should become *Soccer Saturday*'s very own take on referee Howard Melton Webb, albeit a shorter, stockier version, and with a wider range of hair-care products.

At first, I was delighted at being given a whistle and a notebook. 'Pierluigi Collina, Paul Durkin, David Elleray . . . eat your heart out,' I laughed. 'I'm running things now. I am your Jefferee!' Then I discovered that Sky's production team only wanted me to be in charge for a mere 45 minutes, mainly for a bit of a giggle, but also because they feared that I wouldn't be able to keep up with the rigours of running around a full-sized football pitch for three games on the bounce. Well, not without suffering a major injury, anyway. I thought, 'Blow this! If I'm going to become an "Onanist in the Black" I'm going to do it for all three games.' And, unbelievably, they relented. I was to be in charge for the entire tournament.

Then the sleepless nights began. My high-profile appointment raised a couple of worrying issues, the main one being a distinct lack of experience. I'd only previously refereed one game before and that was an under-nines match involving my son when the appointed ref for the morning had blown out with a hangover. As the only vaguely responsible adult present, I had to take charge, but in the end I coped with the task pretty well. However, a warning of what was to come on *Soccer Saturday* arrived when I was asked to run the line for the same team a few months afterwards.

As the game got underway, I had to raise my flag for a blatant offside call almost immediately. Inevitably, someone shouted out, 'Unbelievable, Jeff!', which kickstarted what Stephen Fry would describe as a few moments of 'jolly banter', but the giggles turned to discontent very quickly, especially after my flag had gone up for the fourth, fifth, sixth and seventh time. By the end of the game I had become very unpopular. Parents were telling me what they thought of my flag and where they planned to stick it once the final whistle had blown. Overall, it had been a very unpleasant experience, but it wasn't my most intimidating moment as a Sunday league parent. That came when I took one of my boys to play in the badlands of Southampton, where my first duty as the earliest adult on the scene was to remove a burnt-out scooter that had been abandoned on the centre circle of the pitch. I heard it had been completely trashed by the kids from the local housing estate, some of whom were hanging around the pitches looking pretty scary. When the game kicked off, I then noticed that one of the opposition's players had a massive bandage that covered nearly all of his head, only his face was showing. Anyway, as I got chatting to the parents during the match, it turned out his mum was among them.

'What's up with your lad?' I asked innocently.

'Oh, he fell off the roof of a local carwash the other night,' she explained. 'I'm in the process of suing the manufacturers because there wasn't a sign warning people not to climb on it . . . the b******s.'

Needless to say, I was eager to get out of there as quickly as possible.

When it came to filming the Christmas Special I comforted myself with the fact that there wouldn't be too many disgruntled – or crackpot – parents to deal with, and those that were in attendance would be sitting in the stands and therefore a fair distance away from me. This time, I had Alan McInally, Iain Dowie and Kammy there to eyeball me throughout instead. The only way it could have been any worse was if we'd employed renowned 'ref basher' Paolo Di Canio on the show. Crikey.

In terms of experience and support then, the odds were stacked against me, but the small matter of match fitness also gave me plenty to worry about. As you may or may not have guessed, my days as a marauding, box-to-box full back have long gone. In fact, they never actually existed, and the only marauding I do these days happens around tea time and it usually steers me towards the biscuit tin, so it won't come as a surprise to learn that not one of the panellists fancied my chances of lasting the 270 minutes of action, plus 'Fergie Time'. Their opinions of me were so low that some of them even made the odd disparaging remark about my physique as we got changed for the first game.

'I'd be amazed if Jeff could even get into his referee's outfit,' laughed Charlie on air at one point, thinking I was out of earshot. I wasn't, so I later reminded him that he had been listed in 67th place during a recent poll of Arsenal's all-time greats. Worse, he had been tucked away somewhere between John Jensen and Gus Caesar, which took the wind out of his sails. Nevertheless, I could tell the critics had sharpened their knives before a whistle had been blown in anger. It was my first lesson as a high-profile referee: at the game's top level, everyone's a critic.

Those sleepless nights worrying were made somewhat easier by the knowledge that I'd carried out plenty of homework during the run-up to the tournament; my backside was covered. All of three hours were spent reading the autobiographies by renowned refs Graham Poll and Jeff Winter (whose tome was neatly entitled,

Who's the B*****d in the Black?) from cover to cover. Both books helped me to drift into a deep slumber on those restless evenings, though I must stress at this point that I'm using the term 'renowned' for all the wrong reasons. The only inside information gleaned from my intense research was that it was quite all right to book a player three times in a World Cup before sending him off if you're Graham Poll. More intriguing was the revelation that Jeff Winter believed the standing ovation which followed his last ever game at Anfield might have been for his services to the sport rather than any appreciation for Liverpool's performance.

For the purposes of filming and my own personal safety, Sky had the foresight to provide me with an adviser for the tournament, but it was former ref Dermot Gallagher who arrived on the day and not Winter, which was a shame as I quite fancied a standing ovation or two. Dermot's job was to guide me through the matches and offer insights and technical tips as and when they were needed. I was pleased because Dermot was one of the few guys to have actually managed the game with a modicum of common sense and I always got the impression that if ever a player swore at him during his watch, Dermot would sooner swear back than book the offending party. That attitude had always sat rather well with me, but sadly it's a style that's gone out of the game in recent years.

I first met Dermot while I was in Japan and South Korea for the 2002 World Cup. He was the only Premier League referee to have gone out there under his own steam and at first we passed like ships in the night at two or three different stadiums. I later bumped into him at various Irish bars where together we would lock horns over the state of modern refereeing. I always told him that I thought he had refereed the game in the correct manner, but that was because Dermot was a scary-looking chap (from a distance he could have passed for the post-apocalyptic maniac from 1970s horror film *The Hills Have Eyes*). I certainly didn't want to upset him after one too many pints of Guinness; an outbreak of bad language would have been the least of my worries.

Anyway, on the day, Dermot took me to one side for some last-minute advice, and once I'd warmed up with a series of sprints (to the tea station) and lunges (for the sandwiches), he gave me a list of hints and guidelines. His most forceful point concerned my running style, something that had never been my strongest attribute as Mrs Jeff would attest.

'You do realise that as a ref, you have to move diagonally on the pitch?' he said, which made me think at once of David Seaman's occasionally flimsy performances on the ITV show *Dancing on Ice*. 'You don't just follow the ball around, or zigzag across the field, you run from one corner to the other. In that way you'll always have a linesman in view to give you extra assistance.'

At first I thought he was pulling my leg for the purposes of light entertainment, which would have been fair revenge considering some of the stick I'd dished out to his colleagues during my time on *Soccer Saturday*. But once the first game got underway, I realised that he was right. By jogging in a diagonal pattern I could see a linesman at all times, but assessing the game was a lot harder than I'd ever imagined. Whenever I was at least 25 yards away from an incident, or if there was a player between me and the ball, it was very hard to see what was actually going on. And these were kids running around, remember, not fully grown athletes sprinting at top speed. It certainly gave me a greater appreciation of some of the skills and techniques that go into refereeing a professional game of football. Thankfully, Dermot had very little to knock me for during my first two games in charge; despite my inexperience I showed far more football acumen than anyone had expected. In fact, it was agreed that I'd handled the first two games adequately and I went into the cup final full of confidence.

My self-belief meant that an embarrassing cock-up was bound to follow, but what took place in the final could only be described as a comedy of errors. Midway through the second half there was a fifty-fifty clash between two players on the halfway line. It was a perfectly legitimate tackle, but one of the boys had hurt himself and the ball had been kicked out of play so he could receive treatment. When the physio began to run off the pitch moments later, I restarted the game with a throw-in, which was where I lost control of the situation completely.

Blunder Number One happened when the game got underway: the physio was still on the pitch, although he had jogged some way towards the sidelines. Blunder Number Two took place when the injured player – who I'd totally forgotten to send from the field of play following his treatment – received the ball, centred it and set up what turned out to be the winning goal for his team. I'd always thought that ordering a player from the pitch and then making him wait on the touchline before coming back on was a bit of a farce anyway, but regardless of my opinions, it was one of the laws of the game and I'd totally forgotten it. And in the worst possible circumstances, too. Kammy, as you would expect, couldn't believe it. His team had been on the receiving end of my cock-up and I could hear him going absolutely ballistic from the dugout. He called me just about every heightist insult under the sun.

'Unbelievable, Jeff!' he yelled, during one of his more restrained outbursts. 'How can you have not got that right? Are you that short you can't see over the kids' heads?!'

I suppose Kammy had a point, but he could have cut me some slack. I'm taller than the likes of Shaun Wright-Phillips and Jimmy Krankie, and since my blunder, I've heard of far more experienced referees than myself making even stranger decisions, particularly at junior level. In September 2011 it was reported that a ref had sent a couple of players to the sidelines at the beginning of the game because some of the boys were wearing the wrong coloured underpants, which even by Kammy's high standards seemed a bit of a harsh decision. More embarrassingly, the incident hadn't taken place during a Saturday morning school game or local league. Instead it occurred in an FA Youth Cup tie when the academies of Bath City and Newport County came together in the most prestigious of junior tournaments.

To be fair, the official was applying Rule Four of the Football Association handbook to the letter. If you're not familiar with the law (and I don't recommend you study the FA guidelines, it will only end in narcolepsy), it reads as follows: 'If thermal shorts are worn, they are to be of the same, main colour as the shorts.' Now, I'm all for playing by the book – or at least trying to play by the book – however, I doubt Rule Four had ever been applied in anything other than a televised game before, where it would have been enforced before the players ran out in front of the crowd rather than during the game. On this occasion the ref, who has so far remained anonymous, decided to use it on a kids' team dreaming of FA Cup glory.

As the game kicked off, the ref noticed that two Bath players were wearing the wrong coloured underwear and sent them to the sidelines so they could get changed, in full view of 200 supporters, which would have caused some embarrassment for the lads concerned, I'd imagine. Typically, it was at that moment that Newport scored their first goal in a 6–0 drubbing. Chaos ensued and in the argument that followed, one Bath player was sent off along with his manager. The bad mood continued into the second half and a further three Bath players were shown the red card. Not surprisingly, the ref had to lock himself in his dressing room afterwards, such was the outrage.

'I understand the kit rule, but this was an FA Youth Cup match, not a professional FA Cup game,' said Bath chairman Manda Rigby afterwards. 'The players were made to strip off in front of the crowd, which is quite an ordeal for players aged 16 or 17. That sparked the row which led to the players and the manager getting sent off.

'It is such a shame because players may only ever get one or two chances to play in an FA Youth Cup game. I was in total disbelief. The ref was forced to lock himself in his room after the game for 30 minutes. There were a lot of parents in the crowd who were very protective of the players and tempers were running high . . . It is fair to say that he claimed he was just sticking to the letter of the law. But these players are still children – not professionals.'

In hindsight, that should have been my excuse, too, but I felt really defensive after the *Soccer Saturday* Christmas Special. I knew I had made a mistake in the final (and a bad one at that), but I wanted to blag my way out of it. I pretended that I hadn't realised that the trainer was still on the pitch; I told Kammy that I had made the right decision and that he should accept it. I was being stubborn, but it made me realise just how hard life must be for the guys in the top flight, especially when they have endured a tough game.

In recent years, there have been calls from some quarters of the *Soccer Saturday* panel for referees to come forward and face a post-match interview after Premiership matches. The likes of Le Tiss and Merse would like the refs to explain their more controversial decisions to the public. Well, I wouldn't have done it on that day, I can tell you. I also know that there would be absolutely no benefit at all in getting a referee to explain his decisions after a game. Sure, it would make for great copy in the papers the next day, and *Soccer Saturday* would benefit from some explosive interviews, but the drama would only hang the officials out to dry. Nobody would want to interview them if they had played a brilliant game; the questions from the media would only focus on the negative aspects of their performance. The refs would be on a hiding to nothing every time they faced a camera and therefore exposed to even more abuse from the public. Who would want to do that?

My blunder had been the result of inexperience rather than any legal nitpicking, such as the ref involved in the game between Bath City and Newport County. Nevertheless, the general opinion of my refereeing abilities during *Soccer Saturday*'s Christmas Special were later summed up when Baddesley Park, the winning team, had been presented with their silverware. As I shook hands with the players, their captain lifted the cup, at which point he decided to crack a joke. 'Jeff, stick to *Countdown*, eh, mate?' he said, cheekily.

I laughed, clipped him round the ear and then gave him my copy of *Who's the B*****d in the Black?* as punishment for being lippy. According to Dermot, it was the best call I'd made all day.

CHAPTER TWO

SPOTTING
THE CHEATS

Of course, I was lucky: during the *Soccer Saturday* Christmas Special I only had to referee a few friendly matches for fun and the mood was pretty light-hearted among the kids. But when it comes to the professional game, footballers will do just about anything to nick an advantage. Falling to the floor as if struck by a stray bullet (Luis Suarez), biting (Luis Suarez), feigning injury while simultaneously wafting an imaginary red card in the air (Luis . . . oh, you get the idea); it can be incredibly difficult to spot who's cheating and who's mortally injured in the thick of the action. God knows how the likes of Howard Melton Webb deal with it on a weekly basis.

And it doesn't just happen at the top level. You need X-ray vision in the lower leagues, too. While flicking through 'Jeff's Big Folder of Local Newspaper Cuttings', I stumbled across a 2010 match report on a game between Macclesfield Town and

Burton Albion. Apparently, a bit of a fuss was made when the Silkmen's goalie Jose Veiga brought a 'foreign object' on to the pitch, a description that suggested something really quite sinister – such as a set of concealed knuckledusters or nunchucks – but in reality was nothing more than a golf tee. According to eyewitnesses, though, that one tiny peg was enough to cause a fair amount of drama.

Trouble first started as Veiga began drawing cheers of approval with a series of piercing, accurate goal kicks that consistently soared downfield. That shouldn't have come as too much of a shock. Macclesfield's keeper was an international having represented the mighty Cape Verde since 2004, a team ranked 58th in the world at the time of storytelling (about ten places higher than Scotland[1]). But as goal kick after goal kick rocketed over the halfway line, often to the toes of his team mates, the ref noticed that Veiga had been using a transparent tee to improve his ball striking. While the rest of the players trotted back to the halfway line, the cheeky blighter was secretly placing the ball on top of a plastic peg, which went some way to explaining why his hoofs were gaining such impressive velocity and accuracy. Play was stopped and the tee confiscated, leaving Veiga to rely on good old-fashioned skill and brute force like everyone else.

If Veiga had been playing in Macclesfield, Australia rather than Macclesfield, England, he would probably have been sent off for his gamesmanship. By the looks of things, bringing a foreign object of any kind on to the pitch is seemingly a red card offence Down Under, especially if the foreign object in question is located, well, 'down under'. Which is where I uncovered the curious tale

---

1   Before I get angry emails, that was a joke.

of Aaron Eccleston, born and raised in Macclesfield UK, but a Mansfield Town fan and an amateur footballer living in Australia. Eccleston turned out for Old Hill Wanderers Reserves in Melbourne and during an uneventful fixture against Swinburne University's second eleven in 2011, he received a full-blooded volley to the 'Jacobs' which would for ever place his name in football folklore.

Many men have suffered the pain of a kick to the nether regions – either on the football field or during a heated argument with an offended girlfriend. And like any gent in that unfortunate position, Eccleston rolled around in pain and lowered his shorts to check on the wellbeing of his manhood. Why the referee also felt the need to look was anyone's guess, but during an uninvited Peeping Tom routine, he spotted a shiny piercing attached to Eccleston's wedding tackle. Following the letter of the law, the ref ordered Eccleston, embarrassed and presumably still in agony, away from the field of play to remove the attachment. Matters worsened when, on his return, Eccleston was shown a yellow for rejoining the game without permission, and then sent off when he refused to prove that the offending item had been 'unhooked'.

In his defence, I couldn't blame him. The process would have required a second inspection from the referee, a man who had already been caught peeping once too often. On an amateur video which did the rounds on the Internet shortly afterwards, Eccleston was heard to moan, 'I'm making a complaint, ref. It's not right looking at my c***.'

I felt for the young man. As we all know, officials can get carried away in the heat of the moment. Red and yellow cards are often dished out prematurely; a moment or two of calm and clarity can be the difference between a booking and an early bath.

Sometimes, however, footballers are so stupid that they can find themselves leaving the pitch only moments after arriving on it.

According to *Soccer Saturday*'s Japanese correspondent Matt Le Tissier (well, he is a big fan of sushi), the J-League experienced one of the fastest red cards of all time in May 2011 when Nagoya Grampus defender Takahiro Masukawa cynically hauled down an opponent who was clean through on goal. Having misjudged a quick back pass which arrived straight from the kick-off, he watched with horror as the centre forward capitalised on his blunder, raced past him and homed in on the 18-yard box. Based on what happened next, Ricardo Carvalho's *Little Book Of Ungentlemanly Conduct* must do a roaring trade in the Far East, because an embarrassed Masukawa reacted by applying a sneaky tap to the ankles before adopting Carvalho's now trademarked 'Who me?' gasp of disbelief once the whistle had been blown. The ref was having none of it and ordered him to an early bath. Time on the clock: five seconds.

Further research soon proved that this quick-fire dismissal had been beaten by two incidents closer to home.[2] The first took place when the aptly named Jimmy Pratt of Chippenham was sent off in 2009 after three seconds, having clattered into an opponent during the British Gas Business Premier League fixture against the also aptly named team, Bashley. That feat was beaten only by Cross Farm Park Celtic striker Lee Todd, who was sent

---

2 Actually, both incidents were considerably slower than the red card shown to Sheffield United sub Keith Gillespie who brained Stephen Hunt with an elbow during a fixture against Reading in 2007. Gillespie had only just run on to the pitch as a sub before planting one on his opponent, but given that the game hadn't technically restarted, the Sheffield United midfielder was not in the field of play.

off after two seconds during a match against Taunton East Reach Rovers in 2000. Problems began when the ref stunned players from both teams with some overzealous whistle-blowing as the game got underway.

'F*** me, that was loud,' moaned Todd, one second after kick-off. The ref deafened him again a second later, this time to halt play and show Todd the red card for swearing.

Controversy raged afterwards. 'I wasn't swearing at the ref or anyone else,' explained Todd. 'Anyone else would have done the same. He nearly blew my ear off!'

Every fan likes to think that the ref in charge of their game is crooked, dodgy or a homer. Even I tend to make the odd disparaging remark should Hartlepool concede a soft penalty or suffer a succession of borderline offside calls, but I'd like to point out for legal reasons that all referees are fine, upstanding, honest and law-abiding citizens. Except in Argentina where some of them are reformed murderers, bank robbers and criminal warlords.

Such is the shortage of officials in South America that the Argentine FA has actually turned to inmates in a Buenos Aires maximum security prison for help. There, 20 prisoners have undertaken a course in which they have studied the art of refereeing with a view to working in the professional leagues on their return to society. It's a nice idea. Every time a match between inmates takes place in the prison, these wannabe law enforcers are placed in charge, presumably to instil a sense of responsibility, an interesting facet of the rehabilitation process. The scheme had its hitches, however. Apparently, the first challenge that faced tutors was a lack of literacy among the inmates in black. The prisoners were soon taught how to read and write so they could fill out the match reports after every game, and, one presumes, book all 22 players for violent behaviour, ungentlemanly conduct and shirt theft. It's not just in football that new referees are being developed, either. Tennis, boxing and rugby courses are also taking place in the prison.

'We thought that to allow those who violated the law to now be in a position to apply them on a football pitch was an interesting message for society,' says Alejandro Rodriguez, Buenos Aires' Secretary of Sport.

He's right, it is a smart way of keeping people on the straight and narrow I suppose, but – heaven forbid! – what would happen should one of them make the grade and become involved in an incident as contentious as Diego Maradona's infamous Hand Of God 'goal'? One can only imagine the headlines.

Look, it's easy to poke fun at officialdom. But if we really want to get to the nuts and bolts of what's wrong with the game, then sorting out how our matches are refereed at the highest level would be a good start. As my limited experience on the *Soccer Saturday* Christmas Special proved, even looking after a junior game can be tricky. Sorting out a Premiership game when the stakes are seriously high is much harder, and the refs need a helping hand to get the big decisions right, especially when they're being beamed around the globe and subjected to extreme criticism by the likes of you and me.

UEFA has taken the bold step of introducing officials who stand behind the goals during Europa League and Champions League games, but I think they should go one step further and use actual, real people rather than the cardboard cut-outs that have worked there so far. Have you ever known one of them to make a decision? In fact, have you ever known one of them to move along the line? For the most part, they seem to do a pretty good impression of a tailor's dummy, so why they've been installed there is beyond me. I know in theory that they're supposed to assist the ref when it comes to decisions in the penalty area and goal-line incidents, but so far they've made the scheme a laughing stock, mainly on the basis that not one of them has waved his flag in the past two years.

At times, the assistant referees in the Premier League seem to be just as ineffective. The problems here stem from the fact that they're part-time, whereas the man in the middle – the afore-mentioned Mike Dean or Howard Melton Webb, for example – is usually a professional. One controversial weekend in December 2011 highlighted this issue and the headlines were dominated by two decisions involving the referee and his assistants. The first took place between Newcastle and Chelsea at St James' Park when Chelsea defender David Luiz hauled down the Magpies' striker Demba Ba when the world and his wife could see that he was clean through on goal. Despite Luiz preventing a clear goalscoring opportunity, the ref only flashed him a yellow. Down the motorway at White Hart Lane, Spurs benefited from some equally inconsistent decision-making when Gary Cahill (then playing for Bolton) upended Scott Parker just inside his own half. The incident happened 45 yards from goal; there was at least one other defender plus the keeper between Parker and the goal, yet the referee decided to send Cahill off for denying Spurs a clear goalscoring opportunity. It was madness.

The following day, Newcastle's manager Alan Pardew went on to the sofa for Kammy's round-up programme, *Goals on Sunday*. When it came to discussing the complicated decisions of the weekend, he was chomping at the bit to dissect the referee's decisions, and rightly so, but as a member of the League Managers Association (LMA), he also had one or two salient points to make.

'The answer is for the referees to be better trained and for refs to work together as a unit,' he said. '[Everton manger] David Moyes has made a suggestion that I think the LMA are going to use, and that's to get the refs to come into the training grounds to work with our reserves, our academies and our pros.

'The problem we've got in this country is that the budget for referees is £8 million. That's for everything: the assistants, the assessors, the whole budget. When you think about how much money is thrown at the game, that can't be right. The training for referees costs £35,000, believe it or not. We've got assistant referees who are not full-time, so we're [always] going to have this problem, unless we say the assistant referees are professional, and the referees can then have a unit that's trained, and that train together. They would know each other, they would work with one another, that could help them to deal with [tricky] situations because they're dealing with them together in the week.'

Pardew was right: there is plenty of money swishing around at the top level and it would help if some of it was spent on making the linesmen and women of our game full time. My other simple answer would be to rely on technology, and when I say 'technology' I don't mean the type of gadgetry feared at FIFA HQ, where infrared goal-line sensors and footballs equipped with nano chips have (probably) been the elephants in the room at one of their many sumptuous lunches. No, I'm thinking of a small TV screen positioned on a desk somewhere near the halfway line, in full view of a fourth official who could quite easily cast his eye over any contentious incidents, rather than picking his nose, therefore giving his mates on the pitch a helping hand.

This idea isn't radical, dear reader; all I'm suggesting here is a better use of manpower. At the moment the fourth official is in sole charge of the subs, putting up a board to signify the added time at the end of the match and collecting Arsène Wenger's hurled water bottles from the technical area. How hard would it be for him to review a controversial issue on the monitor and impart some vital information to the ref via his headset? It would take all of five seconds.

'But Jeff,' you might moan, 'won't this undermine the referee's position on the pitch?'

Well no, actually. At present, what has undermined our referees so badly is a string of bad calls and inconsistency in the decision-making process – a card for a two-footed tackle is a straight red one week, it's a yellow the next. My fourth-official idea could sort all of that out. And with the best will in the world, the man on the touchlines wouldn't be undermining the referee, he would be assisting him. Meanwhile, if the fourth official becomes as significant as the guys out there on the pitch, so what? As long as the end result is a great game of football where all the decisions are just about as correct as they could possibly be, then who really cares?

The real crisis hasn't unfolded at the highest level, but at the grassroots where the treatment of referees has become so atrocious that anyone considering becoming a part-time professional official might want to think of a less troublesome vocation. Like a traffic warden, for example, or a job as Mario Balotelli's bathroom designer. As I've mentioned already, I've already seen it at first hand and experienced some abuse as a part-time linesman on a Sunday morning, but on the face of it I was lucky. I've only had to endure the odd insult or cat call. Over the years there have been several cases of serious assaults, threats and general unpleasantness in the amateur leagues up and down the country. Such as when one Sunday league player, Joseph Rimmer of Merseyside, drove his car on to the pitch after being sent off for Lonsdale in a Southport and District League match against Harrington in February 2010. Unhappy with a decision made by referee David Harkness, Rimmer got into his car and skidded into the centre circle where he performed a series of terrifying 'doughnuts' before shouting threatening insults at the ref and his linesman. He was later jailed for 24 weeks and banned from driving for two years, having scared the life out of Harkness who remains one of the many unsung heroes of Sunday League football. The ref had given up his weekends to officiate matches for many years. Unsurprisingly, he quit the game shortly after his run-in with Rimmer.

Closer to home I watched my other son in an under-12s game one Sunday. The ref was not much older than the players – 16 or 17 years of age maybe – but I was shocked to see that the parents in the crowd were prepared to shout insults at the man – or boy – in charge, even at his tender age. It was undeserved: he had played a pretty good game and handled just about every incident correctly, which was great to see, especially when considering his relative inexperience. However, towards the end of the match he awarded a penalty to our team which turned out to be the decisive goal in a 3–2 victory. The parents of the other lot went ballistic and the abuse that was chucked the referee's way was out of order. By the looks of things he couldn't wait to get home afterwards. As everyone wrapped up for the morning and the nets were taken down from the goals, he collected his match fee with a very glum look on his face. Because of the language from some of the mums and dads on the touchlines, that lad suffered a very unpleasant Sunday morning.

It's because of incidents like the ones I've gathered here – not to mention my own experiences of looking after schoolboy games – that I'd refuse to ref a match at kids' level now. It's just not worth the grief. Young refs like the one I witnessed being verbally tortured get paid only pocket money for the 'pleasure' of taking charge of a youth game. If that lad had been thinking of making a career out of the sport, I'm sure the incident would have been very discouraging; referees need to have a thick skin, especially at that age when kids can be easily hurt. But parents on the sidelines don't see them as kids, they just see them as Men In Black and therefore the enemy.

The Respect campaign has worked to an extent at the top level where some protection has been afforded to officials, but because supporters have witnessed the likes of John Terry and Steven Gerrard yelling at referees in the past, they still think it's acceptable behaviour in junior football. But I'll tell you what: the FA and UEFA can have all the touchline tellies and cardboard cut-out officials in the world. It won't make a blind bit of difference if the game hasn't got a ref willing to blow the whistle on a Saturday afternoon at 3 p.m. That's where the real work has to be done.

It's not as if referees are safe from physical harm in the professional game, either. Despite the stewards, CCTV cameras and novelty mascots, the occasional attack does take place, though not so much on our shores, thankfully. In South Africa, for example, the

Orlando Pirates were given a suspended fine of 50,000 rand in March 2011 when one of their fans lobbed a handful of porridge at the ref after the game. Weirdly, Pirates had won easily in Durban, so God knows how the crowd would have reacted had they been beaten. Meanwhile in Holland, an old-age pensioner really lost his rag while watching a referee book six players from his team, FC Oss in the Dutch Second Division. Oss eventually lost 4–3 at home to Almere City in August 2011, which was enough to send this particular fan into a spin – at the final whistle, the OAP drove his mobility scooter on to the pitch and crashed into the ref as he tried to make his way down the tunnel.

There are times, however, when a referee can be smothered as much by affection as he can be intimidated by rage, as happened in Romania where Rapid Bucharest were fined £750 after their manager Marius Sumudica planted a smacker on the cheek of the ref while celebrating a goal against league rivals Gaz Matan. Sumudica had first dived on to the pitch to celebrate in front of the Rapid fans. When he was ushered off the field of play by the official, Sumudica responded by grabbing him around the neck and showing a little 'man-love'.

'I lost it for a moment,' said Sumudica afterwards. 'But he smelled so good. I know it wasn't normal.'

Some refs deal with this type of behaviour and the pressure of making unpopular decisions rather well, others don't; some crumble, others thrive. Take Rod Stewart's brother. While the Scottish crooner has made quite a living from dating leggy blondes and singing 'Sailing' to an audience of middle-aged women, his sibling Don has been happily refereeing amateur football matches for half a century despite undergoing a triple heart bypass operation. Now in his eighties, Don was recently honoured

34

by the FA in November 2011 for his services to the game – duties which include officiating matches and celebrity fixtures organised by his younger, more handsome brother.

'Football has been my whole life, like music is for my brother Rod,' he said. 'Rod often invites teams [to his own football pitch] to come and play and I will always referee. But I've never asked Rod to pay me because he does look after me very well.'

Not everyone is the same, sadly. For every brother of a multimillionaire rock star there is a Babak Rafati, the referee in the German Bundesliga who tried to take his own life during the 2011/12 season. In the same month that Don was being honoured by the FA, Rafati was cracking under the pressure of the game. In the build-up to the league match between Cologne and Mainz 05, he seriously injured himself in a hotel bath in a desperate suicide attempt. Luckily, he was saved by his matchday assistants who began knocking on his hotel door after Rafati had failed to show up for a pre-game meeting. When a member of the hotel staff let them into the room, they were faced with the grisly sight of the referee lying in a pool of his own blood. Some quick thinking and emergency medical procedures saved his life and Rafati was taken to hospital where his condition was stabilised. As he recovered from his injuries it was revealed that the intense stress he experienced as a referee had been a major contributory factor when performing his desperate act.

'Mr Rafati felt a growing pressure to perform, combined with the media pressure and the constant fear of making mistakes,' read a statement in the German newspaper *Bild* shortly after his release from hospital. 'And this was leading to an ever-increasing burden. This burden was even making daily routine problems seem insurmountable and he no longer felt able to cope.

Mr Rafati has decided to go public with the illness and to face up to it. He has checked in for professional treatment to receive therapy for the causes.'

It's worth noting that for three years out of the last four, Rafati had been voted the worst referee in the Bundesliga in a poll of league players by German magazine *Kicker*. Look, I'm not saying that the two incidents are linked, but sometimes the criticism and the haranguing really does go too far. Maybe we should occasionally cut the boys in black a bit of slack. At the very least, UEFA and the FA should be looking to give our much maligned officials some extra support, both for their sanity and ours, because referees and their assistants are clearly not bulletproof.

HARRY REDKNAPP'S TV BURP

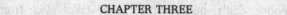

Spare a thought for Rob Palmer, *Soccer Saturday*'s Man in the North West, post-match interviewer and all-round jolly nice chap. Most of the time, Rob comes across as quite an inoffensive fellow, in the best possible way: he's delivered match reports in an ill-fitting Sky Sports blazer for several years now, often without the nonsensical babble associated with some of our broadcasters (one such example, Dean 'Deano' Windass will be dealt with appropriately in the next few pages), and he's always on hand to provide commentary for our Spanish football coverage on a Saturday evening. While I'm slapping on the Brut and preparing myself for a night out with Mrs Jeff in one of Winchester's finest steak houses, Rob often remains in the studio with his sandwiches and Kettle Chips for yet another shift behind the La Liga

37

microphone. Sadly, our coverage rarely takes place from the stands while the likes of CA Osasuna play Real Betis in the Reyno de Navarra, Pamplona. Most of the time commentary comes from Sky's studios in the cooler climes of Middlesex, so apologies if I've shattered any illusions there, dear reader.

Up until a couple of years ago, Rob was completely unknown by most football fans, but then his disastrous post-match interview with Spurs gaffer Harry Redknapp infamously pinged around the Internet faster and more erratically than a Glen Johnson back pass. The chat, which took place after Spurs had lost 1–0 at home to Wigan in 2010 (and around the time the transfer window was due to shut), only lasted 14 seconds but it was enough to make headlines in the sports pages, mainly because of Rob's opening line.

'So, Harry,' he said, the cameras rolling, 'you've made your name as a wheeler and dealer, there's not been much wheeling and dealing . . .'

As if Harry wasn't mardy enough at the result, Rob had seemingly decided to sour his mood further by making reference to Tottenham's lack of transfer activity in the most offensive way: he'd likened Harry's managerial skills to a market trading technique most often associated with Del Boy from *Only Fools and Horses*. If Rob's inference was to be believed, instead of trading international footballers, Harry was buying Russian video cameras and blow-up dolls from Monkey Harris in the local market. Clearly fuming, Harry's face turned a dark shade of red and he stormed away from the camera, shaking his head furiously.

'No, I'm not a wheeler and dealer,' he seethed. 'No, no, f**k off.'

That this incident had happened during a recorded interview rather than a live chat on Sky Sports News was a massive relief and meant that the studio was saved from a general outbreak of pandemonium all round. Then Rob did what any right-minded, post-match reporter in an ill-fitting Sky Sports blazer would do in such a sticky situation: he tried to appease his victim in a high-pitched, girly voice that made him sound like Joe Pasquale on helium.

'Oh, no, Harry . . . I didn't mean it like that . . .'

No good. Harry was storming back to the Spurs' dressing room having treated our camera crew to a blast of colourful language more in tune with a night out alongside Paul Merson and Alan McInally than a post-match interview with one of the Premiership's top gaffers. There was more to come, however.

'I didn't make my name as a f**king wheeler and dealer,' Harry shouted back at Rob, off camera, but sadly not off mic, as the Sky Sports crew desperately studied the floor for something else to film. 'Don't say it like that, I'm a f**king football manager!' At which point the video footage cut out in a style not too dissimilar to the closing scenes of *The Blair Witch Project*, leaving Internet viewers to wonder as to the wellbeing and whereabouts of Rob Palmer (clue: his ill-fitting Sky Sports blazer has not yet been found on a park bench in Pamplona).

Looking back, it was an easy mistake to make and I understood Harry's fury. He had long been regarded as a manager who was capable of making seriously shrewd moves in the transfer market. Interestingly, following the outburst, he then went on to sign Rafael van der Vaart from Real Madrid on the last day of the window for a relatively cheap £8 million. Before his spat with Rob he had always been a great laugh on Sky, especially when it came to doing live interviews. That afternoon, Our Man in the

North West had pushed the wrong buttons. The fireworks had blown up in his face, but in my opinion it was a great TV moment because the football fan had only principally seen one side of Harry. Their view of him was limited to the gregarious, witty, smiling character who once commented on a glaring miss by Spurs' striker Darren Bent by quipping, 'You will never get a better chance to win a match than that. My missus could have scored that one.' During Wheeler-Dealergate he showed the public that he possessed a passionate, feisty streak, which is such an important characteristic if you're going to be a successful football manager.

So far, that strop has been a one-off and I've always looked forward to working with Harry. Thankfully it has happened on a few occasions, most memorably when Spurs turned over AC Milan 1–0 in the San Siro during the Champions League second round in the 2010/11 season. It was one of the great European performances and afterwards Harry was determined to come over to talk to me and our pundits for the evening, his son Jamie and Graeme Souness, who were discussing Spurs' performance in the studio. He was on cloud nine and deservedly so, but of course, his enthusiasm caused a terrible kerfuffle, because UEFA was adamant at the time that all managers in the Champions League should first finish their official press conferences before speaking to any media not in the designated press rooms or 'mixed zone', an area where reporters were free to interview passing players and coaches. Forget about the video technology debate or clarifying the offside rules, this was the issue that really twisted the knickers of Michel Platini and our great European football organisation that year.

Anyway, Harry was having none of it and, flanked by a pair

of UEFA heavies, he came down to see us. We were told that we had been allocated five minutes of studio time and as two overcoat-clad brutes simultaneously eyed their stopwatches and glared across at me like nightclub bouncers (which was quite a trick), Harry relived the evening in his typically forthright and garrulous manner. He was full of adrenalin, which was un-surprising given that Harry's right-hand man Joe Jordan had become embroiled in a spat with Milan's legendary bruiser Gennaro Gattuso at the final whistle. From what we could tell, as the players left the pitch, the Scottish hard man formerly known as 'Jaws' (due to his missing front teeth) went head to head, quite literally, with the Italian hard man known as 'Ringhio', which according to my Anglo-Italian translator (Thommo) meant 'The Growl'. It was a fiery end to a fantastic evening, but as one would expect, Harry made light of it.

'He hadn't done his homework,' he said. 'He could've picked a fight with anyone, but putting his head into Joe's face was crazy. He lost his head.'

The crackling atmosphere in the San Siro was made even more electric by the Wagnerian backdrop of rumbling thunder and torrential rain. Combined, it was a great piece of TV.

Another occasion when Harry and I crossed paths (though I use that term loosely) took place when we were asked to record an advert for a fantasy football game. The plan for the project was that Harry and I would be filmed discussing our team selections on mobile phones – Harry from his home in Sandbanks, Dorset and me from my drawing room in Stelling Towers, Winchester. I sent the message back saying, 'Absolutely no way. I'll shoot it in the studio, but I don't want to have people clumping all over my drawing room and I really don't want anyone to see my presentation cabinet of official *Sky Sports Football Yearbooks* from 1888 through to 2012, I'm really sorry.'

I figured that Harry would have the same attitude, what with him being a top, top drawer football manager and a man of privacy, but lo and behold, the next thing I'd heard was that Harry had allowed the crew to film him at his home at Sandbanks. He'd even got his wife Sandra to make the crew tea and coffee. Apparently they had been there the whole day and had a whale of a time. When everybody got back to the office, they were full of him and how fantastic he was. I knew what they were thinking about me: 'But not you, you miserable sod, you wouldn't even let us into your house, official *Sky Sports Football Yearbooks* from 1888 through to 2012, or no official *Sky Sports Football Yearbooks* from 1888 through to 2012.'

As a rule of thumb, the stereotypical *Soccer Saturday* match reporter in an ill-fitting Sky Sports blazer can be an unruly and unpredictable beast. And then there's Dean Windass: a broadcasting hand grenade with as much grace and subtlety as one of Paul Scholes's tackles. As a player for Bradford, Hull, Oxford United and Boro, Deano was just about as passionate and enthusiastic as you could imagine. I even recall seeing him performing the most exhausting exercises while I was covering Bradford for a Sunday afternoon match some years back. As I prepared for the show, I watched a lone figure running up the steps at Valley Parade, which were very steep. Up and down, and up and down he went; sprint after sprint after sprint. After a time I thought, 'I've got to see who that is.' Blow me if it wasn't Deano trying to get fit. Apparently he had been recovering from a long-term injury at the time and was absolutely determined to get back to match speed as quickly as possible. Sadly, he's rarely shown the same professionalism when it comes to delivering those all-important match reports on *Soccer Saturday*, but at least his bull-in-a-china-shop enthusiasm is very much in evidence.

Anyone who has seen him on the show will know that his football passion is there, for sure, it's just that whenever I've watched Deano on screen, he's scared the life out of me. He attempts to kick and head pretty much every ball, as if he were still playing. Meanwhile, as a broadcaster, his style is cut from the same Spandex as Chris Kamara, but without the eloquence, as I can prove with the following TV highlights:

ON DARLINGTON VERSUS DAGENHAM & REDBRIDGE

> DEANO: 'They've just scored, but the players are so far away, I can't tell you who's scored!'
> JEFF: 'Deano, just give us a clue which team . . .'

ON JASON KOUMAS

> DEANO: 'Jason Koumas has come on as a sub, but I'm not sure who for because it was ages ago.'

ON BORO VERSUS BRISTOL CITY

> DEANO: 'Jeff! Somebody's been sent off! But I can't tell you who because I wasn't concentrating.'

At least he spotted the red card, which is more than could be said for some of our matchday reporters. During a game between Portsmouth and Blackburn in the 2010/11 campaign, I remember receiving news of an early bath at Fratton Park. Apparently, Anthony Vanden Borre of Pompey had been sent off for a second yellow card. Immediately, I cut to our very own on-the-spot expert on the South Coast at Fratton Park, which, very sadly, happened to be Kammy.

'There's been a sending off at Portsmouth,' I said. 'Who's it for? Chris Kamara . . .'

Kammy stared back at the screen with a look of complete bemusement, a look that I knew could only mean trouble: the wheel was still spinning in Kammy's head, but the hamster was very, very dead.

KAMMY: 'I don't know, Jeff, has there? I must have missed that. Is there a red card?'

JEFF: 'Chris, have you not been watching? I have no idea what has happened! What has happened, Chris?'

KAMMY: 'I don't know, Jeff. The rain must have got in my eyes.'

JEFF: 'Chris according to my source, Anthony Vanden Borre has been sent off for Portsmouth for a second bookable offence. Get your fingers out and count out the number of Portsmouth players there are on the field.'

KAMMY: 'No, you're right, I saw him go off, but I thought they were bringing a sub on, Jeff . . . still 0–0.'

JEFF: 'Another cutting-edge report from *Gillette Soccer Saturday* . . .'

Miraculously, Kammy's a fixture on the show and very happy about it, too. Deano, on the other hand, is very keen to get into management, mainly because he had a spell as assistant manager at Darlington and he really enjoyed it, unlike Kammy who has previously managed Bradford and Stoke City with mixed results. Certainly Deano would be an enthusiastic gaffer for whoever he worked for, but I'll tell you what, if his *Soccer Saturday* match reports are anything to go by, it would be a brave club to take a punt on him. He's even texted me a few times whenever the Hartlepool job has become vacant:

'Jeff, cn u put a word in for me? DEANO.'

Well, Deano, you'll be pleased to know that I have put more than one word in for you mate, I'm just not telling you what those words were.

Still, we were all given a bit of a shock when it was announced in 2012 that Deano had been suffering from depression since leaving the game. I knew he missed working at a football club in a full-time capacity. In fact, Deano was so reluctant to hang up his boots that he even made appearances for the likes of Barton Town Old Boys and Scarborough Athletic. He must have been really desperate to have played for that lot because they were teams that were way, way down on the football pyramid.

I just didn't realise how badly his retirement from the game had affected him, not until the news broke that he had tried to kill himself. It was all over the press. In an interview with the *Scarborough Evening News* he later revealed how he'd felt as if he had nothing to get up for in the morning. It was heartbreaking stuff.

'I have cried every day for the last two years since retiring,' he said. 'People outside football think [ex-players] have it all. But I was in a hole that I honestly didn't know how to get out of. Just over a week ago I hit rock-bottom and decided to end it all. I first took an overdose and when that didn't work I tried to hang myself. I felt so alone and believed I had nothing to live for. I need to sort myself out which is why I'm speaking out now.

'People have this image of me as this big strong man who can take anything life throws at him. But I'm not ashamed to say I wanted to end it after a string of setbacks. I knew I'd been a fool but I couldn't shake off the depression at feeling what a failure I'd become.'

It was a real shock. On the exterior, Deano is a joker, a lot of fun and an ebullient character. As is often the way with people who are like that outwardly, inside they can be completely different. Deano's happy exterior had hidden all his unhappiness so we never thought there was a serious issue. I just hope he can get himself better soon.

Soccer Saturday has drawn its fair share of rock star fans over the years, mainly because we've included a number of hellraisers on the panel, 'Champagne' Charlie Nicholas, the late George Best and Rodney Marsh among them. Rock star giants such as Kasabian have even talked up their love of the show, and when Merse – a man who once stayed in the pub rather than travelling to the *Top of the Pops* studios to mime over the FA Cup single, 'Shouting for the Gunners' with his Arsenal team mates in 1993 – met up with Kasabian's football-barmy frontman Tom Meighan for a lads' magazine interview, trouble was bound to follow. Thankfully, it involved a wager rather than a 20-pint bender (or worse) and somewhat foolishly, as the pair said their hellos for the first time, Tom claimed that his team Leicester City were a strong shout for promotion at the start of the 2011/12 campaign, what with Sven being in charge at the time. Merse challenged him to a bet.

'I'll have some of that,' said Tom and the pair shook on it.

How much? A cool grand.

The time it took for them to make the bet after meeting for the first time? All of one minute.

'Bloody hell,' laughed Tom afterwards. 'I've had a bet with Paul Merson. The lads won't believe this.'

God knows whether they've settled it yet, though I'm sure Tom's ebullience would have been soured once Sven Göran Eriksson was sacked a month or two after the wager had been laid. Merse, I reckon, was rubbing his hands with glee.

Another rock star who embraced the show's anarchic spirit as readily as Kasabian was Noel Gallagher, former Oasis song-writer, solo artist in his own right, and a diehard City fan. Noel to his credit has a good set of pipes and writes a catchy tune, though in my opinion he's nowhere near as good as some of Middlesbrough's finest songwriters such as Chris Rea or even that Geordie lass Cheryl Cole. Still, when we managed to interview Noel for *Soccer Saturday* I was absolutely thrilled that we'd got him on the show. But when I saw the clip that was due to go out on air, I was left feeling a little less enthusiastic . . .

NOEL: '*Soccer Saturday*? Whoever came up with that idea is a genius. My favourite pundit? Well, Merson, he hates Man City. He's never got a good word for City. All he says about Man City is, "Nah, I ain't 'aving it . . ." The only reason he's not 'aving it is because he isn't getting paid two hundred grand a week.

'Thommo, I don't mind Thommo, but I wouldn't like to see him in 3D, though, do you know worra mean? I love it when they're giving him stick about Liverpool because you know he just wants to swear. He just wants to lay into some proper, working class swearing, but you know he can't . . .

'Le Tissier, I think he's pretty good, he's pretty level headed, but the man is Charlie Nicholas. He's an old Celtic boy. Anyone who comes with the prefix 'Champagne' in front of his name is all right by me. He'd have been in our band. Apart from the earring which is a little bit eighties, do you know worra mean?

'But how Jeff Stelling is qualified to run that show is beyond me. I've read some of his football columns and he's possibly the worst football pundit in the history of football. He tipped City to go down the first year when Sven [Göran Eriksson, Manchester City manager] first took over and then when we were top of the league at Christmas or summat, I've seen him on *Soccer Saturday* saying, "Well, they're there by merit and he's doing a great job." The man's got no shame.

'He'll be going on now about [City manager, Roberto] Mancini and how he needs to manage all those egos . . . Manage the egos on that panel! They don't respect Stelling. He's the worst man manager I've ever seen.'

I suppose Noel is entitled to his opinions, he's very knowledgeable about the game, he has a lot of interesting views and carries them off with a good sense of humour, but to call me the worst man manager he's ever seen? As Merse would probably say, 'I ain't 'aving it . . .'

CHAPTER FOUR

CLARKE CARLISLE'S A FOOTBALL GENIUS!

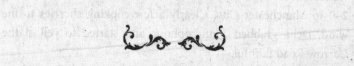

Convincing rock 'n' roll guests to chat with the *Soccer Saturday* crew is an easy job. A lot of bands like football after all, and most of them are happy to discuss on air the various issues regarding their team. The same has applied to *Countdown*, which was my other daytime TV job for a few years until I left in 2011, and made me a pin-up in British Legions and student dorms the length and breadth of the country. We rarely had trouble when it came to convincing the big stars to sit in the studio for a day because a lot of people seemed to enjoy the format of the show, and frankly they didn't come much bigger than celebrity chef, Norwich City's joint majority shareholder and all-round bon viveur, Delia Smith, Patron Saint of Mustard.

I've had a working relationship with Delia for years now and the one thing I've learned about her during that time is that she likes nothing more than to get stuck in, especially if she's entertaining friends at one of her sumptuous pre-match banquets at Carrow Road, which I've heard are often washed down with buckets and buckets of vino. So it came as no surprise when she expressed her interest in tackling a *Countdown* conundrum or two when we asked her in 2011.

As you may or may not recall – or, more to the point, as *Delia* may or may not recall – she once made a bit of a spectacle of herself in 2005 in full view of the Sky cameras when she wandered on to the pitch at half-time with Norwich trailing 2–0 to Manchester City. Clearly a few cooking sherries to the wind, Delia grabbed a microphone and started to yell at the Carrow Road faithful.

'A message for the best football supporters in the world,' she slurred. 'We need a twelfth man here. Where are you? Where *aaaarrrrr* yooooooooo? Let's be 'avin' yooooo. Come *onnnnnn!*'

It all caused a bit of a fuss at the time, but when it came to working on *Countdown*, however, Delia was all class. For months and months we'd begged her to join us in Dictionary Corner. Just in case there's someone out there who's unfamiliar with the show, Dictionary Corner is the infamous spot where *Countdown* place all their celebrity guests and it is a hive of intellectual activity. The role of our guest boffins (if you can call them that) is to assist the show's language expert Susie Dent as she trawls through stacks of different dictionaries in a desperate search for a nine-letter word. They are also given a spot before every ad break to entertain the audience with a witty anecdote or two.

Given that criterion, Delia seemed to be the perfect choice. To be honest, storytellers didn't come much more prestigious or interesting than her, in either the kitchen (and I mean that in a non-sexist way) or the football club boardroom. The only sticking point in getting her into the *Countdown* studios was her schedule. As you would expect from a Norwich City majority shareholder and superstar chef, spare time was a luxury she rarely enjoyed. The Canaries' promotion campaign was under way at the time of recording and there must have been plenty of hot pots simmering away at home. There was also the question of transporting her to and from the studios. Normally guests are paid a rail fare for their journey to the *Countdown* HQ in Manchester; sometimes a car is sent to pick them up if they're very special, like Richard Stilgoe or Les Dennis, but Delia insisted on making her own way there. It was only once the shows had been finished that I learned that she had chartered a private plane out of her own pocket to get her to the studios so that she could fit us into her hectic diary. That act alone pretty much made her the Jay-Z of Dictionary Corner. More importantly it proved to me that she was a very generous lady, which must be a blessing for Norwich. I'm guessing they're very lucky to have her.

We were very lucky to have her too, she was great fun and thankfully everyone managed to behave themselves when she was in the studio, which hasn't always been the case. At times during my three years on *Countdown* there were plenty of reasons to turn off the cameras, usually when some 'S-M-A-R-T-A-R-S-E' had assembled a rude word from the jumbled up letters on the board. During my stint on the show we had 'S-H-I-T-F-A-C-E-D', which you'll not be surprised to learn was spotted by a student. On another occasion, the letters were drawn by my glamorous assistant Rachel Riley in such a way that they spelt out the words 'L-A-R-G-E-B-A-P-S'.

But the most unexpected suggestion came from the TV chef Gino D'Acampo during his time in Dictionary Corner. I forget the exact combination of letters that were placed on the board, but Gino seemed overly keen to reveal a six-letter word that he had spotted as the clock ticked away behind him.

'So, Gino,' I said, 'I believe you have something there?'

'Yes, Jeff, it's a "Minger",' he laughed, beaming proudly as he spelt out the word for those in the studio who might not have heard the term before. Given that most of the audience were pensioners, it was a logical supposition, I guess.

'M-I-N-G-E-R,' continued Gino as I looked nervously at my producer.

'Erm, I don't think we can allow "Minger", Gino. Was there anything else?'

'Oh, OK,' he laughed, undeterred. 'In which case I've got a "Minge", Jeff: M-I-N-G-E . . .'

Unsurprisingly, the cutting-room floor beckoned for Gino's contribution to the intellectual debate that day.

Overall, I think my favourite *Countdown* contestant was the footballer and PFA chairman Clarke Carlisle, a defender for QPR, Burnley and Preston North End among others. Clarke joined us on the show in 2010 which I was very pleased about because he had previously been a fantastic ambassador for the sport. In interviews he came across as intelligent and articulate. Famously he won a competition to find Britain's brainiest footballer in 2002. I quite fancied his chances of doing well on the show, but despite my cheerleading for Clarke, a lot of people in the *Countdown* office were unconvinced when I first suggested him. In their heads they had lumped him in with the incorrect stereotype of the thick footballer, which was a massive under-estimation on their part, because Clarke had already tried to get on the show some ten years previously, but had unfortunately failed the audition.

To be honest, the assumption that all footballers were dim, as held by some of the crew, really got under my skin. After all there have been plenty of intelligent players over the years. Frank Lampard has 11 GCSEs, including an A* in Latin; Crystal Palace player Matthew Lawrence took a degree in American Literature. Even *Soccer Saturday*'s very own Iain Dowie studied for a master's degree in Engineering and worked for British Aerospace. He was reported to have used several inspirational books to help his managerial techniques, such as *Chicken Soup for the Soul*. Though having seen his motivational abilities at first hand during our aforementioned Schoolboys' Cup on the *Soccer Saturday* Christmas Special, I wasn't all that impressed. Iain spent most of the time in his dressing room getting his team to recite motivational power slogans such as, 'What are we? WINNERS!', or, 'What are the opposition? LOSERS!' His players bellowed the slogans for a few minutes before their first game, then trooped on to the pitch and got thumped.

One footballer who might have wrongly been painted as super-intelligent, however, was Aberdeen striker Darren Mackie. Having involved himself in a very worthy scheme in 2011 which encouraged kids in the club's surrounding area to take a greater interest in literature, Darren was voted 'Reading Champion' by his local school, Meldrum in Oldmeldrum. Part of his reward for helping the children with their education was an interview for the school's website, in which he was able to wax lyrical about his passion for books, authors and suchlike. Or maybe not.

'I don't read a lot of books,' said the Reading Champion in pretty much his first line of the interview, immediately dispelling any opinions that he might be the football equivalent of the Richard & Judy Book Club (who are hopefully reviewing *Jeffanory* with favourable eyes at this very moment), though thankfully, there was some good news for the bookworms at Meldrum.

'I read a lot of magazines about cars, health and general interest. I feel excited about the new up-and-coming things in the world. If I did read books it would be autobiographies because I enjoy finding out about things that have happened in other people's lives.

'My favourite book is *Lord of the Rings* [by J.R.R. Tolkien] although I haven't read the book – [but] I have watched the films. The books must be good because the films are so good.' The *Daily Record* newspaper later accused the Reading Champion of 'Tolkien rubbish', which was very amusing.

Thankfully, Clarke Carlisle was a much brighter button than Darren Mackie, and despite some initial scepticism from my producers, I pressed ahead with changing their opinions of him. My cause was helped when I read an interview with Clarke in one of the Sunday papers. He had been going through some difficult personal issues at the time and was recovering from a problem with alcohol; he'd spent a lot of time refocusing his life. At one point in the article he mentioned that one of his new ambitions was to pass the *Countdown* audition second time around.

'Well, Clarke, your dream is about to come true, mate,' I thought, and after getting the green light from the big cheeses at *Countdown*, I found out his mobile number and fast-tracked him on to the show.

To my absolute delight, Clarke accepted immediately and once he was ensconced in the hot seat, I secretly put myself into his corner because a) he was a really nice bloke and b) he was about to fly the flag for a profession that most people considered to be a bit short on brains. I wanted to show to a wider audience that footballers really weren't thick to a man. And besides, Clarke wouldn't have been the first footballer to have appeared on the programme. In 2008 former Notts County player Neil MacKenzie managed to win five games on the bounce, which was more than could be said of County at the time.

When Clarke arrived, he was a bag of nerves. Apparently, the thought of competing in front of an audience of students and pensioners was more terrifying than the afternoon he had made his professional debut for Blackpool in 1997. Well, he needn't have worried because his performance proved everyone in the studio wrong, except me. He won his first two games convincingly and managed an eight letter word: 'O-U-T-S-P-E-N-D'. He really should have won the third, but despite cruising into a commanding lead, Clarke fell away spectacularly and blew it before the final conundrum. His excuses for losing were understandable, however. Clarke had just become a dad and he'd been up all night before his games; in the days before coming into the studio for filming he'd had to train with Burnley, his club at the time. By the time we got to recording his third performance it was nine in the evening and Clarke was cream crackered.

Well, that's his theory. Mine was somewhat different. Clarke had already taken a day off training to play his *Countdown* games, and the club had been very sympathetic to his request. They, like most of our audience, probably figured it was unlikely that he would win a game, let alone take three on the bounce. As he won his first two games at a canter, I think it suddenly dawned on Clarke that he would have to return to the studios for a further day of recording if he won another. That would have meant missing another day at the club. Reasoning with his boss Brian Laws wouldn't have been pleasant because the club were striving to escape relegation at the time; all hands were on the survival pump. My gut feeling was that Clarke threw the game to avoid any confrontations at work. But I guess if I had a boss as tough as Brian, I would have chucked away my chance of *Countdown* glory, too.

Despite his final game defeat, Clarke left the studios in a cracking mood.

'That Rachel Riley, she's an attractive host,' he said. 'When I went on the programme I have to admit I got aroused. Which I was quite pleased about as I'd not got a seven-letter word before.'

So after three happy years, zero nine-letter words and 700 appearances – which according to Opta's stats matches the time spent in the hot seat by both Des O'Connor and Des Lynam *combined* – I decided to walk away from *Countdown* in 2011. The basic reason was that I knew I'd be covering more Champions League football following the departure of long-standing Sky presenters Richard Keys and Andy Gray.

Prior to the changes at Sky, I found I'd been struggling with the *Countdown* schedule as it was. We filmed five shows a day in a three-day block and it could be blooming murder at times. Combined with a hectic European football schedule, not to mention my commitments on a Saturday, the workload had simply become too much for me to handle all of a sudden. Channel 4 wanted me to stay on and sign a new contract, and in fairness they did everything they could to make my life more comfortable. They chopped and changed their schedules to fit around me, but I could tell it wasn't going to work. When I eventually made the decision to turn their new contract down, I actually felt rather relieved.

I did have a great time while I was there, though. My personal highlights included the time when comedian Dave Spikey came on to the show. As part of his routine he brought a bag of funny newspaper headlines into Dictionary Corner (clearly this was a man after my own heart) and throughout the show he would read out the most amusing captions and slogans. When the recording stopped for the day, Dave showed me a cutting from a Canadian publication he hadn't been allowed to display on air for decency reasons. On the back page, as part of a match report on a local ice hockey game, an editor had rather unwisely written the headline, 'Sloppy Beavers Let In Seven!' Dave later had me in stitches when he told me the true story of when he passed Hope Hospital in Manchester. Apparently a signpost there read, 'Family planning clinic: Use rear entrance', which must have been somebody's idea of a cheeky gag.

Dave had made quite a career out of his obsession for newspaper headlines; he even turned it into a stand-up show. Apparently it began when he had driven past an advertising hoarding for the old *Bolton Evening News*. On it, somebody had written the headline, 'Dead Man Weds'. There was no punctuation, no commas or even quotation marks.

'It just made me laugh so much,' he said. 'I concocted this image in my head: "OK, this is Bolton, he might have actually passed away [at the wedding]. I could imagine someone at the reception looking at him and saying, "Well, he's not saying much."' Dave later told me his favourite ever headline came when a llama – and don't ask me how – broke loose in Preston and crashed into a children's playground which sent everyone there into a panic. The *Lancashire Evening Post* delivered the cracking headline, 'Llama Drama Ding-Dong!'

As a fan of the absurd, Dave would have loved some of the correspondence and gifts sent into *Countdown* by the viewers. And they didn't come more absurd than *Countdown* fans, I can tell you. I remember one fan made me a football boot made entirely out of chocolate, studs and all, which must have taken some doing. There was also the time when a viewer sent in an irate letter regarding the 'oversexing' of the show. Now before you jump to conclusions, this complaint didn't concern our maths whizz Rachel who has managed to turn a few heads in her time, such are her good looks. Rather this anonymous fan's ire concerned Susie, possibly the most prim and proper person you could wish to meet.

Dear Susie,

I respect you immensely and you contribute to the show marvellously, but could I please request that in future you do not display your private parts in front so prominently.

Yours,

Countdown Oddball

I couldn't believe it, I'd never heard of the phrase 'Private parts in front' before, and *Countdown* was a family programme, it was hardly *Hollyoaks*, a blur of snogging and racy underwear, which I've always thought was a bit of a pity. I often thought we could have been a bit more adventurous with the show. A rather novel idea would have been to produce a late-night version, where rude words and off-the-wall slang were permitted. Dean Windass and Harry Redknapp could have starred in Dictionary Corner; maybe Kammy could have been our maths whizz. Meanwhile, Gino D'Acampo could have wowed us with his M-I-N-G-Es and M-I-N-G-E-Rs all night long.

All in all, it was a tough decision to walk away. The three years spent with *Countdown* were happy ones. I loved the show and always enjoyed the banter with our studio guests, some of whom were old mates of mine. As well as Clarke Carlisle and Dave Spikey, I managed to spend studio time with John Sergeant, snooker players Steve Davis and John Parrott, impressionist Alistair McGowan and comedian Tim 'King of the One Liners' Vine who delivered these priceless gags:

> 'My friend has got a butler whose left arm is missing – serves him right.'
> 'I was in the army once and the sergeant said to me, "What does surrender mean?" I said, "I give up!"'
> 'I used to go out with an anaesthetist: she was a local girl.'

There's no doubt in my mind that I will miss *Countdown*. The workload was tough, but it was made easier by the fantastic bunch of people who put the programme together both on and off camera. We would work our socks off all day and then go to the bar in the evening, but I always remember the conversation I had with former presenter Des Lynam shortly after accepting the job. He had warned me then that the recording schedule could be demanding.

'Jeff, by the time you're due to make the fifth show of the day, particularly on the third day of the week, you'll more than likely want to kill somebody,' he said.

He was right. It was fun work, but hard work and after three gruelling years, I realised that I had to concentrate on the football. And given the choice of sitting with Les Dennis (no offence, Les) in Dictionary Corner or Graeme Souness and Harry Redknapp in the San Siro, there was only going to be one winner.

CHAPTER FIVE

FAREWELL COUNTDOWN, HELLO ALESHA DIXON

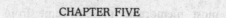

I'll be honest, leaving *Countdown* was emotional. My last show was recorded at the end of November and I'm not ashamed to admit that there were a few tears before the final episode. Like I've said before, despite the heavy recording schedule, I was sad to walk away. I got on well with everyone on the team, from the sound people and camera crew, through to the likes of Rachel Riley and Susie Dent. I think they liked me too, because during my last working shift, gifts arrived throughout the day. There wasn't a horse's head or a 'Chris Kamara Says: "Unbelievable!"' T-shirt among them – though that would have come in handy whenever I had to clean the car.

The most memorable present came from Rachel, who knocked on my dressing room door as I was preparing myself for the last shooting session of the day.

'Come on in, Rach,' I said, wiping the mud pack and cucumbers from my face and putting my glass of sherry to one side for a brief moment.

She shook her head.

'I'm not going to talk . . . I'm going to cry,' she blubbered before running off in tears.

I hadn't expected that at all – people usually break down knowing they're going to have to spend time *with* me. But afterwards Rachel gave me the most fantastic farewell speech in front of the cameras. She then informed the audience that she had found it almost impossible to think of a present to buy me, so what she'd decided to do instead was to prove to the watching millions that I wasn't as short as she had made out during our time together on the show. Kicking off her very high heels, Rachel finally agreed to stand side by side with me in the studio, showing once and for all that we were actually the same height. I thought it was a lovely touch. Now people think both of us are Smurfs, rather than just me.

Because Rachel had started on *Countdown* at the same time as me, we developed a fantastic rapport in our three years together. Obviously both she and Susie must have wondered what the future held for them without me there. It was probably an uncertain time for them, especially as my replacement, Nick Hewer, had previously become notorious for working alongside Lord Alan Sugar on *The Apprentice*, where he often helped his boss to decide upon which hopefuls to fire.

It's funny, part of me felt as if I was letting the pair of them down by leaving, but *Countdown* is an iconic show; it will be for as long as Channel 4 decides to screen it. I honestly think it will go on and on and on. Meanwhile, Rachel's career is in its early stages and she's got a fantastic future in front of her.

Still, it wouldn't be an understatement to say that being the presenter of *Countdown* changed my life in a big, big way. It certainly raised my profile. Stelling Towers is located in a leafy village and it has rather a secluded little community. During my early days on *Soccer Saturday*, I cut a rather anonymous figure in the local shops as I walked to the newsagents in my old Hartlepool tracksuit to pick up the papers. But after my appointment on *Countdown* I couldn't walk down the street without getting accosted, and I had to smarten up my act considerably. Old ladies would jump out of their front door and say, 'Young man! I know who you are now! You've wandered past my door for the last eight years and I didn't know what you did before. Can I have a ticket for *Deal or No Deal*, please?'

Countdown opened me up to a very different crowd to the one that watched *Soccer Saturday*. I wasn't familiar to just a football audience any more, although I know some hardcore *Countdown* viewers became frustrated at the amount of times I mentioned football on the programme. I could see their point, but my biggest problem was that so many contestants were fans that it became next to impossible not to talk about the Beautiful Game. Most of the time they started it.

Anyhow, now I've had a bit of time away from *Countdown*, I've realised that I would like to do something similar in the future. I'd definitely be open to suggestions, especially if the show was of a sufficient quality, so maybe *Family Fortunes* or *Bullseye*, if ever they decided to remake it. Recently I even made an appearance on *Chris Moyles' Quiz Night*, which was a real laugh. I've regularly made a point of turning down a lot of personal appearances over the years because I didn't want to become over-exposed, but also because I was too busy to say yes. I would say no to absolutely everything: *8 Out of 10 Cats* rang me up and wanted to know if I would appear on the show; I was asked to be on *The Xtra Factor* as part of the little panel they have at the end of the programme. I was even asked on to *Celebrity Mastermind*, but strangely not *MasterChef*. I consoled myself in the hope that researchers would have looked at my athletic build and surmised, somewhat accurately, that I was a man of physical dedication and nutritional discipline. They might also have heard through the grapevine that I was just about the worst cook in the world. I can barely make a bowl of cereal, it's really, really embarrassing. I would probably burn Stelling Towers down to the ground if I ever attempted to make beans on toast.

Anyhow, year after year, the researchers on *Chris Moyles' Quiz Night* would call up and ask me to go on as a contestant. As I've said, I always said no because of my time constraints, but I knew that Chris had always been very kind to *Soccer Saturday* on his radio programme, so when I finished *Countdown*, I thought 'What the hell? Let's go for it.' I'd also seen the show a few times and liked it. I reckoned it would be fun and a bit competitive. There was nothing to win, but likewise there was nothing to lose – well, apart from my pride – so I said yes.

My kids were staggered when they heard the news.

'Dad, this show is about modern culture,' they said. 'You know nothing about it!'

They were absolutely right of course, I didn't, but having

brushed up on the latest contemporary musical hits – Adele, *The Best of the Beatles*, Phil Collins' *Greatest Hits* and Jethro Tull's back catalogue – I felt suitably confident I could hold my own. When I arrived at BBC TV Centre for the filming, I learned that I would be sitting alongside three other contestants – Chris himself, Alesha Dixon of *Britain's Got Talent* fame, and comedian Frank Skinner who was a massive West Brom fan – but I sensed things weren't going to go too well when somebody from the programme came into my dressing room to explain the format of the show.

'You're on third, Jeff,' he said. 'That means that you get to choose the topic for one of the rounds. It's a list round and the idea is you name as many things on that list as you can, and when somebody says an answer that isn't on the list, they're out. There are two potential lists, Jeff: there's Steven Spielberg movies and Shakespeare plays . . .'

Well, I fancied Shakespeare's plays. I knew about a dozen off the top of my head, so I told him I'd go for the Bard of Avon.

'Great stuff, cheers, Jeff,' he said, before disappearing. But about ten minutes later, the bloke came back.

'Jeff, I just wanted to make sure you're 100 per cent comfortable with Shakespeare's plays.'

I told him I was happy and that I also happened to think that Alesha might do the best out of the four contestants if I chose Steven Spielberg's films, so I would be able to pick up some valuable points against her. It was a tactical move and hardly in the spirit of the game, but I figured I was on a hiding to nothing in the other rounds.

'Great stuff, cheers, Jeff,' he said, running out of the door again.

Anyway, the contestants went to the green room, everybody seemed really keen to play, and I began running through Shakespeare's plays in my head. Just as I was about to go onstage, the producer tapped me on the shoulder.

'Jeff,' he said, 'I'm afraid you're going to have to go with Spielberg's films. Is that OK?'

I couldn't believe it, the cameras had started to roll and Chris was introducing his guests. Just as I was about to voice my protests, I was announced to the crowd. I felt a gentle push in my back and I was nudged through a pair of curtains and in front of the audience, who were applauding and waving. I was stuck. I had no choice but to wave back while trying to look as cool and calm as I possibly could. So much for making my decision – I had been well and truly stitched up.

Thankfully, when it came to the list round, Frank Skinner was the first to get an answer wrong, but what I noticed straight-away was that Alesha possessed a staggering knowledge of Steven Spielberg films. Maybe she also has a staggering know-ledge of Shakespeare plays, but I had the sneaking suspicion that it was primed in her favour. It didn't end there. The next round featured a giant piano keyboard which was wheeled out in front of the cameras – an instrument not too dissimilar to the one Tom Hanks danced across in the film *Big*; the giant keys which were laid flat upon the floor were played by stamping upon them. We were told that either myself, Frank or Alesha would have to play three tunes on the keys. The other contest-ants then had to guess the tunes. It all sounded pretty straightforward.

When lots were drawn, it was supposed to be Alesha's turn to play the tunes, which, given her musical background was a distinct advantage. However, I thought it actually suited the other contestants because they would have had a better chance of guessing the songs correctly (given her musical ear she would have been able to play them more competently) and I could therefore scoop all the points. That was the theory anyway. Lo and behold, it was decided that because Alesha had high heels on and wouldn't be able to jump across the piano, Frank Skinner should do the round. Subsequently, she got full marks in that round as well; Frank got none.

Amid all this controversy, I was left feeling a little aggrieved, so I decided to get my own back. While Frank performed the first round of songs, I was deliberately left in a booth away from the studio so I couldn't hear Alesha's answers; Frank's songs were piped through to me so I could have a guess when I came back on camera. I was completely left on my own apart from a handful of studio assistants and I must admit, as I heard the tunes I didn't have a Scooby-Doo what they were, but as soon as I was out of shot, I would ask the studio assistants for a bit of help. Brilliantly, they gave me all three answers, so I managed to answer them all correctly (not even I could miss that open goal), which shocked Chris quite a bit.

That round kept me out of last place, which was important because if a contestant finishes last on Chris Moyles' show they then have to sing over the closing credits in front of a live audience. I was pretty keen not to do that. I think the audience were pretty keen for me not to do that either, so by the final round, which was a quick-fire quiz, I was in third place. Alesha was way out in front – which didn't come as a surprise to anyone, least of all Alesha – and Frank was closest to me in last spot. It was squeaky bum time.

Frank managed to buzz in early and got one of the first questions right, which panicked me a bit.

'Oh, crikey,' I thought. 'The pressure's on here. I've got to do something drastic . . .'

Chris asked another question. I buzzed in quickly, but when I got the answer wrong, I thought I'd debate it for ages, not because I believed I was in the right, but because I was counting the clock down. We were running out of time in the studio, so like a good pro – or a Wolves centre half from the kick-off – I began wasting time, seeing out the game in a manner any football manager would have been proud of. In football terms, I was taking the ball into the corner so Frank couldn't get it. Watching Hartlepool for all those years had taught me how to win ugly.

It worked, too. I came in third and Frank had to sing out the show with a version of Queen's 'Don't Stop Me Now'. Overall, the night had been a great laugh. I knew Chris was a big Leeds fan and afterwards he asked me if there was any chance of him becoming a *Soccer Saturday* reporter for the day, on a weekend of my choosing of course. I told him I would put it to the powers that be – I thought it could be a lot of fun. However, after seeing the favouritism dished out to Ms Dixon on his show, I might have to serve him with a cold slice of revenge. Maybe I'll offer Chris the next clash between Millwall and Leeds at their notoriously hostile stadium, The New Den. That'll learn him for messing my questions around.

CHAPTER SIX

WE NEED TO TALK ABOUT PAUL

Long, long ago there was a strange footballer called Paul Scharner, whose madcap appearances on *Soccer Saturday* quickly became the talk of the land. So odd were the antics of West Brom's Austrian international that many people – including me – reckoned he was one stud short of a football boot.

It was easy to see why. During his time in the Premiership with Wigan (2006–10) and, later, the Baggies, Scharner developed into a firm favourite on *Soccer Saturday* because his personality was so crackpot. With every cameo performance on the show (and there were a few) he seemed to become even more eccentric, which made for great telly and went some way to dispelling the myth that Premiership footballers were cardboard cut-outs obsessed with money and devoid of character. I'm not sure what Scharner's bank balance looked like at the time, but I know he had a boundless enthusiasm that would be the envy of Timmy

69

Mallett. He was also very happy to show it off for our cameras, which was a pleasure to see.

One such example of his oddball attitude happened during the 2011/12 season when Scharner called us – that's right, *he* called *us* – and requested that we film him as he travelled into work. Now can you imagine the likes of Steven Gerrard or Frank Lampard offering themselves out for an interview? Of course not, and definitely not one that delivered an interesting insight into their daily lives; it wouldn't happen, not in a million years. Typically, though, Scharner's morning routine didn't involve a leisurely breakfast at home followed by his ride to work in a Baby Bentley. No, it was revealed that his favoured route to training actually involved boarding a 7.30 a.m. train which just so happened to stop at a station near to West Brom's ground. His plan would have taken Sky's camera crew, sound man, producer and reporter on to a carriage full of grumbling commuters. Unsurprisingly, when the club's press office heard about the madcap scheme they put the kibosh on our meeting, but as an example of left-field thinking it certainly confirmed my suspicions that this was not your run-of-the-mill footballer.

The clues were there from the start, though. I had first encountered Scharner when he was playing for Wigan a few years back. I'd been staying in the same Wigan hotel as the team. Before the match I bumped into their then manager Paul Jewell who was an old acquaintance of mine. Paul had appeared on the *Soccer Saturday* panel a few times and we had become pals, so it was arranged that we would have a pint afterwards, along with his assistant, Chris Hutchings.

As we put the world to rights, not to mention Wigan's shaky form, a rather unusual gang of fans sat themselves in one corner of the bar. They immediately caught my eye, not because of their raucous mood, which was at odds with Wigan's defeat that day, but because their attire was so weird: the group comprised a dozen or so men, women and children and all of them wearing T-shirts with Paul Scharner's grinning face printed on the front. It was quite a disconcerting look.

'Who are that lot?' I asked.

'Oh, that's the Paul Scharner Supporters' Club,' said Chris, laughing. 'They're a band of travelling fans from Austria. They fly over for every game, home and away, no matter who we're playing. It's insane.'

At first, I thought it was a wind-up, but the pair of them assured me they were telling the truth and once Paul and Chris had caught the team bus, I went over and chatted to the 'Scharnerettes' for the full story. The Wigan managerial team had not been pulling my leg. It was confirmed that, yes, this mob did follow Paul Scharner, whoever he played for and wherever he played, come hell, high water, or even Hull City. The reward for their loyalty was a chat with their favourite player (that would be Scharner, obviously) after every game, usually in a hotel bar like the one we had been sitting in that evening. The man himself would come over for a quick non-alcoholic drink and a debrief on the match, while regaling his fans with any interesting incidents that had happened along the way. It struck me as the kind of fanaticism most people would associate with a high-profile pop star, such as Justin Bieber or Engelbert Humperdinck, rather than a fairly good Premiership centre half.

Sadly, I didn't get to meet Scharner that evening, but I began to realise that there was quite a circus surrounding his life and once *Soccer Saturday*'s researchers decided that he was worthy of an interview, further evidence of his weird streak appeared. When a meeting was set up, Wigan's press office arranged for the filming to take place at a fancy hotel, which meant there was a genuine lack of enthusiasm for the piece in our offices, mainly because everybody assumed that the cameras would gather nothing more than the stereotypical footballer interview. I figured that at best it would be a bog-standard chat conducted in a neutral venue which displayed very little in the way of individuality or personality. Nothing in Wigan's plans suggested eccentricity on an appropriately large scale – certainly not along the lines of the T-shirt-clad fanatics I'd spotted in the hotel bar during that evening with Paul Jewell and Chris Hutchings – and the piece was sure to be full of the usual platitudes associated with Premiership footballers, the type you see before and after every live game: 'At the end of the day, you know, the gaffer is, you know, happy, so, you know, we've got to keep playing, you know, the way we have been, to be fair. Blah, blah, you know, blah . . .'

We couldn't have been more wrong. When Rob Palmer – aka *Soccer Saturday*'s Man in the North West – and his film crew arrived at the chosen location they were blown away. The hotel in question was a grand, 200-room building with ornate fountains and spectacular statues on a driveway littered with fancy sports cars. Waiting on the steps for them was Scharner, arms wide with a grin to match.

'Welcome to my beautiful home!' he said, hamming it up for the Sky lads. 'Let me show you around, it's a wonderful place I think you'll agree . . .'

For the next hour, Scharner pretended the hotel was his own personal property, complete with swimming pool, lavish bar and snooker room. The staff, who stared at him in complete disbelief, were his 'caterers and butlers'; Scharner was particularly proud of the carpets and furnishings. In fact, he was so convincing that anybody watching the resulting clip would have been completely unaware that the whole thing had been made up for the benefit of our cameras. Even Loyd Grossman and his *Through the Keyhole* team would have struggled to expose his elaborate ruse. The only giveaways would have been the ostentatious reception desk and the gent in Scharner's loo dishing out fancy soaps and towels, which would have been considered extravagant, even by Mario Balotelli's standards.

By the time Scharner had signed for West Brom in 2010, his legend had been furthered quite considerably. During his final appearance at the DW Stadium he sent a message of appreciation to Wigan's fans. The word 'THANX' was coloured on to the back of his skull and the remainder of his hair was dyed blue and white. A transfer to the Baggies did nothing to quell his ebullient streak, however, and shortly after he had arrived at The Hawthorns, a number of newspaper reports did the rounds on Scharner's rather unusual behaviour, where it was noted that West Brom's squad had nicknamed him 'Mr Moanivator', such was his tendency to grumble during games.

'He's a bit of a weirdo,' said his team mate James Morrison. 'He gets on people's nerves, what with his moaning, but he has a lot of experience and you can't take that away from him.'

What I really loved about Scharner's emergence as one of the characters of the game was that he genuinely enjoyed taking the mickey out of himself. Part of this self-deprecation included a series of ridiculous haircuts, some of them even more extreme than the effort shown during his last game at Wigan. His looks included black and white stripes, a red and blue spiky 'do, and one Mr T-style Mohican. Nicky Clarke would have been proud; Ray Wilkins, intensely jealous. Such was the attention lavished upon Scharner's barnet by fans and media that the *Independent* newspaper even described him as 'the eccentric Austrian with the increasingly odd hair', just in case you thought it was only me who had been amused by his chameleon image.

Not everyone was a fan though. Typically, trouble flared when people mistakenly thought that Scharner was taking the mickey out of *them*, which was what happened when West Brom turned over their local rivals Wolves in the 2011/12 season. As the Baggies worked to a 2–0 victory, Scharner decided, rather unwisely, to show fans (some of them from the Paul Scharner Supporters' Club, presumably) the T-shirt he had been wearing under his match kit – a white top with a crude version of West Brom's club crest printed on the front. For some reason, the Wolves players thought that Scharner had taken his celebrations too far, especially as his gesture marked the end of a fiercely contested derby. When the final whistle blew, Wolves' then manager Mick McCarthy was visibly steaming at the ears. One or two Wolves players, most notably Stephen Hunt, confronted Scharner, which made for an ugly scene.

During his post-match interview, Mick was in a pretty huffy mood. 'Scharner had something on his T-shirt and showed it to the lads over the other side of the pitch,' he said. 'There is no need for it and maybe that upset the lads. You can lose but you don't need your nose rubbing in it . . . I get the hump with it. Take the mickey with the ball, that's the game.'

When the dust settled, it later transpired that Scharner hadn't rubbed anybody's nose in it at all. In fact, the shirt had only been flashed at the West Brom fans, and the top was of significance because it had been made by Scharner's son, hence the somewhat crude design. The lad had drawn the club crest on a plain shirt at home and given it to his dad as a present – it had been shown to the fans out of paternal pride rather than a show of chest-beating superiority over their rivals. Mick, in his defence, apologised once he realised the T-shirt had been a bit of harmless fun, but Scharner yet again had found himself at the centre of a rather crackpot kerfuffle. In the West Brom shop, staff even sold a replica 'Paul Scharner Derby Double T-shirt'. Now that wouldn't have delighted Mick and his players, though it should be noted that the shirts were produced for a good cause – 50 per cent of the proceeds went to DebRA, a charity which helps people suffering from Epidermolysis Bullosa, a skin condition which can often lead to painful blistering.

Of course, we loved Scharner's messing around, and after the T-shirt scandal and his aforementioned mock tour of the family 'mansion', I couldn't wait to get him back on to *Soccer Saturday* for another interview. It was almost guaranteed that he would deliver a few giggles, so some months later, Rob called Scharner again and asked him if he would like to do another piece for the show. Unsurprisingly, he was incredibly obliging.

'Of course, Rob! No problem,' he said.

Even less surprisingly, there was an unusual demand attached to the meeting.

'Now, can you meet me on Winding Lane?' he said. 'I'll give you the directions. About 400 yards down that road there's a gap in the hedge. If you crawl through that gap at 2 p.m. on Friday, I'll be waiting for you and we'll do the interview there, OK?'

It seemed absolutely crackers to me, but I knew the rendez-vous carried a huge potential for comedy, so Rob was dispatched in his best rambling gear, an Ordnance Survey map of the Midlands stuffed into the glove compartment of his car.

Locating Winding Lane was straightforward enough, but as the Sky crew battled their way through the branches and thorns at the designated gap in the hedge, they were greeted by the sight of Scharner, who was standing in the middle of a field. Alongside him were two deckchairs – one was for him, the other for *Soccer Saturday*'s Man in the North West – in a setting more befitting *Parkinson* than Sky Sports, should Parky ever decide to conduct his interviews al fresco, that is.

It made for quite a pleasant setting I suppose, but as the interview got underway, filming was interrupted by a shout from across the field. As the crew turned towards the source of the noise, they saw a farmer's wife stampeding towards the cameras with all the grace of a raging bull. Judging by the furious look on her face, she was not entirely thrilled with Scharner's choice of location, or his fancy deckchairs.

'Oi! You lot!' she yelled. 'Clear orf out of our field!' Everyone ran towards the gap that led to Winding Lane fearing a clip round the ear, or worse, a blast of shotgun pellets to the backside.

'Didn't you ask for permission, Paul?' gasped Rob as he dived into the hedge and raced for safety down Winding Lane. Scharner shook his head.

'No, of course not!' he laughed.

Like the day at his 'country home', the venue had all been a joke for Sky's benefit, but this one had backfired rather spectacularly.

No wonder West Brom hadn't exactly jumped for joy when Scharner first suggested his plan to take Sky's cameras on to a busy commuter train. They must have been very aware that his idea of a joke might have involved him dressing up as a ticket inspector. I certainly wouldn't have put it past him to have dished out pretend fines to a carriage full of angry business-men and weary commuters, some of them Wolves fans. It was a shame for us that the stunt didn't come to fruition because it would have made for bloody good telly, but a prank like that could have started a riot.

Scharner was lucky: he wasn't booked for his T-shirt antics in the Wolves game, which is more than can be said for some players. However, when it comes to players getting booked for over-elaborate celebrations, the yellow cards don't come more contro-versial than the case of Liverpool striker Jordan Ibe who was infamously booked in 2011 for hugging some fans following a goal on his league debut (he was playing for Wycombe Wanderers at the time) against Sheffield Wednesday. The referee in question was called Chris Sarginson, and yes, I will name and shame him on this occasion because the decision was insensitive for a number of reasons. Firstly, Ibe was playing his first game in professional football, an overwhelming experience for any player. Secondly, he was 15 years and 355 days old, which made him the youngest ever scorer in the Football League at the time. And finally, after the ball hit the back of the net, he ran to celebrate in front of his family (the fans in question) who had been sitting in the stands, all of them presumably bursting with pride. That could hardly be construed as an attempt to incite the crowd, so why Sarginson felt the need to book him was totally beyond me.

When the news of Ibe's booking came through to us on *Soccer Saturday*, I went nuts. It was another classic example of a referee having no understanding of the game and what a moment like that would have meant to a young man such as Ibe. Furthermore, players like Ibe shouldn't have to weigh up whether they can or cannot take their shirts off to celebrate a goal, or if they can hug their mum in the crowd or not. It's all a bit of fun. Certainly a teenager, who wasn't legally allowed to smoke, play with air rifles, or bed pop stars – all the things that Ashley Cole likes to do – shouldn't have been expected to remain calm in the heat of the moment. Surely, ticking him off would have been enough?

At least Ibe didn't cartwheel and somersault around like an Olympic gymnast. Now, I'm not one to wish misfortune on anyone, least of all a footballer, but how often have you watched Nani – the lovable, charming, not-aggravating-at-all United winger – while performing one of his showy triple somersaults to celebrate a goal and thought, 'Ooh, I do hope you do yourself a mischief, you flash so and so'? I have to admit, the thought has never, ever, not in a million years ever, crossed my mind. But really, there can't be one football manager in the land who hasn't watched one of his super-talented strikers (so not Hugo Rodallega, then) perform a flashy somersault and then angrily promise themselves, 'If that wally injures himself on the way down I'm putting him on the transfer list in the morning.'

'Oh, but it's only a bit of fun, Jeff,' I can hear you cry. 'Stop being such a grumpy old man!' Well, yes, it is only a bit of fun, but what if your star striker ruptured his knee ligaments while celebrating a goal with some amateur gymnastics, rather than in a death or glory tackle for a loose ball in the six-yard box? How would you feel? And have you ever wondered how Nani and Co. get so bloomin' good at their jumps and backflips? My reckoning is they must dedicate at least an hour a week to throwing themselves about like a member of the pop band JLS rather than taking in an extra session of shooting practice or arranging a visit to the local hospital.

Anyone not convinced by my little rant should investigate the injury of Fabian Espindola, an Argentinian striker who currently plays for Real Salt Lake in the David Beckham-sponsored US Soccerball League. Espindola managed to get his head on the end of a hopeful 30-yard volley from his team mate to put his side 1–0 up against LA Galaxy in 2008. Wheeling away in delight, he ran to the bench, hurling his feet over his head in a somersault more reminiscent of a Russian ballet dancer, before landing awkwardly and spraining his ankle. Cameras caught the moment where Espindola frantically waved to the bench, a signal that his game was over. Weirdly, this also coincided with the exact same moment that the ref disallowed the goal. Replays showed that Espindola had been offside as his header pinged into the net.

'I'm embarrassed,' said the stricken striker, having been told he would face six weeks on the sidelines. 'I'm never going to do that again. I don't know what happened. I've done it a million times. If I'd known, I would never have done it.'

Espindola wasn't the first player to have injured himself in embarrassing circumstances, and over the years a whole raft of Premiership stars have slipped up – quite literally – with devastating consequences. Darren Barnard of Barnsley once went bum over boob having put his foot in a puddle of dog pee which had been left on the kitchen floor by his faithful mutt. The resulting ankle ligament injury left him in the treatment room for five months, though at least Barnard's injury was an accident. When Darius Vassell realised he had a rather unpleasant blood blister on his big toe, he decided to lance it, not by going to the club doctors to have it surgically treated as a normal person would do, but by carving through his nail with a power drill. Unsurprisingly, Vassell was struck with a blood infection and had to have his cracked nail removed – not by an electrician with a handy pair of pliers, but by a doctor. Which is probably where he should have gone in the first place.

CHAPTER SEVEN

OFF THE WALL: THE WEIRD WORLD OF THE FOOTBALL CLUB CHAIRMAN

Dear *Jeffanory* reader, for your pleasure, a certain breed of football executive summed up (the succinct version):

Cast your mind back, if you will, to 22 September 2011, when Doncaster Rovers chairman John Ryan made a statement defending his then under-pressure manager, Sean O'Driscoll. Donny had only won three games all year and were rooted to the bottom of the table. Their fans had called for drastic action. Publicly, Ryan promised to stand by his man, and quite defiant he sounded about it, too.

'For the people shouting for the manager's head,' he bellowed, 'I ask the questions, "Who would you replace him with? Who is better?" I can't think of any manager that is better equipped for the job, and those clubs who sack managers willy-nilly end up relegated. The board and I are not going down that path.'

Fast forward 24 hours to Sunday, 23 September 2011, and guess what? Doncaster Rovers had announced that Sean O'Driscoll was officially out of a job.

Funny that.

A certain breed of football chairmen summed up (the longish version):

Not six months before O'Driscoll's P45 had been printed, Fulham chairman Mohamed Al Fayed commissioned the statue of the pop star Michael Jackson and plonked it down at Craven Cottage in full view of 25,700 laughing supporters. There's nothing unusual about the concept: a lot of football clubs have statues outside their stadiums, usually of local heroes done good – Bobby Moore's sculpture at West Ham, Bill Shankly at Anfield, and Kammy at Boro, Pompey, Leeds, Brentford, Stoke, Sheffield United, Swindon Town and Luton all spring to mind. They're all rather good likenesses as well.

Meanwhile, every fan in the land was asking the same question: 'What was Jacko's link to Fulham, again?' Well, as readers of the tabloids knew already, the late singer had once made an unexpected arrival at the club to watch a match against Wigan in 1999. It was all a bit of a freak show at the time, which made Al Fayed's decision to erect a statue to commemorate Jacko's death and that most surreal of days at Craven Cottage all the more stark raving bonkers.

'The last game [Michael Jackson] attended here, he with me, he was running like a child,' said Al Fayed at the statue's unveiling, giving the impression that Jacko liked nothing more than to spend every Saturday afternoon singing, 'We all dream of a team of Barry Hayles' (to the tune of 'Yellow Submarine') from the Hammersmith End, rather than practising his crotch-thrusting moves in a mirror. 'He loved Fulham and wanted to attend all of the matches. People will queue to come and visit it from all over the UK and it is something that I and everybody else should be proud of.'

Good grief! If you think back to all the greats to have played for the club over the years – Bobby Robson, Bobby Moore, George Best, George Cohen, Rufus Brevett, to name but a few – surely the club could have invested in a more worthy alternative? Sure, they already have a Johnny Haynes statue, but I must admit, I thought the Jacko stunt was a belated April Fool's Day joke when I first heard the news. I wasn't the only one. Fulham fans moaned their heads off. Even Rio Ferdinand, elegant commentator on the arts, ranted against the monument on Twitter.

'Did Michael Jackson even like football??!' he tweeted furiously. 'What is a statue of the great man doing outside Fulham FC stadium?!'

Presumably not wanting to go over his 'Tweet limit' of 140 characters, Rio then drew a settling breath before adding: 'Put a poster up not a statue!!! A statue outside a stadium is for people who have achieved great things at that club not for 1lil appearance!'[3]

Having taken the criticism on board, Al Fayed responded in

---

3   I'd like to point out that all grammatical errors, exclamation mark abuse, text abbreviations and spelling mistakes are Rio's own. I am a former presenter of *Countdown*, and was known to find the occasional six-letter word on the show.

the manner adopted by most successful millionaires: he told the haters to stick it.

'If some football fans don't understand and appreciate such a gift this guy gave to the world they can go to hell,' he told the Beeb. 'I don't want them to be fans. If they don't understand and don't believe in things I believe in they can go to Chelsea, they can go anywhere else.'

With that crass statement ringing in the fans' ears, it was left to Fulham's towering centre half Brede Hangeland to deliver the final, decisive verdict from the dressing room. 'Some of our players are Michael Jackson fans, some aren't,' he said. 'And that's the same in the general population.'

So that's that particular argument settled, then.

Now before I go any further, I'd like to point out that I think Al Fayed has done some wonderful things for Fulham since he took over in summer 1997. The success they've had for a club of their size has been unbelievable, and that's mainly been down to the chairman's investment. Only the season before his arrival, Fulham had finished 17th in Football League Division Three (for readers over the age of 30, that's the old Fourth Division; League Two for you youngsters) and to be honest, I thought that was about right for a club of their modest finances at the time. Al Fayed had other plans, though, and while he hasn't exactly displayed great taste in sculpture over the years, he has brought in a string of top-class managers, including Kevin Keegan, Mark Hughes and Roy Hodgson. Fulham later stabilised their position in the Premiership and even reached the UEFA Europa League final in 2010 under Hodgson where they were beaten by Atlético Madrid in extra time.

My issue was that Al Fayed and, to a similar extent, Donny's

John Ryan, had both been victims of an affliction familiar to club chairmen across the globe: Limelight Syndrome, or *Footusin bloodymouthus*, to give its Latin name. Why else would Al Fayed insensitively order fans to switch their allegiance to Chelsea because they wouldn't moonwalk around his Jacko statue in joy? And why else would Ryan have given his manager the dreaded vote of confidence to the press (an act which often sends managers into a panic, much in the same way a rogue wasp unnerves passengers on a packed bus) when keeping his blooming mouth shut would have been a darn sight easier?

You see, my attitude is that the best chairmen should stay out of the spotlight. Wigan's Dave Whelan is a classic example of that. He doesn't interfere, he doesn't shoot his mouth off. A Wigan manager is allowed to organise the team as he wants; he doesn't have to find a place for players that the chairman has brought in. Dave likes his manager to decide how the team should play, not the board, which as some fans might point out, hasn't always been a good thing.

These days, though, there aren't enough Dave Whelans. Former Arsenal and England striker Len Shackleton infamously wrote a chapter in his autobiography, *The Clown Prince of Football*, entitled, 'The Average Director's Knowledge of Football'. I say 'wrote'; what he actually did was to leave his readers staring at a blank page, which spoke volumes. Sadly, that analysis could still be applied to some of the country's current club owners. And while I'm ranting and raving, I should say that I'm very concerned about the wave of super-rich chairmen from overseas buying up English clubs in the Premier League.

Anyone accusing me of turning into Jeremy Clarkson at this point should know that I reckon there have been more rotten

British football club owners than foreign ones. However, I've recently begun suffering from a recurring nightmare. In it, the likes of Sheikh Mansour, Roman Abramovich and the Glazers are sitting together conspiratorially, positioned around a table in a darkened bunker, stroking white cats and crushing cardboard cut-outs of Selhurst Park and Gay Meadow with their ham-like fists (I know it sounds surreal – it's a dream, stay with me).

'So,' cackles Sheikh Mansour, sweeping aside Shrewsbury Town and crushing it underfoot, 'what do you think about my plans to do away with promotion and relegation and therefore kill off the fundamental roots of everything that is good about English football for ever, Mr Abramovich?'

It's usually at this point in the dream that I wake up screaming, my Hartlepool pyjamas soaked in sweat, the Chris Kamara alarm clock buzzing loudly on the bedside table ('It's morning, Jeff! Unbelievable! It's morning, Jeff! Unbelievable!').

Sure, it might seem an unlikely scenario at first glance, not to mention a very, very surreal dream, but my gut feeling is that somebody will seriously present this idea to the Premier League at one stage or another. After all, it's the perfect way in which to protect the financial security of a top-flight football club which is highly dependent on TV money, Premiership merchandising and competition in the shape of Manchester United et al., week in, week out. If you take those lucrative benefits away, the financial pickings can be very slim. And what better way to ring-fence a financial interest in Premiership football than to abolish promotion and relegation to and from the top flight? After all, it's what they do in America, as the likes of Stan Kroenke (Arsenal majority shareholder), Tom Werner (Liverpool chairman), Randy Lerner (Aston Villa chairman), and Malcolm Glazer (Manchester United owner) would testify, as they all hail from the USA. I pray to God that this nightmare scenario doesn't come true.

I'm not the only one who thinks this way. When rumours surfaced that there had been secret meetings in 2011 to discuss this very idea there was uproar from some notable names, including Emperor Fergie.

'I think that it would be absolute suicide for the rest of the [Football] League and particularly teams in the Championship,' he roared to the one journalist not banned from his press conferences. 'You might as well lock the doors. The only place you can make money and realise your ambitions is in the Premier League and you can't take that [hope] away from clubs like Nottingham Forest, Leeds United, Sheffield United and Sheffield Wednesday. All those great teams that formed the nucleus of our old First Division all those years ago. It would be unwise.'

He's right, but I'd like to take his point one step further: if this mad scheme actually becomes a reality in the future, it would mark the death of football in our country.

Some chairmen are all too easy to upset. Southampton's top man Nicola Cortese even had a falling out with the mild mannered Matt Le Tissier, grumbling that he was sick of people asking for free tickets.

'Listen,' Mr Cortese told the *Sun*, 'if I pay for my season ticket then I expect everyone to pay for their ticket too. And I'm not interested in being popular, I'm focused on making this club successful.'

Le Tiss's recollection of events was rather different. By all accounts, Matt had never, at any stage, been after freebies. In fact, he confided in me that he had previously offered to pay for his tickets, which included a cup game against Manchester United in 2010/11. Problems only arose when he was told that, to qualify for a ticket for the cup game, he would have to buy tickets for a match the week before the United tie. Le Tiss was unable to go because he was working for Sky that day; a lot of fans were in a similar position and also declined to go which meant there were a lot of empty seats for the cup match against United, which was a massive shame. A bit of understanding on the club's part could have filled the stadium to the rafters.

I thought it was sadder still that it seemed that Southampton and Mr Cortese couldn't acknowledge the great things that Le Tiss had done for the club in the past. They should have been happy to have him there. Most clubs make a point of celebrating their former superstars: if you go to Old Trafford for a game, you'll see that the stands are full of former players, not to mention their hospitality and executive suites where players turn up either as guests or working ambassadors. It's the same at Liverpool, Arsenal and Spurs.

But there may have been another agenda here. Perhaps Mr Cortese might have had a problem with Le Tiss because of his involvement in a consortium that had previously talked about buying the club. Le Tiss had been the consortium's figurehead chairman and it was their plan to put Kevin Keegan in charge, but for one reason or another the deal didn't work out. I think the damage caused by that scheme had been long term. It might have been one of the initial reasons why Le Tiss and Mr Cortese were at loggerheads.

The most heartbreaking part of this story, dear reader, is that there is no more devoted a fan of Southampton in the country than Le Tiss. I've sat alongside him for years on *Soccer*

Saturday and if ever Saints score during the show he's usually halfway out of his seat, celebrating off camera, which a) sends the crisps stashed under his desk flying across the studio and b) goes some way to doubling the movement he showed during his entire playing career. Nobody could ever doubt his passion for Saints.

Although Mr Cortese was trying to outline the business ethos of a modern football club by saying that nobody – not even the chairman – should expect free tickets, by claiming that Le Tiss was after 'freebies here, freebies there', he was out of order, especially after the service the player had given to his club. On the day of his outburst I tried to put Mr Cortese straight during the show. I even read his comments out live after the final scores.

'Well, Mr Cortese,' I said, 'I do hope you've been misquoted: Matt Le Tissier, 17 years at Southampton, the ultimate One Club Man. He could have gone to Spurs or Chelsea or Liverpool; he didn't. He stayed, he scored 209 goals, he's referred to by fans as "Le God".

'You should give him tickets for life . . . if he was willing to come back. And because he's Southampton through and through, he would be willing to come back. Don't tell me the game's moved on, no Southampton fan will ever forget what Matt Le Tissier gave to that club.'

It needed addressing and I was happy to stand up for Le Tiss. After all, he would have been too embarrassed to have said something on air himself.

I don't want to alienate Southampton here, because I'm a big fan of what they do on the pitch. They've produced some cracking footballers, such as Gareth Bale who looks like a world beater, Theo Walcott and, hopefully, Alex Oxlade-Chamberlain, who has shown a fair deal of potential at Arsenal. My problem with the club stems from how they run things off the pitch, because I've experienced it at first hand. Last year, for instance, I went to see Saints play a Carling Cup second-round game, which was effectively against Bolton's reserves, yet they were still charging £25 a ticket. Elsewhere, the likes of Liverpool were only charging a fiver for their respective fixtures because they were fielding a weakened team and didn't want to short-change the fans for a fixture where the big stars wouldn't be on show.

I also worry that the chairman doesn't understand the traditions of the club and the importance of those traditions. In 2010 there was an event celebrating Southampton's 125th anniversary. Legendary names like Le Tiss, Francis Benali and Lawrie McMenemy were there, as well as Kevin Keegan and Alan Shearer, but the chairman didn't attend. At that point he was already becoming an ever so slightly controversial figure at the club because of a problem that seemed to revolve around the then manager, Alan Pardew. Saints had been placed in administration and the team suffered a ten-point deduction by way of a punishment. That situation caused a lot of problems between the management team and Mr Cortese, as you can imagine. Matters weren't helped when Mr Cortese claimed that the ten-point deduction was irrelevant because the club had spent £2 million to £3 million on new players. He also believed that their appearance in the Johnstone's Paint Trophy was unimportant, despite the efforts made by the coaching staff to get them there.

'We have to get into the play-offs,' he said.

There was a constant friction between the pair of them, which eventually led to Pardew being sacked, but his dismissal was incredibly unpopular with the fans. They loved him down there and they still do – they thought he was doing a great job. So had Mr Cortese attended the 125th birthday celebrations, it would have won so much support from the supporters and the people in the town. I'm not saying for one minute that Nicola Cortese doesn't want the best for the club, because I think that he does and they've been doing fantastically well of late. I just don't think that he understands what the names of Le Tissier, Keegan, Benali and McMenemy have done for Saints over the years and just how much they are loved and appreciated by the supporters.

In the fall-out from the ticket debacle, a number of chairmen of rival clubs got to hear about Le Tiss's situation and began inviting him to their games as a guest of honour whenever their team came up against Southampton. Their South Coast rivals Bournemouth invited Le Tiss and Benali to a game and Brighton's manager Gus Poyet provided Tiss with tickets for the Championship fixture against Saints later that season. Now that can't be right.

The truth is, Le Tiss knows a fair bit about running a football team himself. As the president of his home club Guernsey FC, he's helped to establish the side during their tricky first season in the Combined Counties League Division One, which is basically the sixth level on the non-league football pyramid. Guernsey FC's biggest problem is their location. Given that their Footes Lane Stadium is situated on an island, it costs a hell of a lot of dough for the opposition to fly over for league matches. The club's answer was to fork out for the away team's flights to and from the game, not to mention their overnight stay in a hotel and the parking charges at the airport.

This generosity all added up to a whopping £200,000 over the course of the 2011/12 season (and was part of the league's requirements when they joined), a figure which would probably have covered the cost of Southampton's season tickets for an entire league campaign. Not that Le Tiss cared too much. On the day of Mr Cortese's announcement in the *Sun*, Guernsey FC put nine goals past Sheerwater to go top of the league. As a proper football fan, it would have gone some way to easing his bad mood.

CHAPTER EIGHT

THE GOOD, THE BAD AND THE VEGAN

Ever imagined that the chairman of your football club has begun the working morning in a deliberately controversial and topsy-turvy manner? Of course you have. And when imagining their working modus operandi, I bet the scene in your mind has looked a little bit like this . . .

[STAGE SETTING: THE BEDROOM; THE CLOCK READS MIDDAY]

MR FAT CAT, CHAIRMAN OF HARCHESTER UNITED: 'Hmm, it's a fine day . . . What minor disaster can I unleash on the unsuspecting football public to inadvertently derail my club's slim chances of promotion/Champions League glory/mid-table mediocrity?'

[MR FAT CAT WEARS SILK PYJAMAS; HE PUFFS ON A CIGAR AND SIPS FROM A FLUTE OF CHAMPAGNE. TROPHY WIFE MASSAGES HIS SHOULDERS IN A DISINTERESTED FASHION]
'And how can I conduct this mission while making a complete and utter buffoon of myself in the process? Ah, ha, ha, ha, ha . . .'

Of course I'm joking. I'm sure my nightmarish vision couldn't be further from the truth – everyone knows that champagne is a breakfast drink and lunch begins with the sniff of cognac – but sometimes I do wonder if the football chairman's main ambition in life is to occasionally tickle the hooters of his paying fan base. I say this only because many of them do it so expertly, either by grand design or just through sheer accident. Take the somewhat spectacular example of Mansfield Town chairman John Radford who offered the very glamorous-looking, but previously unknown Carolyn Still a job as his chief executive in September 2011. Now, don't get me wrong: Still was more than qualified for the role. She had worked for a string of top fashion companies such as Gucci and Bulgari and arrived with bucketloads of boardroom savvy. And despite the fact that she was only 29 years of age, and therefore the youngest chief exec in English football, the club held high hopes for her career.

There was a hitch when she became the subject of a debate entitled, 'Is Carolyn Still Football's Sexiest CEO Ever?' (© the *Metro* newspaper). But her talents were in no way questionable and she initially looked set to become the latest in a line of successful women in football, alongside Karren Brady of West Ham and Cherie Lunghi in TV's *The Manageress*.

Feathers among Mansfield's drooling fans were only ruffled once Still had managed to hit the headlines a few weeks after her appointment. According to some of the red tops, it turned out that she had once worked as an escort girl with the exotic name 'Luella'. By all accounts, Still had been 'lured' into 'escorting' and had posed for 'raunchy Internet photos'. She also received 'rave reviews' from 'punters'; it was quite the 'scoop'. Almost predictably, it was later announced that Still, or Luella, depending on when and how you had met her (not that I had, I hasten to add), had become engaged to Radford, which absolutely everybody in the land was ecstatic about. Well, everybody at the tabloids, who tore the pair to pieces.

Very occasionally though, and often through sheer luck, the football chairman might forget about making headlines for all the wrong reasons and actually happen across a halfway decent idea during his midday, champers-fuelled brainstorm. Like at Brighton & Hove Albion, where ground staff once had to suffer the indignity of being pooped upon by the pigeons roosting in the stands at their £93 million Amex Stadium. At the suggestion of one bright spark, the club went out and brought several hawks to scare Brighton's messy dive bombers away from their perches. Somewhat miraculously it worked and now matchday stewards are able to go to games without the protection of a tin hat. Staff even nicknamed one of the sky-high bouncers 'Agro', though I'm not sure where the spelling comes from.

My beloved Hartlepool have been the benefactors of some similarly sharp ideas. Pools' chairman Ken Hodcroft ensures that the club is run on a very strict budget these days, although he can be a bit of a disciplinarian. During one end-of-season club do he waltzed up to me and insisted I swap my rather nice Matalan tie for an official club number, which he then dangled authoritatively in front of my face. I reluctantly agreed despite being rather miffed at the request, but overall, he runs the ship rather well.

For a while we were the worst supported team in the division until Ken and our chief exec Russ Green came up with a scheme to flog season tickets for a cut price. There was a clause to the arrangement, however: basically 4,000 season tickets needed to be bought by 1 July if the tickets were to be sold at a price of £100 (the figure would have risen to £150 per ticket had 4,000 been sold by 15 July; £180 had it taken until 1 August to sell them). The local press ran a campaign, and everyone who purchased a season ticket then encouraged their mates to buy tickets because they wanted to make sure the price stayed at £100. It was a great plan and it seemed to work overnight. Suddenly the attendance figures rocketed from 2,000 to 6,800, and Victoria Park was (nearly) busy for every fixture. It brought a whole new atmosphere to the games, though as Pools midfielder Ritchie Humphreys confessed to me some time afterwards, 'It used to be that we only worried about 2,000 people booing us. Now we might have to deal with 6,800 people moaning about the results.'

On other occasions, the well-meaning club owner can end up with an egg or two on his face, especially the chairman hell-bent on a one-man mission to stand up for whatever he believes in, as the fans of Blue Square Bet Premier League club Forest Green Rovers know only too well. Their particular crusader happened to be Dale Vince, former new-age traveller, owner of green electric company Ecotricity and a devout vegan. To be fair, Dale brought some pretty good eco-friendly ideas to the club. He became mates with my new Sky colleague Gary Neville, and together the pair endeavoured to spread the eco message across football. They even launched a new initiative called 'Sustainability in Sport', which, as the title suggests, is currently attempting to make the business much more environmentally savvy.

Given Dale's passion for the environment, it came as no great surprise when Forest Green Rovers were named as the greenest football club in Britain. The club deserved the accolade: they had submitted plans to build solar panels and a solar tracker into the charmingly titled The New Lawn stadium; the ground even had a stand called the Western Thermal Stand, and when their futuristic, energy-trapping panelling was installed, the club self-generated 10 per cent of the ground's electricity, which was more than enough juice to brew up a half-time cuppa for 4,836 (the club's record attendance for the FA Cup third-round tie against Derby County in 2009). Dale even had the bright idea of spreading cow dung across The New Lawn's pitch, an idea he hoped would result in the Soil Association declaring the ground organic.

'The smell is a bit lively,' said team manager Dave Hockaday. 'But the pitch is looking fantastic.'

If there was one ricket in Dale's eco-friendly blueprints then it was the matchday grub, which everyone knows should comprise all of the recommended five-a-day food groups: pastry, stodge, grease, gravy, and a flash-fried meat from an indiscriminate source. Rather unusually, Dale wanted to introduce a selection of healthier snacks to the fans, so a number of vegetarian dishes were placed on the club menu; controversially he also removed all the red meat on sale. It wasn't long before the grumbling started, especially once the heroic meat pie so loved by supporters around the country became a banned substance at The New Lawn.

Dale's theory was sound: 'You have to feed a cow 10 kilos of soya protein to get one kilo of cow [by cow he meant beef],' he said when we interviewed him on *Soccer Saturday* one afternoon. 'So you can feed 10 vegetarians [with 10 kilos of soya protein] or one meat eater. There is a big environment issue – the planet is overcrowded and we're struggling to feed ourselves. So there is an environmental driver [behind the menu change], but our main drive is health.

'If red meat isn't good enough to feed our players, then it isn't good enough for our staff, fans and visitors,' continued Dale. 'At worst it means once every two weeks watching a football game without being able to eat red meat. Anybody that really needs it can bring a ham sandwich if they wish – that's no problem.'

I suppose this was a nice idea on paper. Fans are for ever moaning about the lack of decent grub on offer at football stadiums and if you've ever had to suffer the balti pies at most football grounds then the thought of tucking into a lentil salad is probably an attractive proposition. The biggest problem with Vince's leaner, greener half-time snacks (and apologies to the catering staff at The New Lawn if this causes offence) was that the vegetarian burgers being served at Forest Green tasted blooming awful. And I know because I ate one.

By way of drumming up publicity for his scheme, Dale sent a selection of his finest veggie burgers for us to try live on *Soccer Saturday*. I could see why he needed the PR. Apparently he was keen for people to eat them because Forest Green Rovers were selling the burgers at cost price and some pretty high quality ingredients were going into them. Well, ingredients that were more expensive than your bog-standard meat and potato pie, anyhow.

'[It's] the kind of stuff that finds its way into your average pie, or burger, or sausage, that shocks me,' said Dale on the show, before we tucked in. 'It would shock anybody to know what parts of the animal are allowed in those products – it's the parts you can't do anything with; the parts that you wouldn't believe are in there. One of the things we're trying to do is to bring our environmental message to this new audience and say, "Look, there are better ways to eat and better ways to live ..." The alternative foods when you try them are really quite wonderful.'

Anyway, as Dale was chatting away, the catering staff at Sky cooked up some burgers for the panel and me to try and, I have to say, they looked good and they smelt good. When we bit into them they actually tasted rather good, but after a few mouthfuls it became apparent that what divided Dale's creations from the traditional meat variety was the texture. The burgers were bloody horrible. When I bit into one it felt like I was sinking my teeth into a block of soggy cardboard. Needless to say, Dale, if ever I'm visiting Forest Green Rovers in the future, I'll be bringing my ham sandwiches.

Still, no matter what Dale and his Forest Green Rovers staff served up to the fans at half-time, at least they had the decency to leave their players out of the crossfire, which is more than can be said for Venky's Chicken – Blackburn Rovers' current owners and purveyors of 'The Chicken Lollipop' (a product that constituted a ball of chicken with a bone serving as the 'lollistick'), perhaps one of the few foodstuffs that might convince me to persevere with Forest Green Rovers' cardboard burgers. At the beginning of the 2011/12 season, the Indian company decided to utilise their high-profile football investment and pushed their players in front of a camera crew for an advert which plugged their wide range of drumsticks and chicken wings. The subsequent TV campaign was so embarrassing that it quickly became an Internet sensation.

Set in the Rovers dressing room, the performance showed Blackburn's first team – Michel Salgado, Morten Gamst Pedersen and Ryan Nelsen included – as they stood in their pre-match huddle. Somewhat surreally, all 11 players marked the sign of a cross on their chests, presumably bringing mercy upon their bowels, before tucking into a plate of chicken drumsticks and thighs lavishly slathered in a sticky, spicy sauce. It didn't end there, though. In the next scene, the team walked on to the pitch suitably stuffed; Ryan Nelsen was filmed licking his lips, such was the joy of his sumptuous pre-match snack.

'I think I came off worst,' moaned Michel Salgado in his *FourFourTwo* column, when recalling the filming session afterwards. 'I'm not a big fan of spices and strong sauces . . . I had to pretend I loved it, but the truth is, one bite and my stomach was in knots!'

Now, I'm no nutritionist, but if this were a common practice in English football, Arsène Wenger – the discoverer of broccoli and inventor of energy drinks – would have run for the hills by now. I can't imagine any of his players eating a bowl of Indian chicken wings moments before stepping out at the Emirates. Well, maybe Abou Diaby, who once confessed, somewhat controversially, to wandering around his house in a Spurs shirt given to him by Tottenham defender Younes Kaboul, which wasn't the smartest of moves.

'It is more difficult to wear in the street,' he said, stating the bleedin' obvious. 'There you are not safe.'

Anyway, I've digressed slightly, but my point is this: even

in the days of pre-match steaks and post-match drinking sessions, this type of nutritional preparation would have been frowned upon. Terry Venables often tells a story of how 1960s goal machine Jimmy Greaves once ate an entire roast dinner (with extra roast potatoes, topped off with a helping of spotted dick and custard) before a big Spurs match. Greavsie then went on to score a hat-trick, but at least he had the sense to wait a couple of hours before kicking a ball around. If the Venky's advert was to be believed, Blackburn Rovers were warming up for games with a bucket feast and a bad case of wind, which might explain why they rarely challenge the upper reaches of the Premiership these days.

Of course I myself know just how much hard work goes into producing a TV advert as I found out to my cost when Carlsberg asked me to be the face – and belly – of their 2010 World Cup campaign. For those of you who haven't seen it, the minute-long film showed a crowd of former sporting legends cheering on the England football team as they walked on to the pitch, which happened to be at Millwall's end-of-the-earth stadium The New Den and just about the furthest away you could possibly get from South Africa, where the competition was being held. Among the cast were Sir Ranulph Fiennes, Sir Ian Botham, Sir Steve Redgrave and Phil 'The Power' Taylor. My job in all of this was to tear my shirt off to reveal the Cross of St George daubed across my manly chest while screaming, 'Come on!' into the camera.

I must admit, when it was first suggested to me, I assumed that the film crew would be using a similarly sized body double, somebody like Hugh Jackman. But no, that was not the case, they definitely wanted to use my full, original, genuine physique in HD. The first problem popped up – quite literally – when I was ordered to take my shirt off for make-up. The crew had decided to film in the dead of winter and my nipples soon stood to attention in the cold like a pair of fighter pilot's thumbs. I really began to panic, however, when the make-up girl took one look at my hairy chest and started to make funny faces.

'Hmm, I'm not sure, but I might have to shave this,' she said, staring at me as if she'd been confronted by Chewbacca in a dark alley.

By 'this' she did, of course, mean my lustrous body hair and there was only one man who could make the final call: the director. Grumbling somewhat, I then had to walk out to the pitch, still topless, to the Man In Charge who was filming Carl Fogarty on a rather fancy-looking motorbike.

'Can you take a look at Jeff's chest?' she said, as I nodded a hello at Carl with a sheepish look on my face. 'Does it have to come off?'

It was heart-in-mouth time. The director stared at me. Arguably the world's greatest Superbike racer of all time stared at me. I looked down at my manly chest. The thought of looking like Cristiano Ronaldo for the best part of Christmas brought me out in a cold sweat. Thankfully, the director could sense my pain and informed the make-up girl that my rug could stay and I was daubed in red and white paint for filming. Sadly, my problems didn't end there. After we'd 'wrapped' for the day, I found that my warpaint was impossible to remove. Warm, soapy water couldn't shift the paint, even methylated spirits failed to do the trick.

I was in a rush to get back to Stelling Towers, so the make-up girl tipped some meths into a water bottle, leaving me to clean up when I got home, but when I eventually got to my seat on the train, people started to stare at me in a very strange way. My shirt was open ever so slightly at the top, and I had smudged red paint around the base of my neck, which must have resembled blood to the other passengers. By the time I arrived in Winchester, the stares and pointing had got so bad that I scurried off the train in a rush and forgot to pick up the bottle of methylated spirits which I'd left on the table. The bottle of methylated spirits that quite easily could have passed for a complimentary refreshment given that it had been poured into an empty mineral water bottle.

'Please God,' I thought as I tried to sleep later that night, 'I hope nobody has consumed that awful concoction. That would be terrible.'

I wonder if Dale Vince or the Venky's have ever whispered the same silent prayer?

CHAPTER NINE

AWAY DAYS

I'm always amazed at the extreme lengths to which some fans will go in order to watch their team in action, mainly because I rarely get to Hartlepool these days. My day job inconveniently begins at 10 a.m. on a Saturday morning when I roll in to make-up for a spot of blusher and lippy. By seven, I'm often finished, which is usually about the time most fans are sinking their fifth or sixth celebratory/consolatory pint of the afternoon. Meanwhile, because of Pools' less than glamorous reputation, the team have rarely made it on to *Super Sunday*, so I don't get to see them on the box; I miss our traditionally early exit from the Carling Cup because I have to cover the games for Sky. So all in all, I make do with the odd pre-season friendly and a midweek away game down south whenever my diary allows it, which always makes me feel really rather guilty.

People often question how much of a fan I really am, so I'm delighted to be able to inform the 'non-believers' that when I was 17, I hitchhiked to Scunthorpe with a mate for an FA Cup first-round replay at Scunny's former stadium, the Old Show Ground, which was pretty much derelict in those days. I stood on the terraces, and as we didn't have enough money to get back home, we planned to hitch back as well. Miraculously, Hartlepool won 1-0 in extra time. My mood was improved further when I began chatting to a few of the Pools supporters as we left the ground.

'Look, we've got spaces on our coach back,' said one of them. 'Why don't you jump on with us?'

Well, we were overjoyed. The driver was fine with it and we took our seats secure in the knowledge that we had a safe journey back to Hartlepool. Well, that was the theory anyway. Despite the fact that we had a police escort to the edge of the town, by the time we had travelled 400 yards from the ground, virtually every window on the bus had been smashed in with rocks and bottles. The occupants of the bus, myself included, were cowering under the seats and the driver had a tin hat on. It's possibly the only time that I've ever considered hitchhiking to be the safest route home after a game of football.

Anyhow, my tales of travels far and wide pale in comparison to the journey made by Kazuaki Kanda, a 21-year-old student who flew 8,000 miles from Osaka in Japan to England (via Egypt), not to visit one of the Premiership's grand old cathedrals such as Old Trafford or Anfield as you'd expect, but instead to watch his beloved Torquay United take on non-league Crawley Town in the FA Cup in 2011. They lost 1-0, which probably made the daunting trip back slightly irksome I'd imagine, but by the sounds of things Mr Kanda had a whale of a time.

'I love Torquay,' he said afterwards. Then putting a halt to any suggestions that he might be completely stark raving bonkers, he added that he'd previously gone to school in the town, hence his support. 'I just couldn't miss this match, I love it here. When I found out the Gulls had made it through [to the FA Cup fourth round], I knew I had to come over. I was so excited.

'My parents and friends back in Japan think it's great, they're all behind me. I'm planning to come back next season to watch Torquay again anyway – the club is in my heart.'

At least Mr Kanda had his course in Sociology and Social Welfare to go back to when he returned home. When Bolton fan Ian Wagstaff was told he wouldn't be able to take time off from his job at a sheet metal company to watch his team take on Stoke in the 2011 FA Cup semi-final, he jacked in his job, which just happened to be in Brisbane, Australia. Wagstaff then spent a small fortune flying around the globe to England. God knows what must have gone through his mind as he watched Owen Coyle's men capitulate 5–0.

'I'm devastated,' he told the papers in one of the understatements of the year. 'But I wouldn't change anything. Apart from the result.' And the decision to quit his £38,500 a year job, presumably.

Still, when I do occasionally get to feel the inevitable pain of travelling to games – both home and away – I seem to suffer more than most. I'm still haunted by the time that Pools made their ill-fated League One play-off final appearance against Sheffield Wednesday in 2005. When I secured a ticket for the game I was absolutely delighted. It was the first time we'd ever climbed to those dizzy heights – the opportunity of qualification to the Championship via the play-offs! Not one diehard fan thought we'd ever have a chance of making it that far when the season started, so getting to the Millennium Stadium was dreamland stuff and I was thrilled to be in attendance.

I must admit, I fancied Pools' chances in the final. We'd beaten our opponents Sheffield Wednesday 3–0 a few weeks previously, but admittedly that game should never have been played. The pitch was waterlogged and it was more like a water polo match. Regardless of the result, though, we still went to the Millennium Stadium as underdogs with the bookies, but I didn't realise just how insignificant Wednesday fans considered our chances until I was questioned during an interview for *Soccer Saturday*'s cheekier 'little brother' show *Soccer AM* the day before the game.

On the show with me that day was actor Thomas Craig, a Wednesday fan who previously had played *Coronation Street* car mechanic Tommy Harris. Craig's main claim to fame arrived when he was murdered on the show by his fictional daughter Katy. It had been rather an apt death, too: Katy bashed him over the head with a monkey wrench.

I'm not a violent man, dear *Jeffanory* reader, but not long after talking to him, I actually began to feel a degree of sympathy for his killer, especially once 'Tommy' had started to run Hartlepool down on the show. In fact, I actually felt like reaching for a tool box of my own at one point.

'Well, of course, we belong in the Championship,' he bragged. 'Unlike a club like yours. For a small team like Hartlepool, an afternoon at the Millennium Stadium is as good as it'll get. You should make the most of a nice day out.'

I fumed, but managed to bite my tongue during the broadcast. The following day, my simmering resentment of Tommy bloody Harris subsided once we'd taken a 2–1 lead with nine minutes remaining; nine minutes to go until the promised land of Championship football. Nine minutes away from a place where, as a grown man, I never thought I'd see Hartlepool play.

Paul Sturrock was in charge of Wednesday at the time and he decided to throw on three forwards to play alongside the two he already had on the pitch. They were last-ditch, kamikaze tactics for sure, but despite his 2-3-5 formation, Pools never really looked in trouble, not until Wednesday's striker Drew Talbot chased after a very hopeful through ball that he barely looked like reaching. As he was on his way, our centre half Chris Westwood suffered a massive rush of blood to the head and bundled him over. To be fair I thought he'd got the ball first and despite the fact that the ball was in the goalkeeper's hands when the incident happened (and therefore there was no goalscoring opportunity in any shape or form), referee Phil Crossley blew for a penalty and showed Westwood the red.

It was absolutely ridiculous. Sheffield Wednesday scored from the resulting spot kick, the game went to extra time and our ten men were outplayed. We eventually lost 4–2. As if that wasn't bad enough, a friend of mine, John Hunt, who had watched the game alongside me at the Millennium Stadium, was getting a terrible earful from his wife, mainly because he'd made a pilgrimage that placed Messrs Kanda and Wagstaff well and truly in the shade.

John had been holidaying with his family in France, and on the morning of the game he had told his other half that he was taking the car to pick up some fresh croissants and pains au chocolat for breakfast. Rather than turning right for the local boulangerie, however, John turned left for the ferry port, where he boarded a boat to Dover and then drove all the way to Cardiff. His ticket for the game had been secretly stashed away in the glove compartment of his car before the family had left for their hols, and during our separate journeys to Wales I received frequent texts informing me of his whereabouts. By the time he had arrived at his seat, the game was only ten minutes in. It was really quite an effort.

John's crusade was a massive waste once Mr Crossley had flashed his red card and ruined Hartlepool's afternoon, however. He drove back to France knowing full well that his wife was waiting to use a stick of crusty bread to attack a very sensitive part of his anatomy. I made the sorry walk to my hotel room in Cardiff at 6 p.m., drew the curtains and got into bed where I dreamt peacefully of cracking Tommy Harris over the head with a spanner. John, meanwhile, was probably praying for divine intervention. Or at the very least a plane ticket to the other side of the world.

Like my mate John, or Tommy bloody Harris, you probably don't know of Dafydd Ryder Owen, banker and Manchester United fan, though, chances are, at least one of those descriptions of his life may have already given you cause to pre-judge him. Nevertheless, Dafydd is a prime example of a particular breed of football supporter: the over-excitable and reckless; the type who has 'Samir Nasri: Arsenal Forever' tattooed on his backside only for Nasri to sign for Manchester City. In this case, Dafydd's particular object of desire was Sergio Aguero – a player who hadn't even signed at Old Trafford when he splashed out on a fancy number plate for his motor, 'KUN 16', the nickname and squad shirt of the multimillionaire striker who then went on to sign for City and definitely not United.

Anyone not feeling a degree of sympathy for a supporter of the Premiership's most successful club and a worker in the industry largely blamed for the global economic crisis might shed a tear at the fact that Dafydd had blown a four-figure sum – maybe 'only' £1,000, or maybe a 'whopping' £9,999 – on his needless number plate. The registration was still proudly stuck to his car when City thumped United 6–1 at Old Trafford in 2011, with 'KUN 16' banging in one of the goals.

'I've got to get rid of it,' he moaned afterwards. 'I'm receiving terrible stick from friends after that beating by City, especially as Aguero scored. I'm gutted United didn't sign him.'

The last I'd heard, Dafydd was intent on flogging the plate and splitting his profits with UNICEF, which just goes to show that not all bankers are bad. Just wildly reckless with their money (and ours). Still, his over-exuberance went some way to reminding me that, sometimes, the game causes us to get over-excited. But even his enthusiasm was dwarfed by Conor Cunningham, a non-banker (a part-time fitness instructor, actually) and Republic of Ireland fan who found himself without a ticket as his nation prepared to take on Estonia in the first leg of the play-off for the finals of the 2012 European Championships. The fact that Conor had not secured entry to the game didn't stop him from travelling to Estonia's capital Tallinn, a journey which took him 24 hours as he had travelled via London, Stockholm and Riga. Once he arrived at the A. Le Coq Arena, he was offered a ticket to the tune of €600, or £515 in real money, which was way beyond his budget, so Conor devised a sure-fire way of getting into the ground: he wandered into an unguarded, open door, where to his surprise he found a bag of match balls and an official Estonian track-suit. Slipping into his disguise, Scooby-Doo-style, Conor then wandered out to the pitch where he handed out footballs to various players from both sides, generally giving the impression that he very much knew what he was doing and looking for all the world like an Estonian trainer, albeit one who didn't speak a word of Estonian.

Perhaps Conor's role as a fitness instructor helped his cause. It's unlikely that a fan with a roly-poly physique would have been passed off quite so easily as one of Estonia's coaching staff, and when Conor decided to embellish his foray into the stadium by sitting on the Estonia bench, nobody batted an eyelid. Not even Estonia's boss Tarmo Ruutli, who seemed so concerned by the 4–0 walloping being inflicted upon his team that he didn't notice the stranger sitting alongside him in a tracksuit with a bag full of balls.

It was only when the final whistle was blown and the Republic had won handsomely that Conor gave the game away. Overjoyed with the victory he wandered on to the pitch and began chatting with the Ireland players as they left the field of play with their tickets for Poland and Ukraine effectively booked.

'When the match was over and Ireland had qualified,' he told a journalist from the *Guardian*, 'I said I'd chance my arm and walked out on to the pitch. I celebrated with the players, shook hands with them all and even asked a few if I could have their jerseys. Keith Andrews said I could have his, but I didn't get to see him again after they went into the dressing room.'

It was a great tale and Conor's adventure reminded me, somewhat loosely, of a time when I blagged my way into a play-off semi-final, first-leg tie against Blackpool, courtesy of the Seasiders' boss, my one time *Soccer Saturday* team mate, the former Liverpool and England titan Steve McMahon. We'd become friends when he was on the show, and to be fair to him, he was a really good pundit – a bit scary at times because he took no prisoners, which was pretty much the way he had played his football, but insightful, really opinionated and also a lot of fun. So when it came to asking for a few tickets for some friends and me, I knew there would be no problem.

The only hitch came when the Hartlepool manager Chris Turner had a right go at Blackpool in the press and claimed his team were getting to the final, no problem. Understandably Steve and his backroom staff were a bit annoyed at this, but before the game they played the role of perfect hosts regardless. We went into the club office beforehand and everybody seemed very laid-back. Around 2.30 he got up and said, 'I've just got to go down to the dressing room, won't be a minute.'

Off he went, presumably to give a lengthy and rousing pre-match team talk, but I noticed in his hand he had a bundle of cuttings which had been given to him by one of his backroom staff, a quiet lad who had been cutting up newspapers from the minute we had sat down in Steve's office.

Anyway, two minutes later Steve came back. I couldn't believe it: the game was probably Blackpool's biggest of the season so far and he had delivered his team talk in double quick time.

'Blimey, that was quick, Steve,' I said, tucking into another beer.

'Yeah, I didn't have anything to do,' he said. 'I just showed them these.'

He handed me one of the newspaper cuttings – it was the article in which Chris Turner had proclaimed, 'Hartlepool are the best side in this division. We'll beat Blackpool, blah, blah, blah . . .'

My heart sank; I knew their lot would be fired up. Indeed Steve hadn't had to say anything, he only had to hand out the local paper to motivate his troops and it turned out to be enough because we were beaten 2–0.

As I mentioned earlier, Steve had a cracking sense of humour, something people didn't normally attribute to him, given his fearless style of play. That day he found it highly amusing to give me tickets that positioned me slap bang in the middle of the Blackpool fans. What a nightmare that turned out to be.

Of course, by that time people knew who I was and what I did for a living. They also knew that I was a Hartlepool fan, so plenty of banter was thrown my way as I sat down to watch the game. The two teams went in at half-time with the score poised at 0–0 and it was the greatest 0–0 of all time, because we should have been 10–0 down. We had been annihilated. It was to get worse, however, because all the way through the second half, a pensioner, who was sat behind me, started punching me in the back.

'There you go,' he shouted, landing a blow on my shoulder. 'Chris Turner said you were the better team.'

Blackpool scored their first.

'What are you doing sitting with the Blackpool fans anyway? 1–0, ha!'

Bang! Another punch.

'What are your lot doing here coming down to this game?'

Their second went in. Bang! He hit me again.

'I told you so . . .'

I'd just about had enough. I turned around furiously.

'If you lay one more finger on me, you stupid old so and so, there will be trouble,' I warned him, very politely.

My mate tapped me on the shoulder. 'Jeff, don't. Think of the headlines: "Sky Sports Presenter Attacks Blackpool Pensioner

(And It's Not Rodney Marsh)!" Calm down, don't do it.'

I knew he was right. So I satisfied myself by scolding the attacker with a few finger wags and the promise that when Blackpool returned to Victoria Park it would be a completely different story. And how right I was. We lost 3–1.

Luckily for me, my friend was there to offer his wise counsel, otherwise there's a pretty good chance that I would have jotted down that story from a prison bed, Johnny Cash-style. At least if the case of 63-year-old granny of 13, Margaret 'Mags' Musgrove is anything to go by. When she ran on the pitch during the Leeds United lap of honour at the end of the 2010/11 season, she was grabbed by a club steward and chucked in the stadium's holding cells.

'I just wanted to shout out, "Lads, I love you,"' she claimed later, which I thought was really rather sweet. Sadly, the long arm of the law cared not one jot for Mags's friendly advances and the pensioner was arrested by the police, released without charge and banned from Elland Road for 12 months.

'It's not like I am a hooligan,' she said. 'People who do much worse than this get the same ban. A suspension from a few games would have hurt, but I already feel like I have been punished enough . . . I had my Leeds United bag across my chest and a United flag tied around my waist. It was hardly threatening.'

Despite the fact that the Facebook group called 'Give Mags Musgrove Her Season Ticket Back Mr Bates' received 350 members and a number of letters were sent to the club, her ban stayed in place.

Maybe Mags should look to her counterparts abroad for inspiration. In countries such as Turkey the locals have developed novel methods for sidestepping stadium bans and the like, and when trouble kicked off in a friendly – a friendly! – between Fenerbahce and Shakhtar Donetsk, the Ukrainian champions, Turkey's football federation decided to punish the Istanbul club by banning men from their stadium for two games. Instead, 41,000 women and children attended the matches for free which, I would imagine, created a very different atmosphere and certainly everyone seemed to enjoy it, particularly the players.

'This memory will stay with me for ever,' said their Brazilian midfielder Alex de Souza. 'It's not always that you see so many women and children in one game.'

But did you see the photos? Well, if all of the women in the ground were actually of the female gender, then Turkey won't be in the running for Miss World any time soon. At least half of the girls had handlebar moustaches and beer bellies; the Sukru Saracoglu Stadium looked more like a drag club than a football ground. Basically, a lot of men had dressed up for the game and while the ground was principally full of women and children there was no question at all that quite a few people weren't entitled to be there by gender. How they got in was beyond me. Security was clearly more in tune with Estonian standards than the US Department of Homeland Security and the scene reminded me of the Channel 4 series *My Transsexual Summer*. Or one of those very late-night parties that occasionally take place at Chris Kamara's house.

Not all fans chance their way into a game of their own accord. In fact, on some occasions, they don't even want to chance their way into a game at all, especially if they're being dressed up as a mascot of their nearest, most hated rival. According to the *Hartlepool*

Mail (you may have guessed by now that I have a lifelong subscription), that's exactly what happened to Shaun Peterson, a Pools fan who had occasionally braved the inferior football at our local rivals Darlington to watch his mate, the former Hartlepool defender Paul Arnison.

October is always a special month for Shaun because it's his birthday and to help him celebrate the event, Paul and a couple of his closest friends clubbed together and treated him to a seat in the Darlington executive box for the game against Newport County. Less thrilling was the revelation – which was only announced once Shaun had arrived at the ground – that they had also arranged for him to be the team mascot, an 'honour' which meant he would be leading both teams out on to the pitch. I honestly couldn't think of anything worse as a Pools fan.

If you're thinking, 'Aah, poor lad,' you'd be wrong. Shaun wasn't a lad at all. In fact, he was a 30-year-old man and quite a strapping one at that, measuring up at 6 feet tall (nearly twice my height), which meant that he stuck out like a sore thumb as he led the Darlington players on to the pitch in his matchday kit – socks and boots included.

'It was about 2.30 p.m. when I was taken downstairs to the dressing room area and handed a bag with the kit in,' he told the *Mail* afterwards. 'By that time, it was too late to bottle out! I led the teams out with Graeme Lee, who used to play for Pools and is now Darlo's captain, then I had to go along the line of players and shake hands. The other Darlo mascot was a kid aged six, and I was getting a few strange looks from the Newport players!

'It was a good day though, full credit to the lads for a good wind-up, and I must admit I was actually quite pleased Darlo won because it was an important game for them and I didn't want their manager or anyone to think I was just there taking the mickey.'

Shaun was right, it's not good to mock your hosts. Though I would advise him to choose his friends more carefully in future. Especially those who might play for 'The Other Lot'.

CHAPTER TEN

'HERE, JEFF, DO YOU THINK IT'S A GOOD IDEA TO STREAK IN HERE?'

As a supporter, I can't think of a more unsettling sight in football than the streaker – especially if the wally in question is tearing off his clothes on a cold February night before racing towards the field of play wearing nothing but a comedy wig. Honestly, brash displays of naturism are enough to make the hair curl, if you'll excuse the pun. I'd imagine it's just as unsettling for the players. Quite frankly, the indignity of watching a blobby belly bearing down on you from afar (and that's just the female streakers) would be too much to bear.

It doesn't just happen in football either, cricket can be just as rowdy. Last summer I went to the Rose Bowl, Southampton's state-of-the-art cricket ground, to watch a match. To my horror it was full to the brim with stag parties, butch men in dresses and male estate agents in ladies' wigs. At times, I thought I was at a Fenerbahce game. Anyway, as I settled into my seat, I did everything that a gentleman is supposed to do at a cricket match. I read the paper and sipped on a pint of real ale; I listened to the radio and fell asleep, only stirring whenever a boundary shot received a raucous cheer. As I really got into the swing of things with yet another snooze I was rudely interrupted by a bloke carrying a tray full of overflowing plastic pint glasses.

'Here, Jeff,' he said. 'Do you think it would be a good idea to streak in here?'

My heart sank at the thought of seeing this fellow's private parts dangling in front of me as I tucked into my homemade cucumber sandwiches. I mumbled something along the lines of, 'No probably not, why?' To which he pointed at one of his mates in the middle distance who was stark b****ck naked, save for a pink wig. This gent was somewhat awkwardly hoisting his legs, and other flimsy body parts, over the wooden fence that divided the Rose Bowl's seats from the pitch.

As our streaker raced towards the wicket, a mildly uninterested cheer went up. He then jogged on the spot and waved back to his mates, presumably expecting an army of security guards to descend upon the field of play and drag him away, but instead a rather amusing situation unfolded: nothing happened. The players ignored him, the umpire ignored him; people in the seats around me returned to the sudoku page in their newspapers. Our pitch invader, somewhat embarrassed by the distinct lack of attention, then returned to where his mates had been standing, whereby eight stewards jumped on him and kicked him out on to the street, hopefully, still in his birthday suit.

As that strange incident played out in front of me, I was reminded of Ashley Vickers, a tough-tackling centre half for Dorchester Town. As a player-manager in the Conference South, Vickers was hardly a superstar, but I remembered reading in the *Dorset Echo* that he'd become a bit of a household name when he gave a pitch invader a clump during a spicy league game against Havant & Waterlooville in March 2011. Trouble had started with 70 minutes played and the game poised at 1–1, when a 'fan' named Alan Young raced on to the pitch. As he danced around the centre circle in socks, Marouane Fellaini-style wig and a skin-tight, bright green mankini which left nothing to the imagination, the players became visibly annoyed.

'What the f*****g hell is that?' sang the crowd as the stewards slowly advanced on Young, fearing the cold might shrink his dignity even further. That wasn't nearly enough action for Vickers, though. The number six decided to take the law into his own hands, manfully bringing the streaker down by grabbing him around the throat and hauling him to the ground.

'The security there were too slow, Vickers caught me quite well,' noted Young, having confessed all on a local radio station the following day. 'He should be a rugby player.'

Sadly, officialdom wasn't in a similarly magnanimous mood that evening. While the crowd cheered Vickers' robust citizen's arrest, the ref responded by sending him off, whereby the cheers soon turned to boos.

'I'm dumbfounded and speechless,' said Vickers in an interview with the *Dorset Echo*. 'A guy ran on to the pitch without any of the stewards getting near him and I thought I was doing them a favour. My only thought was to get hold of him so we could get on with the game. The funny thing was, the stewards actually thanked me for it, but the ref decided to send me off. It beggars belief.'

Luckily, common sense prevailed. Vickers was spared from a three-game suspension by the FA, though that wouldn't have eased the sting of defeat. Dorchester were eventually walloped 3–1. They were even reduced to eight men by the final whistle when Kyle Critchell and Jake Smeeton were sent off in added time. Maybe taking the law into your own hands isn't the smartest tactic after all. Especially if the law is wearing next to nothing and a Marouane Fellaini-style wig.

What footballer hasn't thought about clumping a fan around the chops in a manner similar to the one shown by Ashley Vickers? These days, players and managers have to put up with a lot of stick from the supporters, especially when results aren't going well, but there seems to be a misconception that disgruntled fans are a very modern trend. Some people think that ticket prices or fancy new stadiums like the Emirates are to blame. They argue that the punter who has to pay through the nose for his or her seat will jeer a team off the park more quickly than the fan who watched football in an earlier generation, especially if they haven't seen a glut of goals. 'They're impatient,' moan the players. 'They don't understand the game.'

Well, it may come as a surprise to learn that booing and cat-calling at the full-time whistle isn't an entirely new phenomenon. I remember going to Hartlepool as a kid. The team were in the doldrums (yes, things haven't changed) and they would often leave the field having lost by a goal or five, a cacophony of boos stinging their ears. In the fans' defence it was usually with good reason. Pools couldn't string a pass together back then, but it wasn't just in the lower leagues that jeering took place: it also happened in the old First Division. Former Scottish international and Liverpool defender Steve Nicol once told me that whenever the fans were unhappy with him during the 1980s, they would shout at him from the terraces.

'Get off, Nicol,' they would yell. 'You're crap!'

Steve's biggest problem was that this abuse took place during the pre-match kickabout.

Jeering and whistling isn't my style, but I haven't got a problem with fans who want to boo their team off, though only if all eleven players have performed really poorly. If somebody has paid a lot of money for their ticket and they're not happy with what they've seen on a Saturday afternoon, then they should be allowed to say what they want, providing it's neither vile nor offensive.

Not everyone thinks that way, and I know the players hate it, which won't come as too much of a surprise. I once tuned into a big debate on the radio where a number of ex-pros were discussing how they couldn't stand it when the fans booed them off the pitch. They were absolutely adamant that no fan should ever moan about their own players, but during the debate, one punter called in and made a valid point that took the wind out of their sails.

'Look, we're the fans that go and pay our money,' he said. 'If we haven't been entertained, or if we feel the players haven't tried hard enough, then the only way we can express our displeasure is to boo. Are you asking us to remain silent while we fund Premier League players' lifestyles? Are you asking us just to accept what we're given, when we pay so much money to watch the game?'

I could understand his point: booing, moaning, waving banners with the words 'JEFF OUT!' painted on them (these are just the protesters camped outside my house) have effectively become the fans' only right of reply. Put it this way: if you had experienced a terrible meal in an expensive restaurant, then you could easily complain directly to the people in charge. You could ask to see the manager and demand a refund. That doesn't happen at a football club. It's unlikely a fan would get the opportunity to wander into the stadium at full time, knock on the door of Mr Abramovich, Mr Ashley or Mr Levy and voice their displeasure, not without getting arrested on the way out. So how else are fans supposed to air their views to the people they pay?

Sometimes, the complaints and inevitably colourful language can go beyond the stadium. Last year while taking a peek at the fortunes of Berwickshire side Coldstream FC of the East of Scotland First Division – one of the oldest football teams in Scotland and winners of the Kings Cup in 1968, I hasten to add – I discovered that the club had adopted a strict no-swearing policy after receiving complaints from a number of walkers passing along the footpath by their ground, Home Park. Apparently the language from fans and players inside the ground had got so bad that one resident living nearby even offered a grand to the club if they were able to silence the habitual swearers, such was the abuse heard around the pitch. I'm assuming the language was merely drowning out his television where, dear reader, he would have been happily absorbing the latest scores on *Soccer Saturday*.

Perhaps I should point out here that I have never sworn audibly on air, despite the clips that might have appeared on the

Internet. One person who didn't manage to keep his tongue in check on the show was the late, great Brian Clough who I was fortunate enough to interview back in the days when the panel featured the likes of former Arsenal legend Frank McLintock. In a live feed, Ol' Big Head went on a rant about his relationship with chairmen, which made for great telly, but it had me fidgeting uncomfortably in my chair at times.

'Football is in good nick, it's happy, it's good,' he said. 'I just don't want to see too many chairmen on television, because as you know they're not my favourite lot, chairmen and directors. I feel sorry for them actually. One of them once had the affront to talk to me about football. I didn't mean to upset him but I said, "How can you talk to me about something you know nowt about?" And he looked at me, so I used a little bit of Anglo Saxon stuff that I was sometimes prone to lapse into, and I told him to p*** off . . . I kept my job, but as you see now I'm going downhill rapidly and I'm talking to you. I've hit rock bottom.'

Swearing was the least of Bayern Munich's worries when they signed German international goalkeeper Manuel Neuer in 2011. Before he'd even played a game for the club, Bayern's fans had expressed their displeasure at his arrival, mainly because he'd played for bitter Bundesliga rivals Schalke. The ultras staged several protests, where they claimed that Neuer did not belong at the club, but eventually a strange truce was agreed. A treaty was drawn up by a collective of Bayern fan clubs which stated that the goalie would be accepted by the supporters, but only if he abided by the following conditions:

1. Neuer must not kneel in front of the fans and sing 'The Humba', their traditional song.

2. He is not allowed to throw his shirt into the crowd.
3. He cannot start or join in with the fans' famous megaphone chants.
4. He cannot kiss the Bavarian crest.
5. He must never approach the fence of the South Stand.

Crikey, with supporters like that, who needs enemies?

I'm lucky, I suppose. As a football fan, I have a lot of opinions like everyone else, but thankfully I have a forum on *Soccer Saturday* where I can express a lot of my thoughts and theories. I guess it's only right and fair that all football fans should have their say as well, which is why I rather like the idea of a football phone-in for the car journey on the way home after a game, but if I was a footballer or the boss of a high-profile team, I wouldn't bother listening. Everyone who rings in thinks they could do the job better and some of the flak thrown at managers and players seems pretty misguided at times.

And heaven forbid a professional footballer should brave an Internet forum! It's here that some of the worst bullying known to man can take place. I discovered very quickly in my career that there are plenty of people who take great pleasure in poking fun at football show anchormen who may or may not be of distinctly average height (five foot seven is the national average. Fact) and waistline (slightly less than Matt Le Tissier. Another fact). I know that some people might like me, and some people probably hate me, but I've suffered enough emails at work to know that I don't want to search online for any extra criticism, thank you very much.

Still, none of the complaints regarding my presenting style could possibly match a letter I received a couple of years ago from an irate Fulham fan. At the time I had been writing a column for the *Sun* which appeared in their Saturday edition every week, and at the end of the well-crafted prose I would predict the Premiership scores for the day. It was really meant as a bit of fun. Anyhow, when I mentioned that I thought Fulham would lose 2–0 to Liverpool, it prompted some serious rage in one Cottager who addressed himself on a letter to me as 'Big Neil Sullivan (here on the pen)'.

Big Neil was so angry that he couldn't be bothered to find a suitable pad of paper on which to write his misgivings. Instead he scrawled his thoughts down on the back of a mobile phone bill, and it made for pretty unpleasant reading.

Listen here you podgy, grinning, stupid, slimy, big headed t**t and old codger – you clueless c**t of a man. You, stupid Stelling, with the worst possible Saturday football predictions. You always get them wrong, you f*****g joke Stelling. I support Fulham and yet you always slag 'em.

You always tip them to lose. Stelling says: Liverpool 2 Fulham 0, you c**t.

If you slag Fulham off once more then I'm going to smash your face. We wouldn't even notice you podgy p***k. The next time I read Sun Goals you better have predicted, Fulham 3 Aston Villa 0.

Anyway, the letter arrived on my desk on Saturday morning. 'Oh, crikey,' I thought. 'What score did I predict for Fulham?'

I scrambled around on my desk, desperately trying to locate the latest edition of the paper. Trembling, I tore through the pages and my blood ran cold when I saw the text at the foot of my column: Fulham 0 Aston Villa 1. Thank the stars he didn't write back. Though my mood was soured later that day when I visited the Liverpool website and noticed a thread on the club forum entitled, 'I Hate Jeff Stelling'. Honestly, some days I think I'm better off staying in bed.

Nevertheless, compared to the complaints received by the players of East Fife, I've had it easy. To those who might be unfamiliar with the game north of the border, East Fife are a team that have been generally described by the *Daily Record* newspaper as 'beleaguered'. It's easy to see why. They're not very good and their fans are miserable. Criticism from the Scottish side's unofficial Internet forum 'Away From The Numbers' was so bad during the 2010/11 season that one choice critique of centre forward Steve Hislop even described him as 'The worst footballer ever'. Not having seen Hislop play, I can't actually confirm or deny the criticism, but it seemed pretty harsh to me.

Anyhow, dispelling the myth that professional footballers use the Internet only to tweet their opinions on *The X Factor*/ Cheryl Cole/Dolce & Gabbana's new range of jeans, the playing staff of Beleaguered East Fife actually read the posts from their fans. Even more surprisingly, the players became really rather heartbroken at the criticism. They then wrote an open letter to all 314 supporters attending their next fixture against Peterhead, pleading with them to call time on the insults:

We all understand and appreciate that the ['Away From The Numbers'] forum allows fans to express their opinion and have their say, but, as a team, we firmly consider that some of the posts have become personal and damaging.

We know more than anyone that we have under-performed this season. However, the table does not lie and we are where we are due to poor team perform-ances and not individual performances. We win as a team and lose as a team and that is our philosophy.

The Boys.

Of course, when the fans absorbed this appeal from Beleaguered East Fife's players, their response was typically measured and unsympathetic:

'[Celtic manager] Neil Lennon gets death threats and bullets in the post but just gets on with it. This lot take offence at getting criticism from fans on a website? They're nothing more than spoilt bairns. If they were any good they wouldn't be playing for East Fife.'

George Weir, 54, Methil, Fife, in the *Daily Record*

'If us stewards applied the same rationale as the East Fife footballers ... LOL. I could sue for some of the things I've been called over the years.'

Livibudgie on the Livingston supporters forum, LiviLions

Thinking about it, there's only one footballer in the world who would remain unfazed by the flak delivered by Mr Weir and

'Livibudgie'. And he's currently not kissing the Bavarian crest as a goalkeeper for Bayern Munich.

Still, if there's one recent development that I've found rather strange in the football media, then it's the trend for current pros to man the phones during Saturday early-evening debates on the radio. How they do it is beyond me. They must skip the post-match shower, hop straight into the car (still dressed in their kit and boots) and drive to the nearest radio station to have their ears chewed off by a pack of baying fans (if they've lost), or a pack of baying fans (if they haven't lost). When Robbie Savage was playing he would occasionally show up in the 606 studio on Radio 5 Live. He's since been replaced by Jason Roberts, and while they might be good pundits, I think these roles put them in a very difficult position, especially if they've had a bad result.

Now, this is not a pop at Jason Roberts, I personally think he's a top, top bloke and his game time has been reduced some-what recently, so he has more freedom to involve himself in media work. But if I was a fan and we'd been thumped by someone during the day (and Jason was playing for my team), I'd be thinking, 'Do I really want one of our players going on the radio in a couple of hours?' I might even be of the opinion, at 4.43 p.m. say, three goals down, that Jason might not be concentrating on the job in hand. I'd worry that his mind was focused on what he was going to be doing later on during the radio show rather than what was taking place on the pitch. I've always thought that this was a conflict of interest that could put a player in an embarrassing situation, particularly if they've already had one bad day at the office.

If a footballer is injured, then that's another matter. I remember we invited Jamie Carragher on to *Soccer Saturday* while he was out of action in the 2010/11 season and he was brilliant – it was great to have a current player on the show to deliver his opinions on the modern game. He was passionate, too. Nobody could have been as Liverpool as Jamie. Well, maybe Thommo, who was on holiday that day. And by holiday I mean a guided tour of Anfield with the family.

Jamie was given a Chelsea game to cover that afternoon and as the London side cruised to victory, he offered up several insightful snippets of well-balanced praise. Not that some Liverpool fans saw it that way. In fact, some of them were very angry that he'd even dared to appear on the panel.

I think the problems started when Chelsea scored their first goal. Jamie shouted, 'Goal!' as our panellists are prone to do, but I remember the incident because as he yelled out, Charlie or one of the other boys called a goal at the same time.

'My goal was first!' snapped Jamie, clearly getting into the swing of things, but I think some of the Liverpool fans took offence at his enthusiasm. They were also upset at his assessment of the team. At the time, Liverpool had been having a few problems off the pitch; there were issues with the manager Rafa Benitez and the owners, and inevitably, because he was a current player at Anfield, we had to ask him about the debates going on within the club. He was as honest and open as he could be, but afterwards a number of fans complained that he hadn't defended Liverpool once. Some people were claiming that as a current pro he shouldn't have even been on the show; my view was that because he was out with a long-term injury it wasn't like he was missing an important training session.

Now a lot of Liverpool fans see the world through red eyes. They're biased, like we all are for our teams, and in defence of

Jamie, I think he was trying to be balanced, but I saw one comment which was a bit harsh to say the least. It read, 'I see Carra put in his best performance for 18 months on *Soccer Saturday*.' Thankfully, plenty of other Liverpool sites jumped to his defence. They called him a legend, which he is, and they pointed out he was balanced and realistic and even-handed in his summary of Liverpool's performance. I thought he was fantastic that day, way better than I thought a contemporary pro could be. He's been on shows since then and he's definitely a pundit for the future. Jamie did a great job and we would happily have him back should he ever get injured again or retire from the game. Especially if Thommo ever felt the need to take his family back to the Anfield boot room for a day out. Which hopefully might be pretty soon.

CHAPTER ELEVEN

'WE'RE ALL GOING ON AN ALCOHOLIDAY'

I dread the thought of going away on a *Soccer Saturday* team-bonding break; honestly I couldn't think of anything worse. As much as I love spending my Saturday afternoons with the likes of Thommo, Charlie, Merse, Kammy, Le Tiss and Alan McInally, I wouldn't want to waste any of my annual leave from Sky with that lot. No offence if you're reading this, gents, it's just that sometimes a man can have too much fun in his life.

Not everyone shares that view, I know. I recently heard that the romantic crooner Tony Bennett has an embroidered cushion in his New York apartment. It reads, 'Too Much of a Good Thing is Simply Wonderful'. Well, clearly Tony hasn't spent a lot of time with Kammy, whose idea of a 'good thing' usually involves a karaoke machine and a skinful of alcohol, or

Thommo, a man with two hobbies: Liverpool FC (playing, though that only happens in dreamland these days) and Liverpool FC (supporting).

Kammy obviously falls into the same category as Tony Bennett, but only in philosophical terms because his singing leaves a little to be desired, no matter how hard he tries to convince me otherwise. Nevertheless, Kammy loves nothing more than a weekend away with the *Soccer Saturday* panellists and too much of a football thing is simply wonderful. His joie de vivre was recently evidenced when he arranged a close season charity outing in Tenerife under the guise of the 'Chris Kamara 2011 Golf Jamboree' – a golf-themed event with an open invitation for all the Sky glitterati, myself included.

The plan was to start proceedings with an 18-hole tournament, and with the help of his bulging contacts book, Kammy had secured a cracking list of star players – a cast of thousands; a golfing epic on a *Ben-Hur* scale – including the *Soccer Saturday* panellists and *Soccer AM* presenters, not to mention some pretty impressive figures from the sporting world, such as the retired boxer Ricky Hatton.

It was a nice idea, I admit, and all in the name of charity, but when I first heard the news, my blood ran cold. I had night terrors and bad dreams. In one nightmare I was stuck in a hotel bed, topping and tailing with a sleep-babbling Charlie Nicholas. In the corner of the room was a broken TV. The picture was frozen on *Soccer Saturday*, but Garth Crooks from The Other Channel was sitting in my seat. Meanwhile, on the videprinter, the news of a 10–0 defeat for Hartlepool had just come through. It was hellish.

Anyway, the following morning I thought of excuses,

probably more rapidly than one of Carlos Tevez's many confused translators. I told myself that I couldn't go because I had *Countdown* to present; I was also due to work for Sky at Gary Neville's testimonial at Old Trafford. If the worst came to the worst, I could tell the boys that I had been voted 'Most Stylish Man of the Year' by Tie Rack and had to collect my gold-plated, commemorative tie pin. (Of course, attentive readers will have spotted that one of these excuses was a blatant lie. I no longer presented *Countdown*.) In fairness to Kammy, though, he took my rejection quite well, but a number of my peers later attempted to sway my decision in the run-up to the big weekend. I received loads of calls from mates telling me how much they were looking forward to going. I told them that I was looking forward to the weekend as well. For the first Saturday in as long as I could remember, I was going to be at home, free of Thommo and the words 'Liverpool' and 'The greatest club in the world, if you like,' which felt like a blessed relief.

Now, before you start berating me for not getting into the swing of things, so to speak, I do have one major problem with golfing events: I'm not as good at golf as I would like. Occasionally I've been known to compete in a few exhibition tournaments organised by Sky Sports co-commentator and former player, Ray Wilkins, and I've always thoroughly enjoyed my time at these events. As Ray would probably say himself, 'My word, young man, it really is a smashing day out.' The problem is, I only enjoy myself once I get *off* the course. When I'm on it, I often get myself into a bit of a pickle, normally in the bunkers, ditches, trees and any other hazards that may lie off the fairway.

As you can probably imagine, a golf competition organised by the former England international and Chelsea coach is always a star-studded event. Ray's reputation, plus the fact that a large number of players today spend their time on the golf course – when they're not training, tweeting or lusting after the 'girls' from TOWIE[4] – ensures that the standard of golf at his weekends is also pretty high, with everyone having a low handicap. I always find it extra tough to finish high on the leaderboard in competitions like these because the retired stars are just as good as their modern counterparts. Of the *Soccer Saturday* gang, Charlie, for example, is a handy golfer, Merse plays off a handicap of 18 (24 when it's a money game) and Alan McInally can hit the ball a bloody mile, though rarely in the direction it's supposed to go. Sadly, I have a proper job, which means I only get to play on Sundays when I'm trying to wind down from the show.

Because of my limited fairway time, I've not improved my game in the way that I would have liked, so putting myself in front of a field of footballers, many of whom I might have criticised during *Soccer Saturday*, could only end in jeers, or more worryingly, a golf-related breakdown.

That's exactly what happened when I played in a charity event in Spain with a mate of mine. The event was held on one of those fancy villa-lined courses which roll across the horizon – miles and miles of lush grass stretching out as far as the eye can see with only the occasional lake (or Laguna del Jeff, as I believe they're known on some courses) to jangle the nerves. It was a real treat to play, though that sensation lasted for all of one shot. On the first tee I lined up my drive in front of a modest gallery and curled the ball – with all the grace and power of a Ronaldo free

---

4 *The Only Way Is Essex* for those readers with a life.

kick – on to the balcony of a nearby apartment. Not to be deterred, I drew another ball from my bag, ignored the laughter and catcalls from the crowd and my caddy and played exactly the same shot, to exactly the same balcony. It was soul-crushing.

So, needless to say, repeating that humiliating experience at the 'Chris Kamara 2011 Golf Jamboree' wasn't on my '48 Things To Do Before I Die' list (No. 21: Go for dinner with Cheryl Cole). And thank God that it wasn't! When the boys returned from their little break in the sun and regaled me with their witty, thought-provoking anecdotes, I have to say it sounded less like a golfing adventure and more like a scene from one of those BBC3 documentaries where dozens of drunken British holidaymakers wreak havoc on some poor unsuspecting Spanish resort, revved up by San Miguel and sunburn.

By all accounts the drinking started on the plane. It's a well-known fact that Merse is a very nervous flyer. There have even been times when he's jumped off a flight moments before take-off, such is his fear of being up in the sky. I've always found his phobia to be slightly out of character given that he was often as high as a kite for the early part of his playing career, especially when he was partying heavily at Arsenal. To ease Merse's nerves, Charlie suggested that they should start the weekend with a glass of champagne or two. After that, the boys were up, up and away – especially after they had guzzled their way through four bottles of the stuff.

It was only when everybody landed that they were reminded of the fact that they would have to go onstage during an after-dinner event in one of Tenerife's finest eateries, because Kammy had organised a do called 'An Audience With . . . *Soccer Saturday*'. The tickets had been bought up in a flash, and when Thommo noticed a big poster advertising the night stuck to a wall in Kammy's bar – a pub he'd owned for years – he was taken aback by the size of the event.

'So it's going to be a fancy do is it, Kammy?' he asked. 'What's the dress code? I haven't brought a suit.'

'Oh, don't worry,' said Kammy. 'Wear your shorts, T-shirt, anything you want.'

That should give you an idea of exactly what sort of event, and weekend, it was going to be.

Nobody was too bothered and in hindsight, had I gone with the lads my only major gripe would have been with the sleeping arrangements. You see, I like to relax and sleep in solitude whenever I travel away with work. Not because I have suspicious habits, but because I like the peace and quiet. Footballers these days tend to behave like boy scouts and will happily share a room – and a bed, if some tabloids are to believed – whenever they play football away from home. The old pros are just the same. During their playing careers, the likes of Thommo and Charlie would have spent many an evening in the same room as a team mate or three before matches, though I've since heard that some of the lads had better bedside manners than others. During one Arsenal close season trip, Merse got so drunk that he became embroiled in a fight with his team mate Gus Caesar in a Bermuda nightclub. When he returned to the hotel with defender Steve Bould, the pair decided to trash poor Gus's room. They broke in and hurled his bed out of the window. A bucket of water was thrown around. The place looked like a bomb site. Arsenal gaffer George Graham was not happy and took away Merse's FA Cup bonus money for the season.

Thankfully, the behaviour in Tenerife was much more

civilised. It was only after Kammy's 'An Audience With . . .' and a day of golf (which Thommo won) that things got a little hairy. All the boys went off in different directions – some of them went to Kammy's place, others to various football-themed pubs – and it was in one such establishment that Iain Dowie ran into a couple of scary-looking lads with skinheads and tattoos, one of whom began glaring at him angrily from across the bar.

'You don't remember me, do you, Iain?' he hissed.

Iain shook his head nervously.

'I was a youth team player when you were in charge at Palace. You let me go and told me that I wasn't good enough.'

Clearly, this chap wasn't happy at Iain's business decision and proceeded to stare at him moodily as he tried to drink his pint in peace.

Now, anyone who knows Iain Dowie well will tell you that a) staring at him is a very foolish thing to do, particularly while he's attempting to drink a pint of ice-cold lager, b) he's quite a scary-looking bloke – even I get a fright when his head appears on my monitor during *Soccer Saturday*, and c) he's as hard as nails, as a lot of his team mates at West Ham, QPR and Southampton would testify. So, when his former youth team player popped into the toilet, Iain followed him in, pinned him to the wall and informed him, in no uncertain terms, what would happen if the staring didn't finish, right there and then. Needless to say the angry looks from across the bar stopped pretty shortly afterwards.

After hearing all of those tales, I had to tell the lads, to their genuine surprise, that I wasn't all that keen on committing to an appearance the next time Kammy's charity beano takes place. I've promised them I'll bear it in mind, though the truth is, I'll be secretly praying for another prestigious Most Stylish Man of the Year Award. Failing that, maybe United could be convinced into arranging a second testimonial for Gary Neville?

The excuse of working at Old Trafford was genuine, however. While the lads were away, rucking with former members of their playing staff and getting drunk, I genuinely had the honour of working at Gary Neville's farewell game at Manchester United. It was a cracking evening, the ground was packed and one or two of his former team mates had turned up to play, including David Beckham and Nicky Butt. An hour or so before the game I wandered down the players' tunnel to soak up a bit of the atmosphere and interview some of the players for Sky, one of whom was Gary's brother Phil, the Everton skipper at the time.

'So Phil, you two were once opposing captains when United played Everton,' I said, the cameras rolling. 'And I noticed that you didn't speak to each other once before the game, not in the tunnel, not even when you did the coin toss together at the start of the match. What happened?'

'I know,' laughed Phil, a Sky microphone under his nose. 'To be honest, I couldn't believe he wouldn't say hello to me. I thought, "He's gotta say hello to me. He's got to . . ." What a knob.'

Dwight Yorke, who had been standing next to me and was a pundit for the day, burst out laughing. Countless viewers saw a look of panic flicker across my face as I figured whether I would have to apologise to the public for the admittedly low-level vulgarity. Then I figured that if anyone could get away with calling Gary Neville, Manchester United legend and England stalwart, a 'knob' on live TV, then it was his brother.

Later, as I walked back down the tunnel, I bumped into

Mark Halsey, the Premiership ref who was diagnosed with throat cancer in August 2009. Miraculously, Mark had fought back to full fitness and made his professional comeback in March 2010, during a reserves match between Blackpool and Rochdale, which was some feat, I can tell you. He's since officiated games in the Premiership with aplomb.

By the sounds of things, Mark's road to recovery had been horrific. He told me that a tumour the size of a golf ball had been removed from his throat during surgery. Initially he was informed by the FA that he had to battle his way back to match speed if he was to have any hope of refereeing in the Premier League again. It was quite a challenge given the physical ordeal he had been through during his illness.

Typically for a Premiership ref, Mark loved a challenge and eventually battled his way back into contention. He later admitted that when he passed the fitness test, he blubbered a bit afterwards. I'm not surprised. Part of the physical exam involved sprinting distances of 40 metres, six times on the trot (where each run had to be completed in under 6.2 seconds per run). Then there were 20 runs of 100 metres, which had to be completed in under 30 seconds. A breather of only 35 seconds was allowed between each run. I would have been bawling too.

Sadly, it had been a double whammy for Mark because his wife Michelle was already suffering from chronic myeloid leukaemia when he was diagnosed with cancer. She and the kids were also there for the game, which to his great excitement Mark had been asked to referee. I really felt for them, they'd obviously gone through a lot together, but I was also pleased, because the game obviously meant a lot to the whole family.

To have him back in action was brilliant. I've always thought that he was a top ref and like Dermot Gallagher – whom I've already mentioned in this book – Mark has always been one of the few officials to referee the game in an approachable manner. I've got the impression that footballers can have a chat with Mark when things start to get heated during a match – he won't patronise them or shoo a player away with a dismissive wave of the hand. As I've said before, there aren't too many refs of that ilk around these days, sadly.

Still, I reckon Mark's return to the game wouldn't have seemed real, not until some player had shouted, 'Oi, Halsey! You're f*****g useless!', probably after he had made a perfectly correct decision. A referee needs the players to treat him with a modicum of disrespect if he's to feel accepted; no official wants to be a charity case. Meanwhile, with every 'eff off' and insult, all those tears and lung-bursting sprints in training would have felt more and more worthwhile. Deep down, I bet he loved every second of it. Though I'd like to think that if Phil Neville used the word 'knob' in front of him during a game, he'd flash his yellow card, just to make me feel a little better.

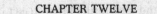

CHAPTER TWELVE

THE UNSUNG HEROES OF SOCCER SATURDAY

Meeting Mark Halsey under those circumstances reminded me that, throughout my 17 years hosting *Soccer Saturday*, I've heard some heroic tales from within the game. Usually they involve a battle against adversity or a good deed done for a worthy cause. Sadly, because of the headlines made at the top of the football pyramid, these stories often go untold, or at least aren't given the attention they deserve. So, by way of a tribute, I've decided to list some of *Soccer Saturday*'s unsung champions . . .

ADAM STANSFIELD, WEST COUNTRY STRIKER

Anyone who's been a friend of *Soccer Saturday* over the years would have been a friend of Adam Stansfield. The one-time Exeter

City, Yeovil Town and Hereford United striker became linked to one of the longest-running gags on the show after I'd noticed his surname was identical to the 1980s pop sensation Lisa Stansfield. For those of you under a certain age, Lisa scored a Number One hit single with 'All Around the World' in 1989 and so whenever Adam scored, I would yell, 'And Lisa will be pleased, Adam Stansfield has got a goal!' Like so many of the other regular catchphrases on our panel – Gary 'High Noon' Hooper of Celtic, for example – the laughs were based on affection and stupidity.

Because of my mucking around, Adam became a cult favourite with viewers and panellists alike. Luckily, I got to use the joke quite a lot because scoring goals was something he did with regularity, particularly in his last ever season for Exeter when he bagged eight goals in 30 league and cup appearances, but his rise to prominence first started after he got a goal for Yeovil back in the day when *Soccer Saturday* was available for next to nothing (if you were smart enough to own a Freeview box). I'm not sure what made me say it, but when his name flashed up on the videprinter for the first time, I pretended that he was related to Lisa. Of course, they weren't brother and sister at all, but my outburst caused such a fuss that, for a while, Adam was constantly asked by fans whether he and the pop songstress were actually siblings. God knows what attention Lisa received from my messing around.

Despite my joy whenever his named appeared, I didn't actually know Adam at all. We never met, but I felt very much as if our paths had crossed; I always followed his progress at all the clubs he'd played for and kept an eye out for any news regarding his career. Sadly, the joking stopped when he passed away in August 2010 after being struck down with bowel cancer. It was a tragic shock to all of us on the show, not to mention his friends at the clubs he'd played for, both in the Football League and the Conference. He had the excellent strike rate of 23 goals in 96 Football League games. By all accounts he was a top lad and I was really moved by Adam's death. Reading out the news was one of the toughest things I've had to do on *Soccer Saturday*.

'I was shocked and distressed, as I'm sure all football fans were this week, at the news of the death of Adam Stansfield at the age of just 31,' I said. 'I didn't know him at all but I felt very much as if I did. He played for Yeovil, Hereford and Exeter, he scored 92 goals in 313 appearances . . . he was never red carded and he picked up just seven yellow cards in the course of his career, which said a lot about his character.'

I hope I paid him a fitting tribute because he deserved one.

His family later established the Adam Stansfield Foundation, an organisation which strives to increase awareness of the illness that so tragically took his life. It also gives aspiring kids the opportunity to develop life skills through football. Because of this worthwhile cause, I eventually met Adam's wife Marie and the rest of his family at a fund-raising night for the foundation in Tiverton, Devon. When I arrived, the venue was overflowing with guests, not just with people who had watched Adam play and were fans of the clubs he'd played for, but with former team mates and managers as well. They had all turned out in their numbers to support the charity, which was great to see.

I suppose you could have called it a bittersweet evening. It was a lot of fun, there were a lot of stories and a lot of laughs, but there were quite a few tears, too. His family were so warm and welcoming to me – they told me how they had loved the joking on the show, and how Adam had enjoyed the attention, too.

Afterwards I felt as if I'd got to know the man himself a little better, what with all the story-telling. But most importantly, the evening raised a lot of cash, which was a wonderful achievement and a testament to Adam's career and character.

As I mentioned in a speech at the end, 'Lisa would have been proud.'

GARY PARKINSON, SUPER SCOUT

As a player, full back Gary Parkinson formed part of an impressive defensive unit for Middlesbrough during the eighties and nineties where he shouldered centre half Tony Mowbray in defence. During his time there, Gary helped the club secure promotion to the top flight on two occasions, before coaching the kids at Blackpool as the head of the youth development programme. Sadly, tragedy struck in the autumn of 2010, when Gary suffered a major stroke on the stem of the brain. The result of this was 'locked-in syndrome', an awful condition which renders the sufferer completely paralysed, but mentally alert. The few people who have recovered from this horrific affliction have likened their situation to being trapped in a coffin.

That hasn't stopped Gary from keeping an active role in the game, however; his keen eye for spotting talented young footballers remains undiminished, and his former Boro team mate Tony Mowbray, now the club's manager, has given Gary a role as a club scout as he attempts to make a recovery from the claustrophobic illness. Every day or so, a member of Boro's coaching staff – usually first-team coach, Mark Proctor – often drives for two hours, over one hundred miles, from the training ground to the Priory Highbank neurological rehabilitation centre in Bury where

Gary is being cared for. They then play a series of DVDs showing potential transfer targets and signings. During each screening, Gary delivers his expert assessment on the players under scrutiny.

On paper this might sound like an impossibility, but with the help of his wife Deborah and 18-year-old son Luke, the former Boro star has devised a way of communicating by blinking, which means he can deliver his opinions and construct articulate reports. Most of the time, Proctor agrees with his assessments – having played in one of the best-loved Boro teams of the last 50 years, Gary is very in tune with the philosophy of the club and is able to spot players with the ability to pass the ball around on the deck and play skilful, attacking football.

It's also a heart-warming sign that team play and bonding can remain strong even after the game has finished for some players. From what I've heard, doctors have been impressed by the efforts of Mowbray and his staff. They hope that the work undertaken by Gary might aid his recovery from the condition. Meanwhile, his former team mates – the manager and coach Stephen Pears, plus Gary Hamilton, Gary Gill and Colin Cooper – and the current Boro squad have raised thousands for the Gary Parkinson Trust Fund, though special mention must go to former winger Stuart Ripley who somehow managed to cycle his way up La Marmotte, possibly the most knackering stretch of the Tour de France route. It was a pretty impressive way of drawing attention to Gary's situation. Fingers crossed, the money they've raised might go some way to putting him on the road to recovery.

PETER REID, SACKED PLYMOUTH MANAGER

Reidy must have been absolutely gutted when he was sacked by Plymouth Argyle in September 2011. He had joined them 15 months previously, having worked as Stoke's assistant manager under Tony Pulis, and almost from the minute he signed up, it was revealed that the club was in a state of financial disrepair. Because of their cash flow problems, Plymouth were forced into administration and were docked 10 points by the League and subsequently relegated after his first season in charge.

Things were so bad during his time at Home Park that Reidy sold his 1986 FA Cup runner's up medal from his time at Everton to help keep the club afloat. He even paid the heating bill out of his own pocket, they were that hard up. Everything had fallen into chaos around him and the players eventually threatened to go on strike because they had worked for nine months on reduced pay. It was a nightmare.

In the first two months of the 2011/12 season, Plymouth picked up only one point from nine games and Reidy was given the boot, which I thought was the crassest sacking of that football year. Under normal circumstances, I would have thought, 'Yeah, the chairman was right. Reidy should have gone because the results had been so bad.' But as the manager, he had been working against impossible odds. He even brought his brother – a former player with Chester City – into the coaching staff to help keep the costs down. Meanwhile, all the decent players had left. It was a really harsh call giving him the heave-ho, in my opinion.

Reidy is also a mate of mine, so I'm biased, but he's a nice fella, a football man through and through, and a bloody good manager. The club should have given him some more time, another dozen games, at least. Who knows what might have happened if they had?

RORY McALLISTER, THE PLUMBING FOOTBALLER

Forget Cesc Fabregas and Carlos Tevez. When it comes to 'Should I Stay, Or Should I Go?' transfer dilemmas, nobody quite touched Rory McAllister's move from Brechin City to Peterhead in the summer of 2011. Hotshot striker McAllister (51 goals in two seasons at Brechin; a Scottish U21 international at the time) had a host of offers from some seriously impressive names – Sheffield United, Charlton and Port Vale had all reportedly shown an interest in his talents, not to mention Scottish Premier League heavyweights St Mirren, Hibs and Aberdeen. McAllister was 24 years of age and the football world was at his feet. What a buzz.

So, did he leave Brechin for bucketloads of cash and a contract that promised thousands of pounds in goal bonuses and image rights? Did he heck. McAllister decided to sign for Peterhead on a part-time deal so he could spend his days away from football completing an apprenticeship in plumbing. Crikey, what an honourable thing to do.

I've heard of players taking on educational and vocational courses but not to the detriment of their football ambition. According to McAllister, however, he had weighed up all the options available to him and sensibly concluded that just about anything could happen to him as a professional footballer. A serious injury might end his playing career, bankruptcy could close down his club. So rather than hoping for the best, McAllister decided to give himself a back-up option, and I for one hope it works out for him, both on and off the pitch. I'd hate to see his talents as a striker go down the drain.

BILLY SHARP; BRAVEHEART

When the then Doncaster skipper Billy Sharp announced the tragic death of his two-day-old son Luey Jacob just days before Rovers' match against Middlesbrough at the Keepmoat Stadium in November 2011, few fans expected him to lead out the team. But lead them out he did, and following a minute's applause before the kick-off, Billy scored the first goal in a 1–3 defeat and was later named as the sponsor's man of the match. In the seconds after his strike, the centre forward lifted his shirt off to reveal a T-shirt with the words, 'That's For You Son' emblazoned on it.

'He wanted to play to score a goal for his son and he was ready to go,' said Donny's manager Dean Saunders afterwards. 'When he said that to me, I couldn't really refuse. You won't score a better goal than that [his strike against Middlesbrough] – it's incredible. I thought: "The story's already been written, he's going to end up with a hat-trick and we're going to win 3–0." It didn't turn out that way but I'm really proud that he wanted to play. It tells you a bit about him as a man. There's not many people who would have done that.'

I had incredible admiration for Billy after his appearance against Boro. It would have taken a lot of bottle to do the job under the scrutiny of the public eye during a time of such grief, and he handled it with a hell of a lot of courage. Billy is a good footballer who is now at Southampton, but from his perspective, the goal and the game wouldn't have mattered at the time. I can't imagine the emotion he must have experienced as he printed that T-shirt on the day of the match. And thank God that for once the referee, Darren Deadman, actually showed some common sense and didn't book him for that most moving of 'celebrations'. There would have been a real fuss afterwards had he flashed a card, and nobody would have wanted to see that. Least of all Billy and his family.

MAX LONSDALE, THE FOOTBALL HOPEFUL WITH BALLS OF STEEL

When the then 18-year-old midfielder Max Lonsdale was rejected by League Two side Macclesfield Town in the summer of 2011, he decided to take the initiative and head for the top, in this case the front drive of Sir Alex Ferguson, where he audaciously handed a DVD of his recent performances to the Scariest Man In Football™. Rather than kicking his backside down the driveway, however, Sir Alex actually took time to watch Max's 'highlights showreel'. Somewhat more surprisingly, he then offered Lonsdale a fortnight's trial at United's fancy Carrington training ground, though sadly the fairytale ended and he was released without a contract.

But talk about neck! It takes a brave – or maybe very stupid – man to challenge Sir Alex, as I found out to my cost when I was asked to interview Wayne Rooney by the Football Writers' Association (FWA) at their Player of the Year Awards in 2010. Rooney had enjoyed a brilliant season up until his injury against Bayern Munich and was a worthy winner of the award. He also looked like being a star during the World Cup in South Africa, so I was delighted when the FWA asked me to chat to him during their very prestigious dinner.

This interview format broke with tradition at the FWA Awards because usually the winner has to stand up and give a speech in front of every renowned football writer in the land, as well as a number of Premier League managers and former players. It can be quite an ordeal. On this occasion, it was decided that Rooney didn't need the pressure and instead he and I sat on a podium and we conducted an informal Q&A session, and I have to say, Rooney was absolutely brilliant. He made people laugh, he was engaging and genuinely entertaining. His incisive wit was made all the more remarkable by the fact that on the top table, not three feet away from us, were his two managers, Fabio Capello and Sir Alex Ferguson, which made for quite an intimidating audience, as I was to quickly discover.

I suppose the trouble started about ten minutes into our chat when I asked Rooney about the goals he had scored during that season and whether Sir Alex had demanded more of him before the campaign had got underway.

'Well,' he said, 'the manager told me that he wanted more goals from me than in previous seasons. But I explained to him that he'd been playing me on the wing. What was I supposed to do? Cross the ball into the box and then get on the end of my own pass?'

Of course that got everyone laughing, everyone except Sir Alex, whose hot breath was burning the back of my neck.

'Come on, Jeff,' he snapped angrily. 'Wind it up.'

I shivered. An angry Sir Alex Ferguson in my ear was the last thing I needed. Everybody in football knew about the Hairdryer Treatment, and I really didn't want to be on the receiving end of one of his infamous rollickings, but I had no option – I had to ignore the Premiership's most fearsome disciplinarian because the Football Writers' Association had contracted me to talk for 15 minutes. I really had no choice but to carry on regardless, like a soldier going over the top of the trenches, or Cristiano Ronaldo announcing he was leaving for Real Madrid.

I looked down at my notes and realised matters were unlikely to improve. My next question concerned Rooney's managers at both club and international level, the two men sitting behind me, one of whom had steam coming from his ears already. When I glanced at the time on a large clock at the back of the hall, I swear the hands were actually ticking backwards.

'So, Wayne, we have both your bosses here tonight,' I said. 'Are there any similarities between the two of them?'

There was another sigh behind me.

'Yeah,' said Rooney, showing the expert sense of timing that had served him so well during a prolific season. 'They both scare the hell out of me.'

Cue more laughing from the audience. Cue more huffing and puffing from behind me.

'Come on, Jeff, that's enough!' hissed Sir Alex.

It was a nightmare, because I knew he was unhappy, but I knew I had to keep going. I asked another question at which point both Rooney and I heard the words, 'For goodness sake, Jeff!' Unsurprisingly, Rooney decided that the Q&A should conclude, for both our sakes.

Afterwards I went to find Sir Alex to explain the situation about the interview and the time demands placed upon me. 'Look, Sir Alex,' I trembled, 'the deal was that we did 15 minutes which was why I kept asking the questions. I'm sorry that you weren't aware of that, but the Football Writers' Association were paying me, so I was obliged to do it.'

He took it well, and I think when Sir Alex looked back at the evening, he would have probably realised that his talismanic striker had done a pretty good PR job. He came across as engaging and witty, a side that not many people had seen before; he clearly had the skills and intelligence to impress his manager, both on and off the pitch. Which, as Max Lonsdale found out at Carrington, is a bloody difficult thing to do.

AL BANGURA, FOREST GREEN ROVERS SURVIVOR

When I've heard footballers complaining about the difficulty of making it through a youth trial, I bet none of them would have endured an ordeal quite like Forest Green Rovers star Al Bangura. The midfielder first fled a violent upbringing in Sierra Leone as a teenager. He then escaped the horrors of human trafficking in Guinea and the threat of male prostitution in France, before securing asylum in the UK and making his Championship debut with Watford in 2005. Bangura later made his first appearance in the Premiership against Manchester United in 2006/07. As a Houdini act, Bangura's story was up there with the likes of *Escape to Victory*, or one of the death-defying stunts pulled off by Benedict Cumberbatch's Sherlock Holmes character.

Sadly for Bangura, the trials and tribulations didn't end with football glory. In 2007 the Home Office threatened to send him back to Sierra Leone because of a legal technicality that meant, basically, his asylum-seeking status had been nullified. What followed was a right old fuss. Bangura was terrified of returning home and frankly, I couldn't blame him. In his home country, the poor lad had been raised in a secret sect where self-mutilation was a ritual act; his father had once been the leader of the same group and was murdered when Bangura was only four. More worrying was the news that his former 'friends' were hardly pleased with him for skipping borders. Bangura was convinced that somebody would stab him as soon as he returned home.

At first, the Home Office decided that he should be deported. That soon changed when an appeal, which included support from Labour MP David Blunkett and Watford chairman Elton John, helped to shine light on the situation. There was even a fans' protest and supporters of both teams during Watford's clash with Plymouth held up signs which read: 'He's Family'. Eventually, a government panel decided that Bangura could stay and allowed him a work permit to carry on with his football career. Since playing for Watford, Bangura has had spells at Blackpool, Brighton, and for clubs in Turkey and Azerbaijan. He later settled down with Forest Green Rovers in the Conference National where I hear that the challenges faced at The New Lawn are comparatively easier than the ones that forced him from his life in Sierra Leone.

'I expect to be given a tough time,' he said shortly after signing. 'But if an opponent attempts to smash me, I will get up and smile at them.'

It's a cracking attitude, but somebody ought to warn him about those burgers.

CHAPTER THIRTEEN

BIG SAM'S HEALTH FARM (AND HOW I NEARLY GOT THE SACK FROM SKY)

If you go down to the woods today (in Hampshire), you might stumble across a lovely little place called Forest Mere, which has been a regular spa retreat for me over the years. Life behind the *Soccer Saturday* desk has occasionally taken its toll on my suave good looks, so to halt the advancing crow's feet and laughter lines brought on by the antics of Chris Kamara, I've often locked myself away in this idyllic, woodland paradise for a few days of hardcore aromatherapy, flotation and 'Manual Lymph Drainage'. It's worked, too. Whenever I've returned home after a Forest Mere weekend, I often resemble a dashing hybrid of Pierce Brosnan and the Ready Brek Kid. My physique glows radiantly and my expression could accurately be described as twinkly of eye, so much so that I was able to empathise with Cristiano Ronaldo when he infamously claimed that people were envious of him because, and I quote, he was, 'Rich, handsome and a great player.' I'm right with you there, Ronnie. Well, at least in the looks department. I've yet to be described as a 'great player', and unless *Soccer Saturday* is taken on by Sheikh Mansour, my weekly wage won't afford me a diamond-studded earring, as worn by the likes of Jermain Defoe, Micah Richards and Charlie Nicholas.

Anyhow, when Mrs Jeff remarked that I might need to lose a few pounds after a couple of hectic working weeks in 2001 I decided to check into Forest Mere for a few days. And what a treat it was, too. Monday was absolutely fantastic, a whirlwind of steam rooms, facial scrubs and stimulating body treatments, like a weekend away with the girls from *Sex and the City*, without the awkward, ill-advised nookie, of course; by Tuesday, I could really feel my body returning to life once more. But on the Wednesday, things took a turn for the worse when I jogged around Forest Mere's grounds and noticed that a large bus had pulled up in the car park.

'That's funny,' I thought, my inquisitive journalistic mind still beavering away, despite a relaxing manicure in the beauty salon that morning. 'They don't usually have coach parties here. I wonder who that could be?'

When I wandered into the resort foyer I quickly found out: Big Sam Allardyce and his Bolton Wanderers squad had just checked in for the night.

'Stelling!' laughed Big Sam when he caught sight of me. 'What are you doing here?'

'Well, I'm in situ for a gruelling SAS-style recovery programme, Big Sam,' I lied, hands clasped behind the back to hide my still sparkling fingernails. 'What about you?'

Big Sam explained that his high-flying Bolton side were up against Portsmouth that night, their rivals from the Football League First Division, as it was known then. It was a game that could set them on the road to Premier League promotion and I could tell that he was buzzing with pre-match tension. It promised to be a cracking match and given that I had been cooped up for over 48 hours in usually no more than a fluffy dressing gown and mudpack, I decided a night of more masculine pursuits might be in order, and I got myself a ticket for the game.

Not wanting to intrude, I went to Fratton Park under my own steam – I even maintained my healthy streak by avoiding the meat pies and pints on sale at the ground – and the uplifting evening was topped off as I watched Bolton secure a fantastic victory, their winning goal arriving late in the game. Like a well-behaved football TV anchorman, I went straight back to the health farm and headed to bed at the sensible time of 11 o'clock, but as I drifted off into Never Never Land, I heard the cough and rumble of Bolton's coach as it pulled into Forest Mere once more.

'Wouldn't it be nice of me if I went down to the bar to say congratulations to the boys?' I thought, already dressed and halfway out of the bedroom as the sound of clinking glasses and merry bonhomie dragged me downstairs. Lo and behold, when I wandered down to the dining area, Sam and his squad were ordering their food for a late dinner.

'Ah, Stelling!' he shouted, patting an empty seat next to him. 'Come and sit here!'

I took my chair and immediately noticed that there was a hell of a lot of booze on the table for a health farm. What I hadn't realised was that Bolton had brought a personal supply of alcohol, which the coaching staff had stashed away in the boot of their bus. Sam then told me he was keen for the team to unwind that night, it had been a hard season for the players and he figured that it was time for a knees-up. Although it hadn't secured promotion for sure, their win over Pompey had put Sam's side in pole position. Even better, he invited me to stay for the celebrations.

'Well,' I thought, 'it would be somewhat rude and unprofessional of me to refuse.' So I agreed to a drink, and when dinner finished around 1 a.m., we were asked, very nicely, to adjourn from the bar and into a secluded private suite at the request of the spa manager. The Bolton lads had made quite a racket as the wine went down and the healthier guests in the retreat were struggling to get their much-needed beauty sleep. Nevertheless, the rabble-rousing was to go on unabated. What followed was an evening of story telling, song and buckets and buckets of fine vino until four or five in the morning, although I do recall that around three, a couple of apprentices got up and tried to escape for the night.

'Goodnight, Mr Allardyce, goodnight, Stelling,' they said, delivering the required levels of proportionate respect. 'We're off to bed.'

Big Sam looked them up and down disdainfully. The kind of glare I later imagined him inflicting upon his one-time striker at Bolton, El Hadji Diouf, when he had been accused of disgustingly aiming his saliva at a Boro fan in 2004.

'Where do you think you're going?' he said, somewhat miffed. 'You two will go to bed when I say you can go to bed!'

He ordered them back to their seats. Clearly, Sam was determined that his players should win as a team and party as a team, a spirit which ran through the senior members of the squad and beyond. My lasting memory of the evening was the sight of defender Ian Marshall clambering on to a table. From his lofty vantage point he told Sam and the coaching staff what was right with the club and what was wrong with the club; he went on about how good Sam was and how wonderful the team was. His eulogy lasted for nearly half an hour and it was a fitting end to a fantastic evening.

Now, I know some fans might feel a little aggrieved if their club had been involved in a night like the one organised by Sam, especially at such a pivotal point in the season, but I thought it was an excellent way of motivating a group of players who had been chasing promotion all year. His impromptu party was their reward for a fantastic performance against their league rivals. More to the point, I know that Sam was a wonderfully high-tech manager at the time. His approach to player energy and fitness levels was top notch. A night like that might have taken its toll on one or two of the older lads in the coming days, but Sam knew how to make up for it on the training ground. But that's why everyone wanted to play for him: they could tell he had their best interests at heart and was more than capable of taking them into the top flight.

I couldn't have looked at a pair of football boots the following day, let alone kicked a ball. When the sun rose and the cockerel crowed, I rose for brunch, my last day in the health farm written off with one of the biggest hangovers I'd ever experienced. Thanks to Bolton's secret stash of booze, I felt utterly and totally wrecked. When I arrived home, Mrs Jeff had the shock of her life. She had expected to see my lithe frame skipping down the drive, my face looking refreshed and healthy, my skin aglow. Instead I was grumpy and weary, my eyes were bloodshot and my face looked as if it had been pummelled by a succession of Rory Delap throw-ins. The Forest Mere weekend had been a waste of time and money, every part of my body ached. Even my manicure looked a little tatty.

It won't come as a surprise to learn that my country escapes have been curtailed for health reasons since then. After Big Sam's boozy rehydration therapy at the spa, Mrs Jeff reckons it's better for my health if I recuperate at home these days. I have to say, I think she's right. Sorry, Cristiano, it looks like you're fighting the body-beautiful war on your own, mate.

Despite our boozy bonding that night, Big Sam and I haven't always seen eye to eye when it comes to football matters. In fact, our professional friendship imploded so badly in 2006 that the resulting argument almost cost me my comfy position in the *Soccer Saturday* studio, which gave me quite a scare, I can tell you.

The nuclear dispute took place when the BBC *Panorama* programme announced it was going to expose a series of bungs within football. Apparently Sam's name was going to feature in the show, which caused something of a controversy among the football media. Around the time that *Panorama* had been on air, Bolton were playing live on Sky in an evening game against Portsmouth and I was the studio presenter. After our night at the health spa, I had developed a great working relationship with Sam and he would often chat to me and the panel live on *Soccer Saturday* during the build-up to an afternoon's action. This time he had agreed to be interviewed before and after the game, and I had a meeting with our producer on how to handle the delicate topic of bungs in football. We basically decided that the best way to approach the sticky subject was not to mention it before kick-off, as we felt that it might disrupt his concentration in the run-up to the match. Instead we agreed that we should approach it afterwards, but in a very sensitive manner.

It was at that moment that Bolton contacted the Sky offices and told the production team that there were to be no direct questions about the allegations. 'They are out of bounds,' said a stern-sounding press officer. My view was that this wasn't a good way to approach the issue because discussing it would have cleared the air. I thought that giving Sam the chance to put his opinions across would be beneficial. It would have made for a nice bit of PR for Sam and Bolton and dispelled all the nasty speculation. I didn't think of it at the time but maybe Sam only appeared because he thought we would steer well clear of this story.

Anyway, the pre-match interview went well, Sam seemed to be in good spirits. He was in even better spirits when Bolton later won the game. As the players left the pitch I was patched through to the tunnel area for our second live chat and it was all going swimmingly as we dissected the major talking points in the match, but before we wrapped up, I decided Sam was happy enough for me to chance one question on the *Panorama* affair.

'Obviously, we've seen the stuff on the BBC this week,' I said. 'There have been some allegations . . . Just to clear things up, have you ever been offered a bung?'

Sam's mood and colour changed considerably. The last time I had seen him in person, he had been helping me to polish off a gallon of red wine, his face had been ruddy with the glow of victory. This time, his cheeks burned with rage and I got the distinct impression that he wanted to shove his Sky Sports microphone into a delicate part of the Stelling anatomy. The word 'bung' had brought the red mist down.

'You're out of order,' he snapped.

As you can imagine the interview finished shortly afterwards, but almost immediately I knew I was in big trouble. I had an earpiece which connected me with the production team. As soon as I had uttered the B-word, I heard a sharp intake of breath; someone in the control room said, 'F**k, why did he ask that?' Hull City's then manager Phil Brown was the guest in the Sky studios that night. When I looked in his direction, I could see that he had gone ashen, which took some doing, given his fondness for a solarium.

I didn't realise just how much of a pickle I had got myself into until after the show when I had said my goodbyes to Phil and the camera crew. The plan was to drive home to Stelling Towers straightaway, but before I could get to my car, I received a call from Sky Sports' producer Steve Tudgay. By all accounts, Bolton's chairman Phil Gartside was absolutely livid and looking for blood. My blood.

'It would probably be a good idea if you beat a hasty retreat from the stadium, Jeff,' he said. 'And don't go anywhere near the tunnel, they're looking for you.'

I figured Steve was right and so, somewhat apprehensively, I snuck out into the darkest Portsmouth night I'd ever known. Then it dawned on me that there was probably going to be a massive storm about my clash with Sam in the press the following day. The papers were sure to pick up on the spat because it had added fuel to the fire started by *Panorama*'s investigations. I was in desperate trouble and there was only one person who could help me: I called Sky Sports head honcho Vic Wakeling.

I knew that Vic had been at the Labour Party Conference that night, but I could tell that his appearance there hadn't safeguarded him from Big Samgate. When he picked up the phone there were no pleasantries, no 'Hello, Jeff, mate.' Instead he snapped, 'What the f**k have you done?' which made me realise at once that Phil Gartside had already been on the blower.

Vic wasn't very pleased to say the least, but we agreed that our first job was to smooth things over with Bolton. Once that was settled, any decisions about my future at Sky could be discussed, an agreement that made me shiver. I was really upset by the situation. I went home and suffered a restless night. In my darkest moments, I feared that if the press coverage was dramatic, I might be about to lose the job I loved most of all. Those joyful afternoons with the panel on *Soccer Saturday* would be finished and my seat taken by an up-and-coming hopeful, like Gary Newbon or Jim Rosenthal.

The following morning my worst fears were realised and the interview with Sam was all over the papers. A few ex-managers thought I'd been out of order and claimed, somewhat unfairly, that I'd been trying to make a name for myself. That wasn't the case at all. I had simply asked him whether he had been *offered* a bung, not whether he had *accepted* one. There was a great deal of difference in the deeper meaning of those two words. I don't think Sam heard the nuance and suspect the reason he got so angry was because he thought I'd gone against an agreement to steer clear of the story.

The controversy raged on and on throughout the week,

though I must say that the papers were incredibly supportive of my situation. A number of columns and opinion pieces were written, arguing it was a question that had needed to be asked. BBC Radio 5 Live even called me up and invited me on air to discuss the scandal, but I thought 'Not a chance, thank you very much'. That didn't stop them from running a major debate on the incident with broadcaster Victoria Derbyshire one morning. During the show, they asked the same questions that I tormented myself with every waking night: 'Should he have asked Sam about the bung?' And, 'What will happen to him now?'

I spoke to a few people to get my head around it all. I called up Phil Brown, who was great. I explained the situation to him because he had Sam's ear, having worked with him before. He told me it would all blow over and there was nothing to worry about. I spoke to Peter Reid and Kammy, I rang everybody I knew who was in touch with Bolton. Reidy was a massive help, he talked to Sam and explained that I was a good bloke, that I wasn't trying to stitch him up and that he should give me a call.

It was probably over a week later that I finally spoke to Sam. I can't remember now who called who, but we talked through the incident and in fairness we were both pretty upset by the way it had turned out. We patched things up and the hatchet was buried, though thankfully not in my bonce. In the meantime, meetings were held at Sky regarding my future on *Soccer Saturday*, but it was agreed that my job was safe. Sam even came on to the panel as a guest one weekend years later, and as was traditional, we had a few drinks in the hotel bar the night before the game. Everything had come full circle.

In hindsight, I don't regret asking the 'bung' question, but at the time I regretted the storm it caused. My inquisitive nature hadn't done anybody any good and in the end, the *Panorama* investigation had no real substance – there was no case for Sam to answer, but because of it, I had put my job on the line, the producer's job on the line, and maybe Sam's job on the line, over a programme that really had no real credibility at all. At the time though, I felt I had to ask it because I'm a journalist and it was – and is – my job to ask. But blow me, if it didn't take months for me to regain my confidence afterwards, months for me to put forward a half-decent question to a football manager or player. For ages I double-checked everything and anything before I said it live on air. The incident gave me a real appreciation for the journalists who put themselves in the legal firing line every day – now that takes a lot of bottle. In theory, what I do should be a walk in the park (or a jog through a health farm car park). Sadly, as my row with Big Sam had taught me, it can be anything but.

CHAPTER FOURTEEN

MONEY, MONEY, MONEY...

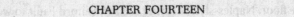

A funny thing happened when Napoli's Edinson Cavani scored his second goal in the 2–1 win over Manchester City during the group stages of the Champions League in 2011: the earth actually moved. Now, I know that sounds just about as far-fetched as it gets, like maybe Charlie Nicholas unveiling a Spurs tattoo on his right buttock, but according to reports from the University of Naples, El Matador's goal prompted celebrations so euphoric that a seismic jolt took place in the region, such was the force of all those Italian fans jumping up and down in unison. It makes you realise just how fattening pasta and deep-crust pizza can be.

Somewhat coincidentally, around about the same time, the earth moved in Manchester too, and not because a goal had been scored against the blue half of town. Instead, when it was announced that City had made a loss of £197.5 million during the previous financial year, thousands of jaws simultaneously crashed to the floor, Naples-style, causing the San Salford Fault to wobble dangerously. Let's just say that number again: one hundred and ninety seven point five million quid. It deserves repeating in words because the figure is so ludicrously huge. City's owner Sheikh Mansour obviously had a lot of cash to throw away that year, we all knew that, but blowing £197.5 million in 12 months was excessive, even by Premiership standards.

So how did City react to the news that they had been perhaps a little exuberant with the credit card as the rest of the world was plunged further into economic misery? (Don't worry, lawyers, I'm not suggesting that those two events were linked.) They did what any club looking to fit into UEFA's Financial Fair Play rules would do: they spent more money and ordered a batch of individually personalised snoods for all of their players, complete with names, squad numbers and national flags stitched into the wool. I'm presuming their mums' addresses were also attached, just in case poor little Samir or Yaya ever left their neck warmers behind in the tuck shop during the increasingly mild winter months.

Look, I'm not just having a pop at City here, I could have chosen any number of clubs on which to land a Stelling 'haymaker': Liverpool, Arsenal or Chelsea could have fallen into my sights for the opening to this chapter. The Gunners especially, because they had the audacity to take a Spanish shop owner to court in 2011 when she dared to name her rather fancy hat boutique 'Arsenale'. It was all incredibly petty. The club first asked owner Alicia Simon to change the name when she registered it in 2007, perhaps fearing that fans would mistake her fancy Sevillano and Cordobes hats for official team wear. When she refused, Arsenal engaged her in a legal battle and won, though Simon – like Barcelona and their ultimately successful quest to sign Cesc Fabregas – later vowed to fight on 'to the end'.

Having learned of City's excessive spending and Arsenal's legal wrangling, it struck me that some football clubs might have started to lose sight of what made them so successful in the first place, namely their unique identities. Arsenal have been regarded as the gentlemanly club for as long as football has existed in this country. Taking a little hat shop to court because it shared a similar name seemed anything but chivalrous to me. Elsewhere, Liverpool have always been considered as a club for the people, which appeared about right given their totem-like presence in the city. However, when Liverpool MD Ian Ayre suggested in 2011 that Premier League TV rights should be divvied up according to a club's popularity, it hardly smacked of the socialist leanings so loved on Merseyside. His argument was that the bigger teams should get a larger slice of the TV cash pie because, he asked, 'Who tunes in in Kuala Lumpur to watch Bolton?' Well, that would be the Bolton Wanderers that spanked Stoke 5–0 that same season. Presumably, the other teams in Ayre's firing line would have included Blackburn Rovers (who beat Manchester United 3–2 at Old Trafford), Fulham (who defeated Arsenal 2–1), and Stoke (who claimed three points against both Spurs and Liverpool). Those results alone would have been enough to kick his idea into touch.

The beauty of football in this country is that anyone from the bottom of the table can beat anyone at the top on their day. That's why the Premier League has become such a globally popular phenomenon. And the fact that clubs like Bolton and Stoke earn as much TV revenue as the likes of Liverpool has meant that they can buy players to help them compete against the big boys. Thankfully Ayre later climbed down from his proposal.

And don't get me started on naming rights. Well, actually do, because the continual chopping and changing of stadium titles that have long made up the wonderful cultural tapestry of the beautiful game in this country has driven me absolutely barmy in recent years, most notably when the owners of Newcastle United announced that they were going to change the name of their ground from the legendary, iconic, not to mention historic, St James' Park to the Sports Direct Arena. I fumed for days; I had spent a lot of time in the North East during my younger years and I'm very aware of the incredible importance that particular football ground holds in the city. After learning of the sacrilegious decision to sell out such a wonderful name to advertisers, I decided to make a stand. Never, ever, not in a million years ever, would I refer to St James' Park as the Sports Direct Arena, not while I was working on *Soccer Saturday*. Sure, the producers would have to put the official stadium name on the bottom of the screen whenever our cameras went there for a live feed – that was all part of the Sky deal with the Premier League – but I was adamant. The words 'Arena', 'Sports' and 'Direct' would never come out of my mouth in the correct order on the show.

Some people might have thought I was being petty, but the renaming of St James' Park was a classic example of football financiers disregarding the emotions of the everyday supporter. Newcastle fans make a pilgrimage to St James' Park – to them it's Mecca. Mike Ashley and his cohorts might own the club, but they don't own its history or its heritage and they never will, and the fans won't refer to it as anything other than its original name. It's a sign of the times that even the aforementioned Ian Ayre stated that Liverpool would never play in a ground not known as Anfield;

Manchester United wouldn't dream of tampering with the identity of Old Trafford, and both those statements, to me, are a stamp of class.

When Mike Ashley's plan was first announced, the current Newcastle owners originally claimed that the name – the one I will not repeat – would be a temporary title. In other words, it was business shorthand for, 'We'll be changing it again as soon as we can find another investor.' Who knows? By the time you've read this, it might have already happened, but if I were a sponsor, I wouldn't touch a famous stadium such as St James' Park with a bargepole because it would turn hundreds of thousands of Geordies against my product overnight.

Look at it this way: imagine, in a moment of madness, I bought up the naming rights to St James' Park from Ashley and Co. and renamed the ground as The Stelling Theatre of Fantasy. I can almost guarantee you that the Geordie faithful would turn their back on the nation's favourite football results show and turn to *Final Score*, Gabby Logan and Garth Crooks instead. The change would probably happen overnight.

It's not just at the top level that drastic personality changes have taken place; naming rights have caused controversy further down the leagues, too. I became embroiled in a dispute with the good people at Wycombe Wanderers when their stadium Adams Park was renamed The Causeway by sponsors for three years from 2003. What annoyed me was that the people who had originally owned the land bequeathed the area to the football club, yet years later the original names have been forgotten or erased. On air I refused to refer to it as anything other than 'Wycombe's Ground'. I had problems in Scotland, too. When Dumbarton changed the identity of The Rock – the name of their home ground since time immemorial – to the Strathclyde Homes Stadium, I refused to acknowledge it as anything other than its original title, despite the snotty emails I received from the club.

Still, the worst one in my opinion had to be Walsall and their much-loved Bescot Stadium. The ground was renamed in 2007 as The Banks's Stadium after it had been sponsored by a brewery of the same name, but what really got under my skin was the identity change throughout the entire club. If you were to wander around the Bescot, you could find yourself watching the match from either the 'Floors-2-Go Stand', the 'Extra Bet Stand', or the 'TXT: 64446 Health Stand'. Now, I'm assuming that this particular part of the ground overlooked the M6 motorway which passed nearby and made for an ugly line in advertising, but were the rest of us really supposed to use those frankly ludicrous names? Whenever Sky went to Walsall, was commentator Alan Parry supposed to say, 'Oh and there's local hero Joe Bloggs watching the game from the "TXT: 64446 Health Stand"? Not a chance. And the sooner we start reclaiming the historical names for our football stadiums, the better.

There ends the rant . . .

And here begins another . . .

If you really want a financial scare, take some time to absorb one of the many surveys that record the average footballer's earnings across all four professional leagues in England. Honestly, it makes my mind boggle whenever I read them. The last time I looked – around the beginning of 2012 – the numbers went a bit like this:

The average League Two player gets around £36,000 a year.
The average League One player gets £70,000 a year.
The average Championship player gets £200,000 a year.
The average Premiership player gets something like £1.6
million a year.

According to a report in the *Sun*, David Beckham earned £33,000 a day in 2010 from his various deals. That's nearly all of an annual salary picked up by someone at AFC Wimbledon. I'm sure those figures would have rocketed again already, especially if the likes of City and Chelsea have had anything to do with them; the only reason I haven't looked at them recently, dear reader, is because I gave up *Countdown* some months previously, mainly on the basis that trying to score well on the numbers game always gave me an intellectual migraine. The last time I studied those numbers, I felt as if a Black & Decker drill had been boring into my skull.

But, bloomin' 'eck, that's a hell of a lot of money at the top level! And what you have to remember is that £1.6 million a year is only an average number in the top flight where the boys at the top clubs in the Premiership are getting a shedload more than the ones at the bottom. The lads on the bench at City and Chelsea are probably getting bigger pay cheques than some of the first team regulars at the likes of Fulham, West Brom and Villa. The amount of money flying around is scary.

Thankfully, Leagues One and Two are doing their level best to keep tabs on the incredible spending taking place. In those divisions a slight modicum of common sense is beginning to take hold. For example, League Two runs a scary-sounding Salary Cost Management Protocol scheme and within the rules, clubs are only allowed to spend approximately 55 per cent of their turnover on players' salaries. League One is bringing in the same restrictions. In the early stages of this plan, clubs will only be allowed to spend 75 per cent of their turnover on wages. This will be reduced to around 60 per cent by 2013/14.

I think it's a sensible way for football to work, but only if it's carried across all four divisions because what teams have discovered recently is that it's very difficult to operate the finances when they drop down a division, even two divisions. Life becomes very hard when a team has been used to operating within a free-wage system in the Championship. Once they have been relegated to League One and, maybe later, League Two, they then have to find a way of trimming the budget overnight. Newly relegated clubs in that position are often unable to fill key positions in their squad because they have blown their entire budget before the season has even kicked off.

It's not as if they can get a huge helping hand from the loan system either, which has become increasingly flawed in recent years. The idea originally was that younger players from the top flight would receive a loan deal with a lower-league club. There they could play regular football, learn their trade and help the loanee club with some great performances. These days it seems to involve top-class footballers hopping from one Premiership team to the next. Emmanuel Adebayor is a great example of that: Man City reportedly paid a large chunk of his reported £225,000 a week wages to play for their Premier League rival Spurs in 2011/12, which is a bit like movie director Ridley Scott paying Tom Cruise half of his salary to star in a Steven Spielberg film.

When the *Soccer Saturday* team investigated the loan system for a feature that same season, we worked out that City had 23 players out on loan, which meant that if you were a youth player hoping to break into the first team group then you had next to no chance. We actually interviewed a kid from City on the show called Mohammed Abu. He was a Ghanaian lad from a poverty-stricken background and possessed bucket-loads of talent; he had risen through the youth ranks at Sporting Club Accra. Abu became one of the rising stars at Eastlands, but was there a worse club for him to be at as a young footballer than City? He was immediately loaned out to a Norwegian club and, on his return to Manchester, he was loaned out again to Eintracht Frankfurt. I wonder whether he'll ever kick a ball competitively for City. At the time of writing, he would probably have been better off joining a club with less money and more modest ambitions. Somewhere like Hartlepool, maybe . . .

If there's a group of people who have no problems when it comes to spending money, then it's Premier League footballers. When Mario Balotelli was sent out to John Lewis in Manchester by his mum to buy an ironing board and iron for the family home in 2011, he returned with a store truck in his wake. Onboard were the spoils of an immense shopping spree: a table tennis set, a trampoline, two Vespa scooters and a Scalextric racing track, not to mention the all-important iron and board. That paled into comparison to Croatian international Vedran Corluka, who gave away his £36,000, diamond-encrusted Hublot watch to a waiter because he 'had complimented him on it'. I've since heard that the restaurant he had been eating in – a fancy place in Mayfair – was good, but not so good that anyone would want to leave a tip equalling the annual salary for a player from League Two. The spending! It drives me bloody mad.

I suppose one refreshing antidote to all that economic frivolity arrived with Corluka's team mate at Spurs, the Cameroonian full back Benoit Assou-Ekotto. In interviews, the Spurs star revealed that he liked to drive to training in a two-seater Smart car (although it does have a personalised number plate) because, 'In London, it is perfect. I can get to training every day for £20 a week. And I don't care if other players laugh at me.'

If ever he travelled to France to see his family, he went via the tube and Eurostar rather than a private jet, and when he sponsored the shirts for a local kids' team in Woodford, east London, he refused the offer of having his name emblazoned on the shirts. Instead he opted for the UN's 'End Poverty Campaign' logo.

I suppose the strangest story surrounding Assou-Ekotto – or Disco Benny, as Spurs fans have christened him, owing to a prominent afro haircut that he wore when his hair wasn't in braids – concerned the odd pair of football boots he took to wearing during the 2011/12 season. And when I say odd, I don't mean pink or Day-glo, but mismatched. Having bought two pairs of boots (he doesn't have a kit sponsor), one blue and one white, Assou-Ekotto was left frustrated when one of the white boots split down the middle during a training session. Rather than throwing the pair away, he took a new blue boot from the other box and carried on playing in the mismatching pair for a few matches.

'Why would I throw away a shoe that was brand new?' he said, by way of a logical explanation.

I'll tell you what, having one blue boot and one white boot didn't stop him from having an absolutely wonderful season that year. 'Disco Benny' managed to turn his career around, because for a couple of years he had been an accident waiting to happen.

He used to give fans nightmares, well Tottenham fans anyway. Now he only gives the salesman from his local Bentley showroom sleepless nights. Who else will buy that Continental Flying Spur on the forecourt? Calling Mr Balotelli . . .

FAN AID

I suppose the unbelievable wealth enjoyed by the likes of United and Chelsea in the Premiership only highlights further the lack of money at the other end of the football spectrum. For every team lavishing their pampered stars with personalised snoods and quarter of a million quid pay packets, there is a Lincoln City, a club so cash-strapped in 2011 that the players had to pay for their own pre-match meals. Or poor old Whitstable Town, who were forced to postpone a league game when thieves broke into their stadium in February 2011 and pinched all the copper in the building. The Oystermen should have been celebrating their victory over Worthing in the Ryman League South. Instead they were counting the cost of an opportunistic break-in. It was heartbreaking stuff and unsurprisingly, their chairman Joe Brownett was furious afterwards.

'I have been at Whitstable Town, a club which I and my family have supported, for over 20 years and this is by far the worst thing that has ever happened,' he said. 'They have taken

181

every scrap of copper they could find. They have stripped the showers, the boiler, taps, pipes, you name it they stole it . . . The people that do this sort of thing are heartless. They do not care about anyone else, just themselves. It goes without saying that we will carry on.'

It's not just the chairmen that suffer when their club is without the financial riches enjoyed by teams at the top level. The fans also suffer, and usually in the most inconvenient of conveniences: the lavs. I can't tell you the number of times I've had to queue for ages at half-time, only to unzip in front of what appears to be a rusty old pigs' trough overflowing with wads of chewing gum, crisp packets and ripped up pages of what could be my column in a well-known newspaper. Going to the loo at a football ground can be a really unsettling experience, especially if I'm performing said ablutions on a photograph of my own face, so it was quite reassuring to hear of a recent competition in which fans were encouraged to vote online for the worst football club toilets in Britain.

The event, which promised a £100,000 toilet revamp for the 'winners' and was named The Best Loosers Competition, drew votes for a number of facilities, including Aldershot Town, Bradford City, Barnsley and Ebbsfleet United, who gathered a whopping 3,287 votes. Sadly the competition was closed due to suspicions of cheating. Apparently, many supporters had broken the 'one entry, one vote' rule, though nobody is sure exactly who resorted to underhand tactics.

'It became clear quite quickly that some fans had managed to get around the security checks and were making multiple votes for their team,' said Best Loosers' spokeswoman Janet Bentick having flushed out the cheats. 'I suppose it is testament to how passionately they feel about having new facilities installed at their clubs, but it breached our terms and conditions.'

However, if there is a date on the calendar that really highlights the gulf between the haves and the have-nots, then it's generally the first week of January when the third round of the FA Cup traditionally takes place. There always seem to be one or two smaller teams that qualify from the non-league sector. It's also the moment when the Premiership teams get dropped into the FA's big bucket of shiny balls for the draw, so during the run-up to this most exciting day in The World's Best Club Competition (but don't tell the sponsors of the Champions League I said that), I scour the newspapers, collecting rich stories regarding our nation's greatest underfunded teams and their efforts to cope with the football big guns.

Generally, these stories fall into one of a few categories, such as the unusual day job of a part-time player, or a club's efforts to play suitable hosts to a team from a far superior league. However, the tales I always enjoy focus upon the rather unusual incentives offered to players in the hope they might then perform some spectacular giant-killing act, such as the fixtures played out by Sutton United who defeated top-flight Coventry City in 1988/89, and bottom of the Football League Wrexham, who turned over top of the First Division (now the Premiership) side Arsenal in 1992.

One such club aiming for a similar result in 2011/12 was the Southern League side Stourbridge. The team had already hit the headlines by beating Plymouth Argyle in the first round, but when they then drew Stevenage in the second, their shirt sponsors Bhandal Dental Practices came up with a very unusual incentive for victory: it was promised that every player in the

Stourbridge squad would receive free teeth-whitening treatment should they turn over their opponents and make it to the third round.

'When we told the boys about their bonus, a few jaws dropped,' said gaffer Gary Hackett, clearly a student from the Stelling School of Comedy. 'A few of our single lads who enjoy a night on the town really fancy getting the Hollywood look!'

Despite the bonus on offer, it was Stevenage who cruised to a 3–0 victory, escaping somewhat comfortably from the coffee-stained jaws of defeat; Stourbridge went home, sucking on the bitter taste of failure (I blame the fluoride). But evidence that a juicy carrot at the end of a stick could ensure FA Cup success was provided in the same year by Ryman League Division One North side Redbridge, the lowest-ranked club in the competition. Their chairman Dan Holloway promised his playing staff a night out in Basildon – or Bas Vegas as it is known to the locals – should they secure passage to the second round. Lo and behold, his motivational techniques worked and following a 2–1 victory over Oxford City, the boys were treated to a night on the not-so-glamorous town. Later, Holloway decided that their achievements deserved a greater reward and he improved their bonus with an end-of-season holiday to Spain for the entire squad. A night in Liquid or Bar Plazma – two of Bas Vegas's stellar nightspots – clearly wasn't enough.

'The lads will now be going on an end-of-season trip to Marbella,' said Holloway in the *Ilford Recorder*. 'That's definitely an upgrade from Bas Vegas! Most of them have been texting me about it!'

Presumably with their excuses, Mr Holloway.

* * *

Thankfully, when a club finds itself in need of a bob or two, fellow fans generally rally round to lend a hand, as is evidenced by Non-League Day, a Saturday afternoon event now organised once a year, often during a weekend when international fixtures – qualifying games for the European Championships and World Cup, friendlies designed to annoy Arsène Wenger and such like – ruin the usual football fare. With Premiership and Championship teams taking a day off so that players can fulfil international call-ups, fans have been encouraged to support their nearest non-league club for the afternoon. So, as England plod to a drab 2–2 draw with Macedonia, or Scotland get thrashed by Cape Verde, the likes of Tooting & Mitcham and Rainworth Miners Welfare can now receive a welcome boost at the turnstiles.

What a great idea! I don't know about you, but I hate weekends without a Premiership game; the thought of a hollow day of international fixtures leaves me cold, mainly because there's no *Soccer Saturday* to present. I never get psyched up for England games if they're friendlies, especially when I know that eight or nine substitutions are going to take place during the 90 minutes, which used to be the case under some managers (that's right, Sven, I'm talking about you). These days there are so many international breaks that weekends involving the likes of England, Ireland, Northern Ireland, Wales, Scotland and Andorra have become the worst part of the season. If I'm honest, I would rather wander out to the park on a Saturday morning and maybe catch a pub game. There's so much more excitement and drama on show, not to mention comedy.

As far as I'm concerned, Non-League Day is a fantastic idea, because anything that helps clubs lower down the pyramid is a good thing. Generally, the standard of football is great in the Conference and the leagues that feed into it; in fact it has been improving steadily for years as a number of former Football League teams have dropped into the Conference Premier (Luton Town, Stockport County, Cambridge United). Sadly that increasing technical ability has come at a price – in order to compete, a lot of semi-professional sides have gone full-time. That change has required an increase in cash at the turnstiles because the players now command full-time wages. Balancing the books has become a real issue.

Non-League Day goes some way to boosting that revenue. It's also a nice idea for fans to experience a different atmosphere – an environment where the supporter can stand a few feet away from the players. It's a completely different vibe to watching a match in, say, the Premier League or the Championship because the fans can speak to the players afterwards if they want to; in the stands they can be only metres away from the action and supporters can even hear pretty much everything that's said on the pitch. That's not always a good thing and I remember watching a pre-season friendly between Arsenal and the current Conference South side Bromley at their Hayes Lane ground in 1996. It was all pretty friendly stuff, the Arsenal team was made up of kids and one or two fringe first-team players such as Glenn Helder, a footballer who later made his way into a fans' Worst Arsenal XI of All Time, but on the day, I think some of the Bromley players weren't too taken by his top-billing status. As a loose ball popped out to the wing, Helder raced on to it, only to be brought down by a lumbering centre half. The referee raced over to flash a yellow and asked, rather sensibly, 'What did you do that for, mate? It's only a friendly . . .'

From my position behind the wooden fence that separated the fans from the pitch, I could clearly hear his rather ridiculous excuse: 'Because I'm a Spurs fan, mate.'

You wouldn't get that in the Premier League.

It's not just at the semi-pro level that charity takes place, it happens at the professional level too, as I noticed during the fall-out from Plymouth Argyle's recent financial difficulties. With the club anchored to the bottom of the Football League and in more financial turmoil than one of Paul Merson's bookmakers, it was announced that the team would be the beneficiaries of a 'Fans Reunited Day'.

Now, I think these events are a great idea on paper: basically, they first started in 1997 when, somewhat ironically, a teenage Argyle fan called Richard Vaughan became so struck by the plight of Brighton & Hove Albion (the club's owners had sold off their ground without an alternative stadium in place) that he organised a day during which supporters of other clubs could rally round and raise money for the Seagulls. It worked too, and fans of clubs from all around the country turned up in their various shirts and woolly hats (well, it can get chilly on the coast) to support Brighton.

I say ironically, because little did Master Vaughan know at the time that his successful scheme would eventually come to the help of his own club some 14 years later. But that's exactly what happened when it was announced that Argyle were in dire financial straits after a period spent in administration. Fans Reunited moved into action and the Save Argyle Fans United page on the Internet rallied together thousands of supporters from clubs up and down the country who descended upon Home

Park, stirred by the website's chilling explanation of how the team had fallen on hard times.

> As anyone with more than a passing interest in football is aware, Plymouth Argyle are in trouble. The imminent danger of liquidation is a daily reality at Home Park. Stories of players not being paid, staff being paid by the manager out of his own pocket, administration, debt and the delays securing the new owners have dominated all news relating to Argyle since March of this year. This nearly came to a head in the first week of September 2011 when there was talk of the players and staff going on strike and refusing to play a game away at Burton. Fortunately strike action was averted when the players and staff agreed to receive 40% of owed wages now and the remainder on completion of the long overdue takeover by Bishop International Ltd on the understanding that the takeover will be completed by the 31st August 2011. Distressing times for a club and its fans who just two short seasons ago were playing in the Championship by winning two promotions between 2000 and 2008 . . .

It says a lot that fans of all clubs were willing to get into a scheme like this one in order to help Plymouth. On the day, apparently there were scarves on show from all sorts of teams, from the Premiership down. It was also a day that would have taken a hell of a lot of effort to attend. It's not as if Plymouth was a town located slap bang in the middle of the country, it's a long hike to get there, wherever you live. All in all, it was a top,

top effort from everyone involved and helped to raise a few quid for the club.

There was one serious question that nagged away at me as this very admirable and charitable event took place, however: it wouldn't happen in the Premiership, would it? I couldn't imagine Chelsea fans turning up at Anfield to support Liverpool should they ever find themselves in serious financial trouble. Would supporters of Sunderland or Fulham make a pilgrimage to the Etihad Stadium if ever Sheikh Mansour walked away and left Manchester City in financial difficulty? Unlikely.

I don't know why that is, exactly. Maybe it's because the stakes are that much higher in the Premiership, therefore the divisiveness and hatred of rival clubs is much more intense at the highest levels. Sometimes I almost feel as if Premier League football is more tribal than elsewhere – fans support Arsenal and hate Spurs. They don't necessarily appreciate the good things about their rivals. Supporters of Championship or League One sides would probably argue it's the same in other divisions, but I really think there's an unbridgeable divide at the top, a divide that would prevent a City fan from helping out United in any shape or form, and vice versa.

I think further down the leagues, fans are unified by their shared experience of adversity. A fan of Torquay would have understood exactly the hardships and emotional traumas a Plymouth fan might have been going through as their club faced financial collapse; they would have related to them. Meanwhile, in the lower leagues, I think everyone appreciates just how much effort the fans put into supporting their clubs without enjoying the spoils of the Premiership or Europe, and I don't mean that in a patronising way.

Fans seem to mix more easily away from the Premier League and Championship, too. There are a lot of lower-league games where I've seen home and away fans meeting up for a pint and a laugh in the pub beforehand. I've travelled with Pools to Cheltenham and been in their social club in the ground for a pre-match pint and a packet of pork scratchings. The Cheltenham fans and Hartlepool fans had a beer together before the game and it was a fantastic atmosphere, everyone got on. It's hard to imagine that happening at many games at the highest level.

Look, I'm not saying the mingling of fans wouldn't happen at every game in the Premier League, and there are certainly several worrying flashpoints among the lower-league games too, but there's more of a togetherness about third- and fourth-tier clubs. I guess a preservation society of goodwill exists because nobody wants to see a team go to the wall. The fear among fans is that their team could be next, so there is a genuine unity against financial struggle among followers of clubs like my own, and long may that continue, because it can make for a great atmosphere, as evidenced by Fans Reunited Day.

Well, not for everyone, and here comes a word to the wise: you really don't want to be the opponents on a designated Fans Reunited Day because the team in trouble is lifted up by the support; their rivals that day are generally crushed by the inevitable sensation of being the pantomime villains for the occasion. I remember when Brighton were being helped out during the inaugural event. The old Goldstone Ground was absolutely heaving, packed to the rafters with fans from all over the country, cheering on the home team. Overnight, Brighton & Hove Albion had become Cinderella, Fans Reunited Day was their ball. And who the hell were the ugly, wart-ridden, fat-bottomed sisters that day? Bloody Hartlepool, that's who.

If the Goldstone had a roof, it would have been lifted off, such was the noise from the home stands and Pools got absolutely stuffed. Just to prove it wasn't a fluke, Plymouth picked up their first win of the season when it was their turn to enjoy a Fans Reunited Day all those years later. So my advice to any kind-hearted supporters would be this: by all means, help your fellow man, travel the length and breadth of the country to pluck your rivals from financial plight and deliver emotional support. But just make sure you check the bloody fixture list first, because being an ugly sister is not a pleasant experience. Not if football fairy tales are anything to go by.

CHAPTER SIXTEEN

SUNDAY, BLOODY SUNDAY

If you were to put down *Jeffanory* for one brief moment, click onto the encyclopaedic website Wikipedia, and type in the words 'Jeff + Stelling', you might discover some really rather interesting facts about me and my career. Apart from the shocking stat that I am in my late fifties (rather than the fortysomething spring chicken that I know you still think I am) and how I've run the London Marathon eight times (my PB is three hours and 28 minutes), there is a tale of how, many moons ago, I was an apprentice at Newcastle United before my career was cruelly shot down by injury, not to mention the emergence of Malcolm Macdonald and such like in the first team.

What a load of tosh! There wasn't a cat in hell's chance of my ever making it as a pro, though I do like to play up to the rumour every now and then, especially if I'm propping up the bar with Georgie Thompson and the Sky Sports News girls. The truth is, the closest I ever got to being a youth team player for the Magpies was when I used to walk past the ground during a lads' weekend to Newcastle. As a teenager, I was always going to be a journalist rather than a footballer, partly on the basis that I had two right feet (I was left-footed), but also because both of those were in such a state of disrepair (I blame the marathons) that I could barely run around a football pitch. So sadly, Wikipedia fans, Hartlepool Sunday League was only ever going to be my level, despite my best attempts to make it in the game as a pro.

But can you imagine if I had been an apprentice at St James' Park? My time at the club would have coincided with legend-making appearances by the likes of Frank Clark and Mickey Burns. I would have had a great time, mainly because I could have spent years kicking a permed Phil Thompson around the pitch whenever Newcastle played at Anfield. And just imagine it: after a glorious career in top-flight football, rounded off by a failed stint of managing my boyhood club Pools, I could have become engaged in a very different role among the *Soccer Saturday* crew. Rather than being the highly respected, award-winning and witty anchorman of Saturday afternoon's most popular show (after the re-runs of *Monk* on another less exciting channel), I could have taken on an ex-player's position; I could have been the next John Salako. Sadly that wasn't to be. The truth is, I wasn't much cop as a Sunday league footballer, but boy, did I love it. I have plenty of fond memories from my days of kicking a ball about with a stinking hangover and up until I was 30-odd, I played in a lot of pub leagues.

Now, believe it or not, when I was younger, the standard in Hartlepool was really rather good. Some of the guys I used to compete against certainly had the potential to play professionally, albeit in the lower leagues, but sadly, they just didn't have the dedication when it came to the training. It didn't help that they couldn't stay out of the pub on a Saturday night – or a Monday, Tuesday, Wednesday, Thursday and Friday night either, for that matter. My only problem was that playing Sunday league football was quite tough in those days. Hartlepool was a hard place, so black eyes and bruised ribs were common complaints come Monday morning. I remember one game where the team I was playing for were in a cup fixture against a side from the town's roughest quarter. From the kick-off to the final whistle, challenges were flying in all over the place. In fairness, I did like a tackle myself, and in the first minute, I threw myself into a fifty-fifty tussle which rapidly turned into a scuffle. Suddenly and unwisely, I was standing nose to nose with the captain of the other lot, which was a mistake because he had at least a foot in height on me – it's one of the reasons why I know how Craig Bellamy feels every time he squares up to a Premiership centre half. Though I suspect that Craig Bellamy doesn't feel a sense of bowel-clenching terror every time he squares up to the likes of Jonny Evans, like I did that particular morning.

I was petrified.

'Oh s**t,' I thought. 'What have I got myself into here?'

In those days I was a newspaper reporter, nobody would have recognised me from my job and I had yet to reach the dizzy heights of the World's 96th Most Attractive Man (thank you, readers of a well-known crossword puzzle magazine). But as my newly found nemesis stared me down, his expression suddenly softened.

'Jeff?'

I took a step back, wiping the mud, grass and God knows what else from my eyes.

'Brian!' I shouted, recognising the face. 'How are you, mate?'

It turned out that the bloke readying himself to deck me was my cousin's husband. Luckily, we had recognised one another before the blows had rained down (from him, not me) and my cheekbones remained intact; a violent scuffle had been averted.

Of course, that has rarely been the case in other leagues around the world and I had to chuckle when I saw the video footage doing the rounds of a German amateur footballer called Matthias Hilbrands, who was playing in a game between amateur sides SV Sem Jemgum and Fortuna Veenhusen. As play went up one end of the pitch for a corner, Hilbrands, a centre half by trade, was called to the touchline because the manager – clearly not from the Fabio Capello school of discipline – noticed that his mobile had been ringing. Untroubled by the action on the field, Hilbrands took the call and was filmed happily chatting away, that is until the ball broke loose and a fleet-footed midfielder raced towards him. Still holding the phone, the defender lumbered into action and scythed his opponent in half before hanging up and receiving a yellow card from the ref. As British Telecom once noted, 'It's good to talk.' And to hack, chop and maim as well, by the looks of things.

At least there was only one card. Things got more confrontational closer to home during a game between Chorlton Villa and International Manchester in 2009. Having awarded International Manchester a penalty and seen it saved, the ref (who later asked not to be named by the national press) ordered a retake because one of the Chorlton players had broken wind as the kick was about to be taken. Apparently the noise had knocked the taker off his stride. A further stink was kicked up when he booked the guilty party and when an argument broke out, the keeper was sent off when he claimed that the ref 'was the worst he had seen in years'. It wasn't enough to take the wind out of Villa's sails, so to speak, because they went on to win 6–4, but the ensuing kerfuffle did earn the club a £97 fine.

'My gut feeling is that someone made the noise with his mouth,' said Villa boss Ian Treadwell. 'This club had an exemplary record before this game. [But] it was a mistake for any of my team to get involved. The referee has applied the letter of the law to the absolute button. What you would hope for is that there can be room for some common sense as well.'

A similar incident happened when Portsmouth rivals AFC GOP played Aspley House in a Sunday league game. As the teams were preparing to kick off, a 30-year-old player from AFC GOP called Levi Foster broke wind in the face of the referee as he was having his boots checked. The official – the brilliantly named Bunny Reid – took offence at the little outburst and threatened to send Foster off, until he was eventually talked down to a yellow by players from both sides who presumably found the incident so hilarious that they were quite happy to prevent a red card before the first whistle. In hindsight, that was a schoolboy error. AFC GOP won the game 5–0 and Foster was named man of the match, which was probably a result of his pre-match meal (as was his booking):

'I had a curry the night before,' he confessed afterwards.

It won't come as a surprise to you, dear *Jeffanory* reader, that my own run-ins with Sunday league officialdom have been just as aromatic, though thankfully not as blustery as the incidents involving Chorlton Villa and Levi Foster. When I first started playing for pub teams, I turned out for a Hartlepool side called St Joseph's. Before I signed, they had lost their first four games 20–0, so it was figured that anybody, even me, would have been an improvement to their struggling outfit. Anyway, a minute into my debut I managed to score and St Joesph's were 1–0 up. 'Fantastic!' everyone thought. 'That boy can play!'

How wrong they were. After 90 minutes and a series of blunders on my part, we managed to lose 1–20, so though it was an improvement of sorts, it hardly ushered in a new era of Sunday league dominance for St Joseph's.

Anyhow, as the goals were flying in against us during our next match, I noticed that the ref was a little unsteady on his feet. Every time he trotted past me, I could detect the strong whiff of alcohol on his breath, and when I fluffed an easy chance, he ran over to where I was lying face down on the turf. The reason I knew he was there was because I could smell the intoxicating pong of booze as he tottered up to me.

'Don't worry son,' he said, pulling me to my feet. 'A drop of this'll put it right.'

He pulled a hip flask out of his pocket and unscrewed the top. I caught the smell of whisky and took a sip, and boy was he right! Immediately I felt better; my miss was forgotten. As was the miss after that, and the miss after that. Every time I fired one wide, the ref gave me another hit from his flask and by the end of the game I was really quite enjoying myself.

One of my greatest Sunday league moments took place back in the day when I was a cub reporter for the *Hartlepool Mail*. I'm not sure who came up with the idea, but when somebody discovered that our great town was twinned with a place called

Hückelhoven in Germany, it was decided that we should go over there on a football exchange trip. Now, for those of you not familiar with the area, Wikipedia describes it as 'a town in the district of Heinsberg, in North Rhine-Westphalia, Germany', which may or may not be true (probably not, if my own entry is anything to go by), but I can tell you that it was located in the industrial heartland of the country. Anyhow, when our German counterparts accepted the offer of some friendlies with their local teams, we hopped on a single-decker corporation bus and drove into Europe, like Stoke City on a slightly more comfortable and less annoying Europa League fixture.

It was because of our adventure that I now know all too well why so many teams come back from the nether regions of the Continent with a hangover. For starters, the journey was disgusting. Our bus was nothing like the fancy jets used by the modern teams of today when playing Dinamo Whothehellareyou? in the outer reaches of Ukraine, and the 20-odd hour journey across mainland Europe was purgatory. There was no air conditioning and the bus stank of 16 beer-soaked men with wind and dubious hygiene, and that was before we had even set off on the road. By the time we had arrived in Hückelhoven a day later, the overwhelming aroma was a heady mixture of BO, rotting cauliflowers and Deep Heat.

Because of our long journey and typically tardy arrival, we were due to play the first of three fixtures almost immediately, and as our driver pulled up at the ground we were bowled over by the sight of our opponent's home stadium. From what our quickly cobbled together research had told us (a few phone calls – this was the pre-Internet era, remember), the teams we were facing were the German equivalent of the Dog and Duck pub, but their stadium suggested they were more Bundesliga hopefuls than also-rans from the Rhine Combination League South. The pitch was immaculate. It was ringed by four stands, complete with a snack bar and fancy toilets and their dressing rooms were better than some of the hotels I'd stayed in, though that wasn't saying much. I did work for the *Hartlepool Mail* at the time.

'Blow me,' I thought. 'This lot must be good, we're going to get stuffed.'

How wrong I was. Fears that our opponents might have been a secret Bayern Munich reserve team were quickly dispelled when we scored our first goal after five minutes. It was one-way traffic from then on and we walloped our German rivals 7–0, despite the fact that I was suffering from deep vein thrombosis brought on by the journey and most of my team mates were still high from the fumes on the bus (though actually that might have explained why we played so well). The stadium had been a complete smokescreen, too. Our lot were used to changing in the nearest car park before a game, such were the inadequate facilities in our league, but it turned out that a lot of German Sunday league teams were very well organised, so much so that they could afford to build fancy stadiums like the one we had played in that day. Thankfully for us, the gulf in wealth and luxury was not indicative of a gulf in footballing prowess.

The hosts did not appreciate our superior ability one jot, however. There was supposed to be a celebratory dinner that evening and on paper this was set to be a joyous affair, the football-mad contingent of two towns coming together to celebrate a shared love of the Beautiful Game, but what actually unfolded was an event as one-sided as the match earlier that day. Our hosts refused to talk to us. At dinner they sat at one end of the hall and we sat at the other. Our attempts to communicate with them were rebuffed and it was only after a few beers that one of them admitted that we had insulted them with the number of goals we had scored. Apparently in mainland Europe it was considered the height of good behaviour to go easy on the hosts if you are a much better team. We had done completely the opposite and inadvertently created a minor diplomatic incident.

Luckily we managed to make up for it in the following two games by getting comprehensively spanked, but that wasn't because the sides we played were that much better than us, it was just that our team selection was carried out with two criteria in mind: first, 'Can you stand?' And second, 'Can you run 20 yards without throwing up?' Everybody in the squad was absolutely wrecked because we spent the remainder of our trip getting plastered. As part of the exchange scheme we were asked to stay with the families of our opponents, which was something I would have genuinely appreciated in my later years, but I was in my mid-twenties at the time. I didn't want to spend my evenings with the family, stuffing my face with bratwurst and küchen. I wanted to hit the town, meet the local fräuleins and down steins of Dunkel Bier. So that was what I and the rest of the team did, usually not stopping until we had all fallen over or been sick in a bin.

Isn't it great that the British are so culturally giving whenever we travel abroad?

Like the first German team on that fateful cultural exchange trip, I know how it feels to be a loser. I've been on the end of some rather humiliating drubbings during my time as a Sunday league player and I understand only too well the sting of relegation and the poisoned kiss of football stultification. However, one of the rites of passage in life is learning how to accept defeat and disaster. It takes a man to lose well, and over the years I've developed near superhuman qualities given that I am a Hartlepool fan – a team with the unenviable quality of being able to snatch defeat from the jaws of victory.

Because of Pools' affliction, my skin is like rhino hide, toughened from the slings and arrows hurled at me from gloating supporters of other, more successful clubs. My vision is so myopic that Arsène Wenger would lose in a battle of touchline blindness. I also have buttocks to match the best superhero actors – Hugh Jackman, Christopher Reeve, Rowan Atkinson – given that I've had to clench my way through countless periods of 'squeaky bum time' during a seemingly never-ending duel with relegation. It's been a rite of passage though, because losing is something that every man should experience if they're to learn the values of honour, valour and blissful ignorance.

So I was dismayed to discover that some smartarse had tried to do away with the concept of humiliation, and briefly tampered with the scoring system in the Telford Junior League, a group which looked after thousands of players from the under-10 level to the under-16s. In a somewhat strange move, it was decided that only three scores could be published in the weekly results lists and divisional tables – 0–0, 1–0, or 1–1 – the idea being that any embarrassment suffered by kids on the wrong end of a heavy beating would be spared. I remember my son Robbie played a cup tie the weekend that the Telford Junior League announced its crackpot idea and he thought it was a lot of rubbish. Two hours later (when his side's goalie hadn't turned up and a team who were table leaders in the division above had scored 15 goals against them), he was all for it.

Having watched a lot of kids' football with my sons, I understand some of the morals behind the Telford Junior League's decision: nobody wants to see the kids getting demoralised or embarrassed. However, if every game ended as a draw or a 1–0 win in English football, we might as well pack up and move over to Italy where they pride themselves in stalemate and jaw-grinding, defensive boredom. Personally, I think junior football should be refereed like a boxing match. If a side is cruising to victory by eight or nine goals, then the final whistle should be blown and the game should be restarted, with the remaining time played out as a friendly. That way it would stop the match from becoming a completely demoralising affair for the losers. I've watched when teams have whipped their opponents by a dozen goals. All the lads want to score hat-tricks, everyone wants to notch up a record score. But if you're on the wrong end of a hiding, it can be pretty depressing.

It's not just the kids that are vulnerable to a 20-goal spanking; sometimes the grown-ups suffer too. While surfing the world wide web for football gossip, I once visited a site called Who Ate All The Pies? (something in the name appealed to me) and I couldn't believe my eyes when I read the tale of a Cornish side called Madron, who were widely considered to be the worst team in the Mining League Division One. Their reputation hadn't arrived without good reason: a quick glance at the table showed a series of stats that even the boys on *Soccer Saturday* would have struggled to comprehend. At the start of the season, Madron had played 10 games, lost 10 and carried a goal difference of -203. Minus 203! When they turned up to play league leaders Illogan Reserves they brought a very un-Man United-like squad of seven players, the keeper was a complete stranger, and they were beaten

55–0. As the reliable Who Ate All The Pies? stats man later confirmed, their defeat took place at the rate of one goal every 100 seconds.

'We paid Madron a lot of respect and just got on with the game,' said Illogan assistant boss Mark Waters, somewhat unconvincingly. 'They came into the bar afterwards and were as good as gold.'

Of course, if you have been on the right side of a 55–0 scoreline, then that must feel absolutely fantastic, but it does make a mockery of the league somewhat. I was reading about a kids' team called Ickenham Youth FC who had won 18 trophies in 2010/11 and bagged 602 goals along the way. In one match, they scored 22 and their goalkeeper claimed four – that's two more than Chris Kamara scored in his entire career. I'm not knocking the players or the team, I hear some of the lads are really good and have attracted scouts from Arsenal and Fulham, but the opposition couldn't have been that much cop, could they? And what does a manager do when he's in charge of a side like that? Does he leave out his best players when they're about to face a team from the bottom of the league? Or does he find a league where the standard of competition is a lot higher?

Ah, the dilemmas of the modern-day manager. Though it should be noted that all of the boys on the team are under the age of seven.

I hung up my boots when I was 41 years of age. The kicking and the scrapping was too much to bear, especially when the hangovers became harder to deal with as I got older. Raising myself on a Sunday morning to get changed in a car park, before running around a muddy pitch in the pouring rain, didn't appeal to me any more, so I retired.

Sometime after that, when I hadn't played for ages, my son's school hosted a dads' match against the fathers of their rival school, a local centre of sporting excellence. They were renowned for being very competitive and in the run-up to the game it was made clear to me that my son's XI were short of players and could I help them out with a cameo appearance? It was the crunch game of the year and there was a lot of pride resting on the fixture. I could tell that the pressure was on.

'Look, if you're really in trouble for players then give me a call the day before,' I said.

Of course, the call came. A teacher rang me 24 hours before the kick-off and asked me to play, but I readily agreed because it had been tipping it down with rain for the best part of a week and there wasn't a game in the land that was going to be played that weekend. When I woke up the following Sunday morning, I was delighted to see the lakes of water on my lawn and a biblical gale shaking the trees outside. The match was sure to be a write-off.

'Fantastic,' I thought, 'I can turn up, look keen and feign disappointment when the game is called off. Then I can go to the pub.'

How wrong I was. Given that I was playing in a fixture between the two most competitive schools in the area, it really shouldn't have come as a shock when the pitch was declared playable and the two sides were sent out to warm up. Despite the apocalyptic conditions, the grudge match was going ahead and I was very much in the manager's plans.

'I'll play as a holding midfielder,' I explained when he asked me where I wanted to start. 'I'll sit in front of the back four, so I won't have to move too far. Give me 15 or 20 minutes and then I'll come off, the sub can come on and play the rest of the game.'

I thought it was a great plan, and when we kicked off, I started OK. I got a few good, early touches and sprayed some passes around like a shorter, less agile version of Glenn Hoddle (or maybe a slightly rounder, more mobile version of Jan Molby) when, all of a sudden, our centre half fell to the floor clutching his hamstring. He then began rolling around in agony.

'Oh, blow me,' I thought, not because I was concerned for his well-being, but because I knew our only sub would have to come on and I would have to play for the next 75 minutes or so. And what a trial it was. The pitch was a bog, the rain had turned the turf into a gluey, ankle-deep slime and running around was next to impossible, which actually did me a favour. No amount of speed from a lightning-quick striker was going to catch me out. The minute any player turned their heels, the mud reduced his pace to walking speed.

In the end, I managed to finish the game and we secured a 1–1 draw against our younger, fitter, more determined rivals. But the next day I was in agony. I could not walk. It made me wonder how those 50-something players in pub leagues around the country do it. They must get up and down the stairs of their houses in a chairlift most Monday mornings, because I couldn't get up and down mine without the assistance of Mrs Jeff or one of my sons. I'd never experienced pain like it before, not even after one of my eight London marathons. It was official: Sunday football was over for me, and no amount of whisky in the world would ever get me on to a football pitch again. However, if Newcastle should ever need an apprentice . . .

CHAPTER SEVENTEEN

A HISTORY OF VIOLENCE AND FOOTBALL FISTICUFFS

Once upon a time, and a very good time it was, when pigs were swine and dogs ate lime and monkeys chewed tobacco, when houses were thatched with pancakes, streets paved with plum pudding, and roasted pigs ran up and down the streets with knives and forks in their backs crying 'Unbelievable, Jeff! Come and make a bacon sarnie out of me and watch some football on the telly!',[5] I got into a punch-up, a scrap, a ruckus. Take a deep settling breath: I know that particular revelation might have come as a shock to some of you. Maybe put *Jeffanory* down and spend

---

5   With apologies to Katharine M. Briggs of 'Jack the Giant Killer' fame.

an hour or so watching *Football First* or *Super Duper Soccer Sunday* to calm yourself.

Good. That should ease the nerves . . .

Right, so where were we?

Oh, yes.

The fight. I don't want you to think badly of me here, dear reader, so before I get into the nuts and bolts of how my little outbreak of fisticuffs began, I'd like to point out that I've hardly been a brawler in life. Scrapping with drunken strangers at kicking-out time has never appealed to me. I was a teenager of the sixties and I've always been more in tune with flower power, free love and origami (man). Though for employment purposes I should stress that the closest I have ever got to Woodstock or free love was a quick kiss and a fumble in the back of the cinema with a local lass. I didn't inhale any wacky baccy with mates, and I definitely didn't dance naked around Hartlepool town centre in a stoned haze.

Nevertheless, while I've always been a lover, I've also been aware that sometimes in life a gentleman has to raise his fists in the face of danger. He has to search for the hero inside himself and hopefully discover his inner Sylvester Stallone, Steven Seagal or Simon Stainrod (as evidenced by my minor Sunday League scrap in the previous chapter). Well, that was my excuse anyway, and the embarrassing kerfuffle in question took place a couple of Christmases ago when the *Soccer Saturday* crew went out for our now traditional festive dinner. It was decided that we should go to a restaurant on the Fulham Road in London for food and drinks, and a really rather nice affair it was too. Christmas crackers were pulled, wine was consumed and Kammy organised a group singsong at the request of the owner who wanted to clear the bar area for our arrival. Anyway, the restaurant was built over three floors and to get to the toilets I had to wander up a flight of stairs, which took me past a function room where a rather rowdy bunch of teachers were also enjoying their festive celebrations. It was during one such visit that I noticed that several of the boys, clearly bored by my attempts to organise an impromptu game of table *Countdown*, had joined the other party.

'Jeff,' shouted someone who may or may not have been Merse, I can't remember. 'Come and have a drink with us.'

'Why not?' I thought. 'I might learn a thing or two.' And so I joined education's finest for a glass of sherry.

What struck me immediately was that all of them recognised me from *Countdown* (I was still presenting the show at the time). That shouldn't have come as a shock because teachers have long had the privilege of clocking off at three o'clock – I guess they were able to watch the show whenever they wanted (I know, I know: they do a lot of marking, too. I'm only kidding). The second thing I noticed was just how drunk they all were. My word, some of them could barely stand. Anyway, the collision of two incredibly different worlds was very convivial at first, and both parties mingled spectacularly for an hour or so. That was until one of the women who had been drinking with the teachers' group (from the minute the school bell had clanged at three, by the looks of things) stumbled over to where we were standing.

'My purse has been stolen,' she slurred, glaring first at me, and afterwards at Le Tiss, who was also standing there. Then, having decided that I was the most suspicious-looking member of the group, she pointed in my direction.

'Have you stolen it?' she snapped.

I couldn't believe it. I smiled politely and explained very firmly that, obviously, I hadn't.

'I am Robert Jeffrey Stelling,' I told her, 'the face of *Countdown*. I am an Honorary Doctor of Professional Studies at the University of Teesside. I have been granted the title of Honorary Freeman in Hartlepool alongside the Sultan of Spin, Dark Lord Peter Mandelson. Why would I have possibly stolen a purse?'

In hindsight, perhaps mentioning 'Mandy' wasn't the best idea. In fact, it only confirmed her suspicions that I was as crooked as they come and she began chucking insults and accusations my way. Almost immediately everybody turned on me, including Merse and Le Tiss who were quite enjoying the complimentary drinks that were being dished out at the time, and I was hounded from the bar. I couldn't believe it. Still expressing my innocence, I returned to the *Soccer Saturday* party, but as I approached the bottom of the stairs, I heard one of the teachers proclaiming to anyone who would listen, 'Jeff Stelling: what a w****r!'

Well, that was it. I went potty. I turned and charged, head down, like an enraged bison from the BBC documentary *Frozen Planet*, and scaled the steps at a speed Theo Walcott would have been proud of.

'What did you say?' I roared at the offending party, striding purposefully towards him and rolling up the sleeves of my brand-new shirt, ready for action. It's funny, people had always said to me that being in a fight could be a surreal experience. Apparently, the senses go into overload and the adrenalin races around the body. The passing of time becomes an almost surreal event, everything slows down, and it can resemble an out-of-body experience. Well, let me tell you, time didn't slow down nearly as much as I would have liked because as I stormed towards my intended target, nostrils flaring, elbows and fingers pointing (think Robbie Keane after being flagged offside), I noticed with a sinking heart that the teacher who had called me a 'w****r' was clearly from the PE department, and quite possibly a rugby coach with some experience of pummelling heads. Nevertheless I could feel my inner Stallone, Seagal and Stainrod coming together, and the hero inside me was determined to press ahead. Then one thought at the back of my mind came to the fore.

'A bloody barman better get here quick to break this up, otherwise I'm in trouble.'

I prayed to a higher force and dived in, but what followed was hardly a volley of Rocky Balboa-style punches and jabs. Instead, onlookers were treated to a classic football melee: the coming together of a group of grown men who should have known better, the mob pushing one another, swearing, throwing insults, and tearing at shirts, none of them really wanting to throw a punch for fear of getting a whack back. This went on for a few seconds, though it felt like minutes, until I felt the blessed, wonderful, protective grip of a barman's hands on my shoulders and I was dragged away to safety. The two warring parties were separated.

I was embarrassed at first because it had been quite a scene. Afterwards, somebody bought me a drink to settle my nerves, but I wasn't interested. As I've said, I'm a man of peace 99.9 per cent of the time. I'm usually only driven into a black mood whenever Hartlepool lose, and that only lasts for a few minutes, so the *Soccer Saturday* advertising break at 4.45 is usually a suitable time for me to swear and kick chairs around the studio. For the most part, I'm a picture of calm and tranquillity. You could compare me to the Dalai Lama, or even Ray Wilkins.

I'm also a sensitive soul, so I made my excuses and left – I was genuinely upset by the incident and I didn't need the grief. I later heard that the missing purse was never found, so the issue was unresolved, but I couldn't have cared less. In the taxi home I remember thinking, 'I wish that lot weren't in charge of the educational future of our youth.'

But then I'm sure they were probably thinking something equally unflattering about me. The sore heads in a west London staff room the following morning would have been just as disillusioned.

'I wish he wasn't the smiling face of my long afternoons in front of *Countdown* as I pretend to do the marking,' one of them may or may not have thought. 'Jeff Stelling: what a w****r!'

I'm not the only one to have embroiled myself in an ill-judged bout of fisticuffs. Footballers and soppy outbreaks of violence often walk hand in hand, though for the most part these brawls rarely go beyond the pushing and shoving stages in the Premier League. With cameras trained on just about every player on the pitch, it's impossible for a scrap to break out without somebody filming the rather girlie flailing of fists between two blokes with £200 haircuts and Alice bands. The trouble really only starts when the cameras aren't around. Or if Craig Bellamy has been named in the starting line-up.

In the lower leagues, it can be a different story. Like when Northern Premier League Division One South outfit Ilkeston FC took on Blue Square Premier side Mansfield Town. With only a handful of hardcore fans in attendance on a tranquil August afternoon, the players were free to hurl themselves around the pitch like Uma Thurman in *Kill Bill: Volumes One and Two*. Video evidence was not going to capture any off-the-ball incidents and Mansfield Town were bullied for the best part of 73 minutes, at which point their manager abandoned the game because it had been so violent. In hindsight, he made the right choice. Before the game's collapse, three of his players had already been taken to hospital, all of them having been involved in what the papers later described as 'incidents' with Ilkeston's Gary Ricketts. When news of the brawling hit the national press the following day, the *Independent* raised the question as to whether the match had been 'The most violent non-league game ever?' They had a point. One of the injuries, to defender John Thompson, was so bad that he required 40 stitches to a wound in his face. Mansfield's physio was later recorded as saying that Thompson had a 'chunk of skin missing, [which was] probably still on the advertising hoarding.'

I think two points are worth making here. The first was that Ricketts had been Ilkeston's player-coach, though he was later suspended by the club and fined two weeks' wages. The second was that Ilkeston and Mansfield Town were supposedly playing in a summer friendly. Blimey, if that was a runaround to bring the squad up to speed for the start of the season then God knows how they must have played when it got to the business end of the league campaign.

Maybe the English game should take a few hints from our pals in the Bundesliga. Not content with occasionally kicking our backsides in World Cups, the Germans have also developed a novel way of settling disputes. While watching Borussia Mönchengladbach beat Cologne 3–0 from my telly in Stelling Towers in 2011 – a game that carried the whiff of a one-sided hiding – two Mönchengladbach players, Mike Hanke and Marco Reus, became involved in a squabble over who should take a free kick. Having bickered for a few seconds, the pair didn't snatch the ball out of one another's hands like schoolgirls, they didn't push one another in the chest. Instead they settled the debate with a quick round of rock, paper, scissors – a playground game familiar to most people and a far more civilised way of coming to a decision than the usual volley of swear words and personal insults. (For those of you unfamiliar with the game: on the count of three, the two competing players make a hand symbol denoting either a rock (closed fist), a piece of paper (flat hand), or a pair of scissors (two fingers); paper beats rock, rock beats scissors, scissors beats paper. Got it?)

If only all arguments were settled in that way. If I'd had a pound for every time I've watched players bickering over a set piece, well, I'd be richer than QPR's majority shareholder Tony Fernandes by now, most probably. Players have always fought over who should take penalties and free kicks. Harry Redknapp often tells a tale from his West Ham days of how the mercurial (for mercurial read crackers) striker, Paolo Di Canio, once got into a ruck with Frank Lampard over a penalty. Lampard was the designated taker at West Ham, but Di Canio wanted to take it instead, and a right fuss he made about it too.

According to Harry, his lot had been playing Bradford City at home and were 2–4 down; Di Canio had seen three blatant penalty appeals rejected by the ref and was a bit miffed, and rightly so. I had watched the match on the telly and each incident was clear cut; the ref had an absolute nightmare. Di Canio was obviously a bit upset about the way the game had been played out and gestured to Harry that he wanted to come off after his third appeal was waved away. When Harry ignored his request, Di Canio ran over towards the bench, sat down on the pitch cross-legged and folded his arms as the West Ham coaching team begged him to get up and carry on.

'I no play, 'Arry,' he said, burying his face in his hands as the Bradford players started passing the ball around him like a training cone, nearly scoring a fifth. It was at that moment that the Upton Park crowd started singing his name: 'Paolo Diiii Can-eeee-oooooo/Paolo Diiii Can-eeee-ooooo.' The chanting did the trick. Di Canio jumped up, received the ball, went around half the Bradford team to set up a chance. Not long after Hammers midfielder Joe Cole pulled one back. A few minutes later West Ham, finally, won a penalty. Frank Lampard grabbed the ball to take the spot kick, but before he could put the ball down, Di Canio came over and snatched it from him.

'It was unbelievable,' Harry said. 'They were both pulling the ball, but Paolo wouldn't let go. In the end Frank gave up. It lasted for a minute, the two of them wrestling for the football.'

As Di Canio stepped up to take the penalty, I could really sense the tension.

'Let's hope he doesn't miss it,' said the commentator, stating the bloomin' obvious.

Di Canio stepped up and fired the ball home, before Lampard scored the winner in a 5–4 thriller.

'He was mad,' said Harry of Di Canio. 'He used to come in singing with his sunglasses on one day, another day he'd come in and he'd have the hump. I used to have to put him in the winning teams in the five-a-side games. I'd always put him in the same team as Stuart Pearce and Nigel Winterburn – anyone who might kick him because I didn't want him to have an argument.'

Harry was right, he was mad. As a player, Di Canio was a wildly individual character who caused drama all over the shop, most notably when he pushed over referee Paul Alcock during a game between his former employer Sheffield Wednesday and their Premier League counterparts Arsenal in 1998. Forget the great goals he scored during his seasons in the Premiership; close your eyes for a second, think of Di Canio, and what do you see? That's right, the wild-eyed Italian flicking his wrists into the chest of Alcock; the ref tumbling to the ground with all the grace and dignity of an off-licence bag blowing about the pavement. Like Thierry Henry's handball against the Republic of Ireland in France's 2010 World Cup play-off game, Di Canio's one heinous act of unsporting play overshadowed large chunks of his good work for a while.

Di Canio was a scrapper, but it was good to see that he hadn't changed upon his arrival at Swindon Town as manager in 2011. Everyone expected some more pushing and shoving, and typically it kicked off almost from his first day on the job. First came the news of his bizarre training regimes, in which Swindon's players were hardly given a day off. 'In terms of commitment, I want 100 Paolo Di Canios,' he explained, but I don't think that his players shared the same enthusiasm. After a 3–1 defeat to Southampton in August 2011, striker Leon Clarke and Di Canio became involved in a scrap when the striker refused to leave the pitch following an argument with Swindon's fitness coach, who was presumably trying to get him to perform a series of post-match push-ups ('It's what Paolo would want!' he may or may not have ordered). Di Canio was clearly not enthused by the public show of dissent and dragged Clarke down the tunnel, where a flurry of argy-bargy took place. Leon Clarke was no Paul Alcock, however.

He definitely wasn't going down without a fight, and club stewards were forced to separate the duelling pair.

Clarke was promptly shipped out to Chesterfield on loan where he scored goals for fun, which was interesting given that he couldn't score for toffee under the regime at Swindon. Di Canio, meanwhile, was determined to stamp his personality on the English game. Presumably having learnt from his experience against Bradford as a player, he later encouraged his players to dive during matches, a decision he announced to the press, surely alerting every single hawk-eyed official and fan in the country.

'It's not fair but it's the only way to receive something,' he said. 'With some players, if he has a chihuahua character I can't make a chihuahua into a rottweiler. He could be a proud chihuahua but he remains a chihuahua. So many of the players at the moment are chihuahuas away from home – this is the truth.'

It was an incisive assessment of his Swindon team. Di Canio later claimed an FA Cup scalp when his team turned over Premiership side Wigan in the third round in 2012. When asked who he would like to face in the next stage he answered, 'Barcelona.' Shouldn't we make him England manager?

Sometimes footballers can take their frustrations out on the wrong guy; they kick the cat, often almost literally. In Barranquilla, Colombia, however, they take matters one step further and kick the owl.

In case you think I've gone mad, it's probably helpful if I explain to you the importance of the owl to fans of Atlético Junior, a side from Colombia's Primera A division. There, the owl is as important to Atlético supporters as it is to the fans of Sheffield Wednesday. It is to them what the Gunnersaurus is to Arsenal fans, or Cyril the Swan is to Swansea fans. Though there were some differences with Cyril given that, first, Atlético's mascot is a real-life nocturnal bird rather than a man who probably should be doing something better with his time, and second, Cyril once infamously grabbed the head of Millwall mascot Zampa the Lion and booted it down the touchline before a game. A Dutch TV station later interviewed Cyril and asked him what he had said to Zampa during the incident, to which he is reported to have responded, 'Don't f*** with the Swans.' He later released a pop single ('Nice Swan, Cyril') and appeared in panto (in *Aladdin* at the Grand Theatre in Swansea). When it comes to nutty mascots, nobody ruled the roost quite like Cyril.

Anyway, I've used the word 'is' when describing the Atlético Junior owl, but their living, breathing, 'proper' mascot is actually dead, and boy did he snuff it in controversial circumstances. When Atlético took on Deportivo Pereira in a league game, the owl accidentally strayed on to the pitch. As it waddled around the penalty area like a feathered, more attractive Luka Modric, it was struck by a football, which sent it into a bit of a spin. Further insult to its injury was added when Deportivo defender Luis Moreno then gave it a swift kick, sending it flying – not of its own accord – off the pitch, much to the horror of the watching fans who began chanting, 'Murderer! Murderer!' at Moreno from the stands. He was later given a police escort from the ground, such was the very real threat of immediate vengeance.

The owl was rushed to the vets where it was diagnosed with

a broken leg, but it soon went into shock. A couple of days later, it was pronounced brown bread, much to the disgust of the Colombian public.

'The owl died at about 2.57 a.m.,' said a vet on national telly, microphones shoved under his nose. '[It] went into shock and we weren't able to recover him from that stage.'

Moreno soon received death threats, and several terrifying phone calls promised him a terrible fate, not too dissimilar to the one that had befallen the Atlético Junior owl.

'My family is very worried about what happened,' he said afterwards. 'And even more because there is an entire country against me, and I think that's not fair. I believe that what happened is regrettable and I apologise to the entire country and I believe it's time to let the issue go. I believe that there's not much more to say.'

The Colombian government had different ideas and hit Moreno with a fine of 26.78 million pesos, which sounded on paper to be around the going rate for a reasonable Premiership striker, but actually equated to around £9,080. That was followed by a fine of a further 600,000 pesos which, it was reasoned, would cover the costs of the owl's treatment; a public apology was later made and Moreno served out his punishment by performing community work in a local zoo.

Still, Moreno's actions seemed insignificant when compared to Rapid Bucharest defender Marius Constantin who once tried to throttle his manager, our old friend Marius Sumudica (he of ref-kissing fame in Chapter 2). An argument had broken out between the pair when Sumudica made a comment on the training ground about Mrs Constantin. Mr Constantin responded by trying to squeeze the life from his boss with his bare hands, a highly illegal option we've all considered at some point in our lives.

'Sure I made a joke about his wife,' said Sumudica afterwards. 'But he's a punk. He stinks of beer and smokes. If you go in his room, the smoke is so dense you could leave a bike standing upright, unsupported. He likes the mini bar and uses gum to clean his breath. You know, I don't care for him.'

He might have been incredibly unpopular in his manager's eyes, but Constantin sounded like the perfect *Soccer Saturday* pundit to me – he drank and smoked. Given his fondness for fisticuffs, he might come in handy should we get into any trouble at the next Christmas party. Or, at the very least, be on hand to share out some Wrigley's gum for the long journey home. Sign him up!

CHAPTER EIGHTEEN

WATCH OUT, GAZZA'S ABOUT

A great while ago, when the world was full of wonders; a time when the studio walls wobbled on *Soccer Saturday* and Rodney Marsh's motor mouth was free to offend the football world, a rumour did the rounds about a prank that had been played on one of Newcastle United's foreign employees. The goalscoring sensation – who cannot be named for reasons of dignity, slander and threats of physicality so horrific they would make Tony Pulis blush – arrived at the club amid a flurry of hype. He had also cost the board a hell of a lot of money, which was why it was suggested to the senior players at St James' Park that they should help their new signing settle into Geordie life. Moving from hotter, faraway lands to the Toon was quite a culture shock after all, and the pressure was on for Newcastle's latest recruit to score goals. And fast.

The lads readily agreed. Together they talked to him about

the best restaurants in town and listed the coolest places for him to hang out in the evenings. They showed him around the local golf courses and leisure clubs. The squad even advised their new team mate – we'll call him Señor X – on the local fashions, telling him where to shop for the snappiest threads. It was hoped that with this advice, their exotic counterpart would settle quickly, helping them to push on in the league.

Typically, these kind-hearted gestures didn't pass without a joke or two, and neglecting to inform the management team, Newcastle's squad decided to wind up Señor X by way of a team-bonding exercise. During a guided tour of the Toon, it was claimed that the height of sartorial elegance in Newcastle were garments bought from the Disney Store, the global brand renowned for its Tinker Bell T-shirts and Mickey Mouse cufflinks. The players lied through their teeth: everyone in England had been wearing 101 Dalmatians clobber in nightclubs, they said. They even told him that the UK's flashy lifestyle magazines had proclaimed Disney Store as the next big thing, a brand to rank alongside Ralph Lauren and Global Hypercolor. Señor X fell for it, hook, line and sinker and lo and behold, when Newcastle United's squad went out on the town, en masse, for the first time since his arrival, the poor chap appeared wearing a Mickey Mouse tie and Donald Duck socks. Unsurprisingly he was then laughed out of every club and bar along the quayside.

By the sound of things, Señor X was not the only member of the Newcastle squad to have been stung by a prank or two. In fact, horsing around seems to have been a major tradition at St James' Park for decades, which may or may not explain why they have won so little over the past 40 years. As Señor X discovered to his cost, many of the pranks involved new faces at the club, especially those who might have faced the challenge of overcoming a language barrier.

For example, when German international Dietmar Hamann joined Newcastle United in 1998, he was a player of some repute, having arrived from Bayern Munich. That didn't stop the Newcastle team from presenting him with a copy of Hitler's book *Mein Kampf* at the team's Christmas party.

'It's true,' he told *FourFourTwo* magazine when asked about the stunt. 'People made up stories that I was offended by it, but I'd been in England for six months and really enjoyed the English humour and mentality, so it was not offensive to me at all. I actually left the book on a bus because we went straight from the Newcastle training ground to a pub . . . I haven't seen it since.'

A generation earlier, the joking had been even worse, and during the 1980s, when the likes of legendary midfield whizz-kid Paul Gascoigne played on Tyneside, Newcastle brought the first Brazilian to English football, the mercurial Mirandinha. The samba star was already a troubled soul: he was nicknamed 'The Greedy One' because of his tendency to ball-hog like a school captain in the playground; he infamously swapped shin pads rather than shirts with Gary Lineker at the end of a game against Spurs ('It was a great deal! My pair were old and rubbish, and his was shiny and brand new,' he explained). The Toon Army even penned a charming little ditty to sing to him from the terraces: 'We've got Mirandinha, he's not from Argentina/He's from Brazil, he's effing brill!'

Trouble really started for Mirandinha when – like Señor X – it was decided that his team mates should help him to settle at Newcastle. That was the moment when Gazza offered to teach him English. Not aware of Gascoigne's madcap streak, the

Brazilian midfielder readily agreed and the pair set to work, often with hilarious results. The main problem for Mirandinha was that Gazza – unbeknownst to his pupil – had decided to become wilfully creative with the use of our wonderful language, much to the amusement of the Newcastle playing staff. During lessons, he would deliberately exchange everyday phrases for insults and swear words, which got Mirandinha into all sorts of trouble, as you could imagine. At the club canteen, he would obliviously ask for 'Hairy fannies' rather than chips, a social faux pas that made him very unpopular with the cooking staff.

Judging by his portly physique at the time, Gazza was having no such problems ordering his own hairy fannies by the plateful. It is worth noting that after two years in the North East, 'Wor Mira' (as he was nicknamed) used the cash he had earned in England to buy a pig farm just outside Sao Paulo. His home-cooked sausage, egg and hairy fannies is, presumably, a right hit with friends and family.

Typically, that rather crude translation wasn't Gazza's only score. During one early game for Newcastle, Mirandinha made a rash tackle as he attempted to clear the ball from the edge of his penalty area, sending an opponent to the floor with a thump. The ref was having none of it and with all the swiftness of a modern-day official, he flashed Mirandinha a yellow card. Struggling to make amends, the Brazilian drew on his limited reserves of English and remembered the phrase Gazza had taught him for 'sorry'.

'Mr Referee,' he said, nervously reaching for his best apology. 'F**k off.'

Oh, Gazza, the football world would have been a poorer place without you.

* * *

What these tales of Geordie japes are supposed to prove, dear reader, is that footballers, given too much time, can get bored, often with disastrous consequences. To kill the hours between dead-ball sessions, head tennis and kicking Gareth Bale into Row Z, your average pro likes nothing more than to behave like an absolute rotter to his team mates. This unpleasant behaviour usually takes place at the training ground. And if stories are to be believed, the nation's prestigious centres of footballing excellence most resemble circus rings, or rehearsal rooms for the Chuckle Brothers – that's Ian Rush and John Aldridge, as they're more commonly known to the rest of us.

While flicking through my extensive newspaper library at Stelling Towers of late, I've come to realise that the most common focus for a professional footballer's 'joke' usually involves the personal property of his peers. Merse told me a horrific story of how he once went to the toilet in the pillow of his Arsenal room mate Perry Groves. I daren't divulge any more information for fear of making you ill, though I do remember that when he first regaled me with the story it got me thinking: 'In what other workplace would it be acceptable to trash a colleague's personal property willy-nilly, with no concern for the consequences, other than the extent of their revenge attack?' In my day job, I couldn't possibly imagine cutting the tie of Matt Le Tissier as he delivered a match report. I certainly wouldn't pass any fluids on to Alan McInally's bed sheets. The pair of them would kill me, probably with their bare hands.

In the world of professional football, however, anything goes. And I mean *anything*. During the cold snap of 2011, a lorryload of snow fell from the skies and the UK ground to a standstill. Railway lines were shut down and the roads became packed with drifts and icy patches. More alarmingly, football matches were called off up and down the country and children bunked off school to throw snowballs at smartly dressed TV presenters who might have been grumpily clearing their driveways at the time. Among the worst-hit areas was the Midlands, but luckily the ground staff at West Brom's training ground managed to clear the pitches so that their players could happily frolic around on the grass.

There was still enough snow around to play with though, and as the team showered after a hard morning's session, goalkeeper Scott Carson returned to his car to find a snowman strapped into the front seat. To add insult to injury, the culprit had taken the time to stick a carrot nose to the head and place a wonky grin made from stones across his chops.

'It was good banter, to be fair,' said Carson later, through teeth more gritted than the roads.

His calm demeanour was probably aided by the fact that there was no permanent damage to the upholstery. Not everyone has got off so easily, however. When Manchester City travelled to America for a pre-season tour in 2011, some of their players decided to play a prank on our old mate Mario Balotelli, which carried the whiff of permanency about it. Balotelli is a footballer who could best be described as 'unpredictable'. I could dedicate a whole book to his displays of eccentric behaviour, which were regular and uncontrollable. During his early months at Eastlands, the Italian international eschewed the Premiership footballer's traditional holiday destinations, such as Vegas and Barbados, and went to the Lake District instead. He set his bathroom on fire after letting off a mini-fireworks display indoors. And during a UEFA Cup defeat against Dynamo Kiev (or Kyiv, as we have to get used to saying now) his face swelled up to such an extent that he had to be substituted. It was later reported that he had suffered an allergic reaction to the grass, a complaint not dissimilar to an Olympic swimmer suffering from an allergic reaction to water.

Balotelli is a headline writer's dream. Even my old mate Noel Gallagher fell in love with him. 'He's the absolute greatest living human being on the planet at the minute!' he proclaimed on *Soccer AM*. 'He's not of this world. He's not like the rest of us. When he eventually leaves – like when [Kevin] Keegan left Newcastle and had to get lifted off the pitch in a helicopter – Mario's going to get fired out of a cannon and back into space where he came from! We all love him.

'The thing about him is that if he played for any other club in the country, we'd all still love him, because he's a great character. And the word from City is that when they go on these kids' days, all the kids flock to him because he's like the naughty schoolboy or something. There's a little bit of Mario in all of us as well, because I've been sat in my bathroom sometimes thinking, "It would be great to set this on fire, wouldn't it?"'

Now, by the time you read this, Balotelli might have left the Etihad Stadium given his run-ins with controversy. He might be in Manchester, sure, but he might also have disappeared to Spain, Italy or the dark side of the moon. Given his fiery temperament it was only natural that his team mates should be happy to set Balotelli's high-maintenance personality ablaze, and as the squad prepared to hop on a plane and travel to the States for a pre-season tour, somebody placed a sports holdall stuffed with kippers on the back seat of Balotelli's Maserati sports car, which was worth a whopping £150,000. When the squad returned to Manchester two weeks later, the sun and summer heat had suitably warmed the fish enough to create an unimaginable pong. The smell was so bad that, on opening the car door for the first time, poor old Balotelli was very nearly sick on the spot; his motor was packed with flies. Reports later claimed that his car was an insurance write-off and impossible to drive, such was the stink. Still, it wasn't as if the striker had cared for the vehicle during his time in the city. Having been impounded 27 times while gathering £10,000 in parking tickets, it was probably for the best that his Maserati was off the road.

The closest I've got to being involved in an on-air prank actually took place on *Countdown*, which was hardly a breeding ground for anarchy and chaos, but the staff behind the scenes on the show were great fun. Our producer Damian Eadie was an out-and-out Blackpool fan and was also the man who devised the conundrums for the programme, which was quite an art form because making something amusing from nine jumbled-up letters could be a tricky business – a bit like Merse trying to pronounce the name of former Newcastle striker Shefki Kuqi ('Shef-keee Coo-keeee, is that right, Jeff?').

One of Damian's great gags came at a time when Preston North End – Blackpool's fiercest rivals – were suffering a bit of a slump in form and the two sets of fans had set about one another with a series of pranks. At its peak, Blackpool fans cobbled together enough money to hire a plane, which they flew over Preston's Deepdale stadium trailed by a banner that read, somewhat rudely: 'We are superior. Love Blackpool FC.' I was very aware of the spat – it was all the fans of Blackpool and

Preston could talk about whenever I met them, and it all seemed like a spot of good-natured fun to me.

Around the same time, I began recording a string of *Countdown* episodes and in one studio session I announced the final conundrum of the day. Up flashed the letters, which were jumbled in such a fashion that they disguised the word 'Priciness'. Somewhat annoyingly for any Preston fans watching, Damian had muddled the vowels and consonants so that they actually spelt out the phrase, 'PNECRISIS'. When the letters flashed up, all I could hear in my earpiece was Damian in fits of laughter. I don't think Preston fans were too enamoured, but any Blackpool supporter watching would have been over the moon.

When it comes to working at Sky, however, we've always played it straight because we're experienced pros. Nevertheless, I'm always hearing of great pranks old and new through the grapevine (aka the Former Professional Footballers' Association of Drinkers) and when the pundits get together, they love to reminisce and the tales usually include a rogues gallery of chancers and wind-up merchants. One such raconteur is Gary Neville, who joined the Sky team in 2011 having retired from his role as Manchester United's moaner-in-chief. As a player, Gary gave everything. He was United through and through, but because of his ultra-professional nature, fans of the opposition didn't take to him too kindly. In fact, a lot of supporters couldn't stand the sight of him. One such person was Piers Morgan, the lovable, in no way smug, newspaper editor turned TV host. Morgan, an Arsenal fan, had been so rattled by Gary during his playing days that he took a pop at him when he finally hung up his boots in 2011.

'Farewell to the most annoying player in the history of world football,' he tweeted, strangely forgetting Robbie Savage and

Dennis Wise. He later expanded his vitriol in a column for a national newspaper which brimmed with unnecessary anger and loathing.

'My own hatred of the rat-faced weasel ran so deep that the mere sight of him would make me come out in blazing boils of fury,' he wrote. 'As his former colleague, Jaap Stam, so memorably observed in those ill-fated memoirs a few years ago, Gary and Phil were "a pair of busy little s***s". And the Dutchman didn't mean they were always occupied.

'From the moment Neville walked out on the pitch, puffing out his small chest like a stunted peacock, he'd irritate me. He was like the worst kind of office block shop steward. An officious little numpty with delusions of grandeur, a haughty overestimation of his own talents and a relentless ability to wind everybody up at all times with his sheer presence.'

When I first read Morgan's assessment of Gary's personality, I was quite taken aback. It certainly didn't chime with the person I had met, although he once admitted to laughing his head off at me when I fell from the stage during the launch of the Respect campaign in 2008 – a programme introduced to halt the increasing harassment of refs by professional footballers during games. This embarrassing incident happened after I'd been asked to host the televised event alongside a string of football guests, but as I'd prowled the stage, the crowd eating out of my hand, I lost sight of the edge and tumbled gracelessly to the floor. Gary, who had been watching on the telly at home, laughed so hard that he had to wipe the tears from his eyes. Maybe, Morgan's assessment had been accurate after all.

Still, if Gary was a 'busy little s***' as claimed by Stam then he applied his worst trait with a positive spin on Sky Sports. In his first season, he proved an excellent addition to the *Super Sunday* show and delivered excellent insights and tactical nous in his analysis section on *Monday Night Football*. He also expressed the opinions of a top pro who had only recently retired from football at the highest level. What I liked about him was that he delivered a fresh insight – he had been in the dressing room with some of the players we were talking about, he had been on the training ground and talked tactics with the likes of Sir Alex Ferguson. He had been in the thick of things.

Being an analyst is not an easy job to do. I told him before he started that he would have to stick his neck on the line with his opinions. He would also have to criticise some people who might have been his mates, or opponents, and that can be pretty tough. But to be fair to him he's done it. He was even critical of the Manchester United team after their Champions League final defeat to Barça in 2011, that despite the fact that he rode to and from the game on the team bus. Elsewhere, he hammered Chelsea's David Luiz when he infamously claimed that the defender had played as if he was being 'controlled by a ten-year-old in the crowd with a PlayStation', such was his erratic display of defending during the match against Liverpool. The comment caused a right fuss, most prominently from Luiz's then manager, Andre Villas-Boas.

'Gary Neville was a fantastic defender,' he said upon hearing the comments. 'But it is a stupid approach to an opinion. If that's the way he wants to take the game that is ridiculous.'

The only person not fussed was Luiz himself and on Twitter prior to Chelsea's Champions League game against Bayer Leverkusen he was reported to have said (in broken English): 'Good morning GEEZERS, go to Germany now! Gary Neville I love u!'

He later expanded on it in an interview with one of the papers when he said, 'I don't feel anything about it, I just laugh about it – because I am a very simple and laid-back guy. I also made sure that I replied to Gary Neville through Twitter and I told him that I loved him. It's normal.

'He was an excellent player who played for many, many years for Man United. Any player needs to be prepared to face this sort of criticism, because if you are not, then don't play football, play something else, or just stay at home and play on the PlayStation!'

Luiz isn't the only fan of Gary's analysis; the TV and sports critics seem to think he's been a cracking addition to the team as well:

'Neville has solidified in recent weeks,' wrote Barney Ronay in the *Guardian*, 'losing his ferrety callow quality, turning towards the camera instead a full-face belligerence, a relentless and moreish zeal. I think we can say it now: there's a new sheriff in town, a new king-pundit. And maybe the pundit is about to enter another of his furtive growth spurts.'

From what I could tell almost immediately, Gary was a sociable chap and happy to tell a story or two. During his time at Old Trafford I suppose he must have watched many a joker come and go, one of whom was his former team mate from the 1992 FA Youth Cup-winning side, Nicky Butt. Always a source of fun in the dressing room, Butt once decided to play a prank on Manchester United's fearsome, man-mountain goalkeeper Peter Schmeichel, though the gag nearly backfired spectacularly.

Gary told us that as the United squad showered and changed after training, Butt decided it would be funny to dangle a boiling hot kettle behind his team mate, the scorching hot steel suspended centimetres from the exposed flesh of Schmeichel's buttocks. The United dressing room fell about laughing, but when Schmeichel turned around to see what all the commotion was about, the roasting hot kitchen appliance brushed against his nether regions, burning them instantly.

'Peter went mad,' said Gary's team mate Jaap Stam in the papers. 'He wrapped a towel around his hip and went after Nicky who had to run for his life as Peter chased him around The Cliff [United's old training ground] a few times, leaving us in tears from laughing.'

Footballers, eh? What a pain in the arse. In fact, what a pain in the 'Jacobs'.

CHAPTER NINETEEN

WIN OR LOSE, WE'RE ON THE BOOZE

Footballers, as we know, can be creatures of habit. It's an occupational hazard, I suppose – the daily routines and drills that come with a life as a professional sportsman often create the need for familiarity. After all, to play at his best, a footballer needs to be in the right frame of mind. A chaotic schedule or periods of unpredictability and uncertainty, no matter how small or seemingly insignificant they might appear to the rest of us (a different meal, a new bed, a different Page 3 model from the previous week), can often be the short cut to disaster, a poor performance and a hairdryer from the gaffer.

One such player to thrive on routine is Phil Jones, Manchester United's centre half-cum-midfielder and a player of great promise. Quite recently, Jones happily admitted to being a sufferer from borderline OCD. That he announced it to Manchester United's official TV station seemed odd enough. Odder still were the details of his pre-match rituals, a series of actions so convoluted and eccentric that the most fastidious of footballers would probably have considered him stark raving bonkers.

Jones's habits run as follows: before kick-off he puts on his socks and boots in an order dependent on whether United are playing home or away. If United are playing at home, he'll put on his left sock and left boot first because the words 'Manchester United' appear on the left-hand side of the fixture list. If United are playing away (with their name positioned on the right-hand side of the fixture list), he reverses the routine. It doesn't just apply to his socks and footwear, either. Whenever Jones crosses the white line to run on to the pitch, he plants his first foot – left or right – according to where United are playing that day, home (left) or away (right).

'This will sound proper over the top,' he said in possibly the most understated sentence of the decade. 'But you know when you go to a hotel room and there are two towels hanging down? When I was on international duty last week, I picked the towel on the left because we were at home against Spain. I know it's weird, but I can't help myself. Nobody knows about it so nobody has ever noticed – although I guess the secret's out now.'

Phil Jones isn't the only one. Former England keeper David James once argued that all footballers are, by their very nature, obsessive. He compared players to autograph hunters and trainspotters. In his view, the oddball at the end of Warrington Bank Quays train station with a notepad and pen was linked by the same psychological drive as a footballer, such as Cristiano Ronaldo, who was compelled to hit a ball 500 times a day, every day, in training. The mindset was the same, only the area in which it was performed was different. James also admitted to a routine as unusual as the one followed by Phil Jones: before games he would go into a public toilet, or the dressing room loos, and then wait for them to empty, at which point he would spit at the wall. Why exactly, he didn't say, though he also pointed out, somewhat shrewdly, that what most footballers would consider superstitious activities or lucky routines, others would probably view as obsessive behaviour, or just downright unpleasant habits, as was the case with James's toilet routine.

It's not just the players that struggle with this syndrome either; managers can fall foul of the same psychological conditions. One such sufferer is Manchester City manager Roberto Mancini, who apparently runs through a series of bizarre acts should he or anyone in his company ever drop a glass of fine vino.

'If you spill wine, he [Roberto Mancini] has to stick his fingers in it and dab it behind his ears, like perfume,' explained the superstitious Italian's assistant David Platt. 'Apparently, that wards off the bad luck. So we're in his office after the Liverpool game and I knock over a glass. There's nothing in it, really, but a drop comes out and splashes on the table and he's over, from the other side of the room, finger in the wine, dab, dab. And not a word of explanation to anybody. I can see Kenny Dalglish and [Liverpool assistant] Steve Clarke looking at him as if he's mad.'

I guess if I had to work with Carlos Tevez and Mario Balotelli for an extended period of time, I'd probably exhibit the same behavioural patterns, though Mancini's bizarre superstition brings me on to the very subject of this witty and entertaining chapter, dear *Jeffanory* reader: a habit that a number of footballers have shown a fondness for over the years. Namely drinking, a vice so irresistible that many a player has fallen foul of its sweet, intoxicating, frothy, ice-cold, fizzy, mouth-watering charms.

One such victim was our very own Paul Merson, a man who at the height of his fame was so in thrall to booze that he would knock back pints and pints of electric lemonade on the night before a match. So bad was his habit, that when advertisers recently produced a promotional video for a football memorabilia website, they put together a funny spoof that highlighted his drunken excesses. In it, Merse and his former Arsenal team mates Ray Parlour and Alan Smith were filmed sitting in an auction house as items of football memorabilia – boots, signed photos, old kit – were paraded for the bidders by none other than former Arsenal full back Kenny Sansom. As the auctioneer held up a shirt from the final game of the 1990/91 season, Merse turned around to his friends with a confused look on his face.

MERSE: 'What's so special about that then?'

SMITH: 'We won the title that year, Merse, don't say you've forgotten?'

[A second shirt is held up on display.]

AUCTIONEER: 'Shirt number two is from the League Cup final of 1993.'

MERSE: 'Did we get to the final that year?'

PARLOUR: 'Course we did! You scored, you muppet.'

[A third and final shirt is held up, this time from the

1994 Cup Winners' Cup final. Merse looks back at his mates, confused.]

SMITH: 'Copenhagen, Parma. 1–0. I got the winner after 20 minutes.'

AUCTIONEER: [Holding up a very long receipt]: 'And to round off the lot . . . the Arsenal bar bill from the Copenhagen hotel after the game.'

MERSE: 'Oh yeah, I remember that. Twenty-seven pints, 16 vodkas and a bottle of brandy. And that was just me.'

Sometimes I wonder if he isn't still knocking back 16 vodkas at a time. Whenever he comes on the show, he's for ever tripping over his words and stumbling over his pronunciations. I've already discussed at length some of Merse's most famous blunders in my bestselling (well, in Hartlepool at least) first book, *Jelleyman's Thrown a Wobbly*, but the cock-ups and blunders happen at such a rate of knots that I've decided to update his greatest moments of recent years. The list is topped off by the time when, during the build-up to the game between Manchester City and West Brom at Christmas 2011, the panel began to discuss the importance of Gareth Barry in a team brimming with superstar names.

'Oh, he's top drawer,' Merse declared. 'Different class. I played with the lad when he was a teenager and he was a proper player then and a top, top lad. He's the sort of lad you wouldn't mind your daughter bringing home . . . Well, maybe not now. She's nine.'

We fell about laughing, it was classic Merse. Thankfully those giggles weren't a one-off. Take a look at the latest examples of 'Mersonisms' . . .

ON AN EVERTON GOAL

MERSE: 'And it's a goal, 2–1 to Everton. What a header!'

JEFF: 'And [Denis] Stracqualursi is the goalscorer?'

MERSE: 'Yeah, the super-sub.'

JEFF: 'My goodness, well that's his first goal in English football . . .'

MERSE: 'Oh no it's not, it's [Apostolos] Vellios.'

ON A GOAL

MERSE: 'Oh, it's an absolute worldy, Jeffrey . . . Jeff . . . Jeffrey? Jeff! I think I'm your wife!'

ON THE ART OF MANAGEMENT

MERSE: 'Someone said to me when I was manager [at Walsall], write your best team down on a piece of paper and put it in a drawer. Whenever you're struggling, go back to that team. It never worked for me . . .'

ON A MANCHESTER UNITED GAME

MERSE: 'At the moment they don't look like scoring, Man United. They are on the attack at the moment, but it's 1–0 and the goalkeeper hasn't made a save . . . Berbatov! 1–1! I didn't even know Berbatov was playing, seriously.'

Possibly his biggest blunder arrived at the beginning of 2012, when the panel came to discussing the fortunes of Newcastle, in particular the form of their striker Demba Ba who had been on fire at the time. We raised the point that he might have attracted the attentions of some of the bigger boys. I must admit, I was thinking about Man United, Spurs, Chelsea and the like, so when Merse mentioned that Villa would be a good destination for him, all hell broke loose . . .

JEFF: 'Why would he want to go to Aston Villa from Newcastle?'

MERSE: [Long pause] 'Bigger club.'

THE PANEL: [Sharp intake of breath] 'Woah!'

JEFF: 'Every Newcastle United fan is currently reaching for their PC, their laptop, their phone to complain about that. Aston Villa are a bigger club than Newcastle?!'

MERSE: 'Have Newcastle won the European Cup?'

JEFF: 'No . . .'

MERSE: 'Oh? How many times have Newcastle won the League?'

JEFF: 'When did Aston Villa last win the League?'

MERSE: 'Aston Villa have won a lot of stuff since Newcastle last won anything. [He was right too, Aston Villa won the League in 1981, the League Cup in 1994 and 1996 and the European Cup in 1982. They also won the European Super Cup in 1982/83 and the Intertoto Cup in 2001 and 2008, though nobody outside of Villa Park really cared about that.]'

TONY COTTEE: '1969 was the last time Newcastle won anything [which was the Inter-Cities Fairs Cup; they also won the Intertoto Cup in 2006, though nobody outside of St James' Park really cared about that either].'

MERSE: 'Right, so where shall we start with Aston Villa? The League, the European Cup, the Carling Cup . . .'

JEFF: 'Is that solely what makes you a big club, then?'

MERSE: 'They hold exactly the same [number of fans in the ground] as Newcastle as well, they get the same gates [er, they don't Merse. St James' Park is bigger by 10,000 seats], but let's put both of them in perspective. Unless you live in Newcastle or Villa [and why Merse believed that Villa was a town is beyond me], nobody else is wearing their shirts, so they're only really big clubs in their cities, if we're being honest. But Villa have won a lot of stuff. I think Thommo will go with me here . . .'

THOMMO: [Looking terrified] 'Don't implicate me!'

Thommo made a shrewd move by removing himself from the debate, because within minutes the Internet came alive as a volley of abuse and criticism was hurled at Merse, some of it justified, too. I'm not having a pop at Villa because their fans are incredibly passionate, but in Newcastle football is a religion. If the team wins on a Saturday they have a great night followed by a great week. It affects everybody's life from the moment they get up to the moment they go to bed and I'm not sure if it's like that at any other club. If you're a dyed-in-the-wool Villa fan you probably hate me right now, but that's just the way I feel. Look, I know it's a school playground argument, a bit like the my-dad-is-bigger-than-your-dad debate that goes on with children up and down the country. Well, all children apart from mine, because they know they're on a hiding to nothing. A bit like Merse and his Villa-are-bigger-than-Newcastle debate.

Merse hasn't been the only *Soccer Saturday* panellist to have found himself in trouble with the demon drink. The late, great George Best was also fond of a tipple or 20 as we all know. I recall one time in particular when he fell victim to a heavy night on the sauce, mainly because I didn't see him in action the following morning when he was supposed to be on the panel. Instead his bender had been so wild that he ended up taking a couple of girls (who later turned out to be of the 'professional' variety, though he told us he didn't know that at the time) back to his hotel room, where they stole two grand off him as he slept. George unsurprisingly called in sick the following day.

It wasn't the first time a woman or two had got George into

trouble either. When he was a player with United, George once charmed a lady into bed in the hours before he was due to play against Leeds United in the 1970 FA Cup semi-final. Apparently he had managed to chat her up on the stairs of the team hotel. Man United boss Wilf McGuinness apparently caught George in the act and wanted to send him packing, but Manchester United's then director Sir Matt Busby intervened, which turned out to be a mistake.

'We drew 0–0 again,' said Wilf. 'George had the chance to win it but fell over the ball in front of goal.'

Thankfully George didn't hurt himself during the aforementioned ill-fated drinking session, at least not physically. The same can't be said for matchday reporter and former player Peter Beagrie, who injured himself quite badly during a pre-season tour of Spain with Everton in 1991. Having got a tad tipsy following a friendly against Real Sociedad, Peter had some difficulty in waving a taxi down. Instead he convinced a local to give him a lift on the back of his motorcycle. Once the unusual-looking pair got to the front of his hotel, Peter was annoyed to discover that the main door was locked; the night porter had fallen asleep behind the reception desk and no amount of banging or shouting would wake him. In a moment of madness, Peter jumped back on the motorbike, much to the horror of his newfound mate, revved up the engine and drove through the glass front of the hotel. There was glass and blood everywhere; the cuts on Peter's back were so severe that he later needed 50 stitches. That wasn't even his biggest cock-up either. As he gathered his senses and took stock of his wounds, Peter realised that he had crashed into the wrong hotel – the Everton squad were actually staying in another building down the road.

The one man who seems not to have got himself in trouble with the grog has been, somewhat ironically, 'Champagne' Charlie Nicholas, the only panellist with a type of booze stuck to his name.

'The nickname used to bug me when I was a lad,' he once told me. 'But only because I couldn't afford the stuff. I used to only be able to drink shandy and "Shandy" Charlie Nicholas didn't sound so good, so I didn't correct anybody.'

Good idea, Charlie. Yours, Jeff 'A pint of Hoegaarden, if you're asking' Stelling.

CHAPTER TWENTY

TWITTER YE NOT (#IJUSTDONTUNDERSTAND THEINTERNETSOMETIMES)

[WARNING: This chapter contains grammatical errors, abbreviations and the occasional 'WTF?' moment. They have nothing to do with me. I'm a former presenter of *Countdown*, don't you know. LOL. Cheers, Jeff.]

The other day I went to the supermarket in my Hartlepool pyjamas. I bought broccoli, toothpaste and a box of Dairylea Triangles. Later in the afternoon I watched *Neighbours*, quoted some Freud to Mrs Jeff and ran a competition to win a date with Chris Kamara – a prize you could only claim if you had been the 1000th person to message me that day. To round off a hectic 24 hours, I then threatened to punch a Grays Athletic fan on the nose after some rather cheeky criticism of the neckwear I'd been wearing on *Soccer Saturday*; by midnight I was unceremoniously sacked from Sky for making an inappropriate comment about my former *Countdown* co-presenter, the easy-on-the-eye Rachel Riley. Phew, what a day.

Of course, I didn't really do any of these things, and certainly not in public. Well, the part about those Dairylea Triangles was halfway true, but as far as I know my job at *Soccer Saturday* is still safe. However, had I actively used a Twitter account while under the influence of a) alcohol, or b) egotism, I could have potentially felt the need to deliver the kind of banter listed above in order to engage with an audience of stalkers, trainspotters and tabloid journalists; the juicy details of my life rolling through the Internet from the minute I got up in the morning to the moment I kicked back in my drawing room at midnight, tumbler of whisky in one hand, a copy of the *Non-League Paper* in the other.

Now some of you might not be aware of Twitter. You may well have been working your way back from a football game in the Faroe Islands rather than surfing the net for the past 12 months. Or perhaps for the last few years you've preferred to entertain yourself with more intellectually challenging stimuli on a weekday afternoon, such as *Countdown*. Regardless of your reasoning, I can reveal that Twitter is a website and often a silly one at that. On it, members – or 'tweeters' – can post succinct messages of a length no longer than 140 characters, the idea being that the forum gives anyone – you, me, Barack Obama, Jordan – an opportunity to express their thoughts to the world. As if anyone really cares. I mean, honestly, what right-minded individual wants the rest of the world to know what they've been doing in the garden centre, or what particular member of the *Loose Women* gang has annoyed them that day (my guess: probably all of them)? The mind boggles.

Weirdly, though, one group has taken to Twitter with gusto: the modern superstar footballer, a breed of celebrity who, on the one hand, seems perfectly comfortable with issuing legally scary super-injunctions to protect their privacy, but on the other, appears strangely happy to tell the world and his wife exactly what they think of the results rolling in on *The X Factor*, or what they'd quite like to do to Scarlett Johansson given half the chance. Which seems odd when you think that several of them have spent millions in legal fees to prevent football fans from rummaging through the finer details of their saucy bedroom secrets in the newspapers.

Really, I'm surprised that footballers have got involved with it at all to be absolutely honest. The one thing I wouldn't swap with the modern player is his lack of personal time, especially as he goes about his daily business. Even walking down the high street can be an exercise in high-tech counter-surveillance these days. A mobile-phone camera or paparazzi photographer is usually dogging his every move, whether he's clothes shopping with the girlfriend, eating a nice meal in a fancy restaurant, or urinating on a pool table in a Leeds city centre pub. Surely the pressure of a life in the limelight must get too much? Once the front door is shut and the curtains drawn after 'work', a barrier could be erected between the public and his private life and nobody would begrudge him at all. But that ain't the way it works, strangely.

And this is where Twitter comes into play. From what I can gather, based on my limited foray into the site, it's away from the club canteen or the football ground that large numbers of the Premiership's elite tend to impart vital snippets of information on a wide range of subjects, such as how their dog got on at the vets, or where they bought their favourite underpants. The result is largely a cacophony of anodyne tidbits and virtual, verbal diarrhoea that has absolutely no bearing on the football world. For example, can you guess which deep thinkers wrote the following?

1. 'Today was the official revealing of the wax statues of me and my wife. We're very proud! Do they look like us?'

2. 'Dogs have no sense of time and cant [sic] eat chocolate. No need 2reward [sic] ur [sic] dog 4being [sic] patient with some Kit Kat. U'll [sic] kill him 4nothing [sic].'

3. 'Surely farmers can get up an hour earlier if they want to work more? It's not like putting the clocks back gives us an hour more light?'[6]

It's hardly enlightening stuff and really not enough to interest the most diehard of football fans like myself. Nevertheless, one argument for Twitter I've heard rattling around the saloon bar is that the forum allows the fans to get a little closer to their heroes, just like they could in the 1960s and '70s. In those good old days, First Division players would join a legion of mutton-chopped fans in the pub for a few pints of flat beer after a match; everyone rubbed shoulders together and your run-of-the-mill, top-billing footballer was happily in touch with the common man, mainly

---

6   ANSWERS: 1. Rafael van der Vaart; 2. Louis Saha; 3. Michael Owen.

because the common man was buying him mild and bitter by the gallon. A lot of people reckon that Twitter does a similar thing today: it links the untouchable, multimillionaire footballer with his supporters.

What a lot of rubbish. In those halcyon days, players would only drink with fans of their own club, not with rival supporters. If somebody played for Liverpool and popped into a pub by Goodison Park for a few pints after the game, they'd probably expect to have their head examined afterwards, as well as every broken bone in their body. And herein lies the problem: on Twitter, professional footballers have opened themselves up to a barrage of criticism and abuse from just about anyone with a laptop or a smartphone and half a brain. I've read dozens of reports on professional footballers who have signed up to Twitter in the morning only to close down their accounts by the evening, such was the torrent of abuse from fans, both from rival teams and their own club.

Probably the most disastrous example of how Twitter can be a fickle mistress regards the story of Darron Gibson (or @dgibbo28 as he was known on the site), then a fringe player at Manchester United (he now plays for Everton), so therefore a spare part at one of the most disliked clubs on the planet. In a nutshell: a prime target. Unsurprisingly, having logged on, Gibson found himself on the receiving end of an Internet 'earful', of which I've listed some of the nicer comments:

'@dgibbo28 the biggest compliment i can give you is that you are better than Carrick.'

'@dgibbo28 hasn't tweeted yet. Seems somewhat fitting after

the countless anonymous performances we've seen from the "footballer".'

'@dgibbo28 nothing would make me happier than if we sold you this summer, you're probably a nice bloke, but an awful footballer.'

Two hours after logging in for the first time and posting his personal details, @dgibbo28 had closed down his account, never to brave the cruel world of Twitter again, which must have generated a fair deal of stick down at the training ground the next day. Though probably not from Rio Ferdinand, whose grammatical expertise on the website appeared to match the ball-playing prowess of his team mate. In an analysis of footballers' linguistic skills on Twitter, an English-language expert reckoned that 88 per cent of the words used by Ferdinand were 'basic'. Unsurprisingly, the former England skipper was a bit put out at the accusation. Luckily Rio was already familiar with the perfect platform from which to stick it to the boffins in his usual eloquent and poetic manner, of course.

'So if u shorten words to get wot u want in within 140 characters it makes u a twit?!' he tweeted. 'I think that's working well within the 140 boundaries!'

To further prove his advanced grasp of the English language, he added: 'I swear down, we need more than 140 characters on ere, I want to get tings across wivout avin 2 use numbers 4 words!'

Nice work, Rio. Still, if any good came from Gibson's foray into social media, it was that he'd shown the dignity to at least turn the other cheek and walk away, which is more than can be said for defender Danny Gabbidon. During West Ham's calamitous 2010/11 season – in which Gabbidon played a part before he moved to QPR, and the east London side were relegated to the Championship – the defender was blamed by fans on Twitter for his team's collapse against Aston Villa. Gabbidon lashed out: 'U know what f*** the lot of u will never get another tweet from me again u just don't get it do you. Bye Bye.'

Days later, however, the *Guardian* newspaper noted that Gabbidon had imparted some rather contradictory – and altogether more sophisticated – opinions on the club's official website.

'The fans here have always been unbelievable,' he said. 'They've been really patient, they could have been harsher to us. I'd just like to thank them . . . they've been fantastic.'

Blimey, not only is Twitter a virtual world, it's a bloody shameless one as well.

From my own experience, I've noticed that the Internet can be a scary place. When I'm getting my notes ready for *Soccer Saturday*, I'll often read fans' online forums, just to get an idea of how the supporters of a club feel about a certain manager or their chairman. Often I'm staggered by the high number of nutters who are roaming free out there. Some of the people that contribute to these sites have extreme views that really shouldn't be taken seriously. They certainly shouldn't be used to represent how the majority of fans feel about a particular subject. Well, at least that's what I tell myself as I read the notes from posters banging on about how they 'really, really hate my guts'.

Of course, these aren't the only crackpot stories to have emerged from Twitter since it first opened for business. Among the countless tales of bitter, former employees hacking into their boss's accounts and angry girls administering revenge on their cheating boyfriends, footballers have delivered a fair amount of hilarious, shocking and downright stupid posts, all within the designated 140 characters. These include . . .

#1
@Joey7Barton

Mr Barton has spent large chunks of his time getting up the hooter of managers, fans, opponents, and just about anyone in a vague position of authority during his career, which rather unpleasantly included some time in Strangeways for assault and affray. In somewhat impressive circumstances, the midfielder showed a marked desire for self-improvement during the latter stages of his time at Newcastle and then QPR. More unexpected was Barton's fascination with Twitter, where he vented his spleen on just about anything and everything, from the work of German philosopher Friedrich Nietzsche to the latest series of *I'm A Celebrity . . . Get Me Out Of Here!* ('The watching of "I'm Not A Celebrity . . . Or If I Was I Don't Have Any Semblance Of Self Respect Left . . . Get Me Out Of Here" should be banned . . . I'd rather lose every one of my vital organs than appear on this pile of sh*te. Enjoy simplifying ur selves watching.').

The most surprising rant, however, took place when Mr Barton decided to lash out at the Labour Party. Clearly bored with embroiling himself in spats on the pitch with the likes of Arsenal's Gervinho – with whom Barton had a flimsy bout of fisticuffs when Newcastle met the Gunners at the start of the 2011/12 season – the midfielder turned his attentions to the leader of the other Opposition, Ed Miliband.

'I've nothing against lisps in everyday life just authoritarian figures having them, especially elected ones,' he tweeted. 'Labour no chance next election. They should of [*sic*] put his brother in charge, better front man. Also he stabbed his brother in the back for top job. Ed is a helmet.'

#watchoutjeremypaxman

#2
@rioferdy5

I don't want people to think I'm having a pop at Rio in these pages, because I think he's a cracking footballer who's done wonders for England and United, it's just that he sometimes seems to do himself more harm than good when it comes to representing himself online, which is why he's received more than one mention in this chapter. But putting aside the criticism of his basic language skills for just one minute, Ferdinand's most embarrassing tweet took place during his coverage of United's 2011 pre-season tour of America, which included a prestigious trip to the White House.

During this adventure, @rioferdy5 was on hand to deliver a blow-by-blow account of his date in the world's most famous building of influence (apart from Old Trafford, of course). It made for painful reading . . .

On landing:

> @rioferdy5: 'Just landed in Washington, kinda hot still! A guy of huge importance has just DM'd me + asked me to visit him . . . just checking my schedule!!'

@rioferdy5: 'Yes boss I got 1/2hrs so I'll pass through in a bit, will be good to catch up + put the world to rights! Do you have tetleys tea bags?!'

During the visit (when Rio thought it would be a good idea to take some pictures of security staff):

@rioferdy5: 'The security needs beefing up here at the White House . . . !!!'

And then the inevitable:

@rioferdy5: 'Whoa . . . some1 has got into my phone + taken down my pics off twitter . . . this is deep . . . is Jack Bauer in Washington?!'

@rioferdy5: 'My pic of the security was #removed quick, rapido, sharpish, fast . . . they don't play here in DC . . . I feel like I'm on *24* right now #baffled.'

Sometimes, words speak louder than actions.
#whatdoyouexpectwhenyoutakephotosinthewhitehouse

Now I can imagine what's going through your mind right now, dear *Jeffanory* fan. You've no doubt absorbed the first part of this chapter, laughed at the jokes and nodded appreciatively at the well-crafted prose. Chances are, though, you're probably thinking, 'Hang on, it's all very well for Jeff to knock Twitter, but it's a bit of a cheap shot, given that he's not even on it.' Well, to be honest, I did once sign up for Twitter in the Christmas of 2011 and the experience was initially so horrific I closed my account within days, a bit like the aforementioned Darron Gibson.

To be honest, the main reason I actually signed up for Twitter was to stop the countless fraud @jeffstelling accounts that currently exist. There are loads of them, none of which are actually me. Before those fateful few days at Christmas, I had never logged on or posted; those pages were just the fictitious work of somebody with a warped sense of humour, or too much time on their hands. A lot of them were very clever, which ruled out any of them being put together by Chris Kamara; however, whenever I've enquired as to how I could get them removed, I've always been told by Twitter that the onus was on me to prove my identity, often by emailing them a scanned copy of my birth certificate or passport, which is a bit like being burgled, calling the police to your house and then being asked to prove that you actually live there before anything is done to investigate the crime.

So far, 'I' have tweeted the following online:

@jeffskysports: 'In the office. Just had a serious bagel – salami, rocket and cream cheese.'

@jeffskysports: 'Out seeing Harry Potter. Don't hold it against me!'

@jeffskysports: 'Massaging my camel.'

Anyone who knows me will tell you that a) I'm more a steak, chips and onion rings man for lunch, b) I've not once watched a Harry Potter movie (well, not unless I've fallen asleep on the sofa during the Boxing Day evening game and woken up hours later) and c) the closest I've ever got to massaging a camel was when I walked past the donkey ride at Blackpool beach. How anyone comes up with this stuff is beyond me.

There have been times when this joking around has gone too far, however. Not long after manager Phil Brown left Hull City in 2010, an Internet spoof did the rounds online. Whoever had put it together had cut up clips from *Soccer Saturday*, taking shots of me talking into the camera. They then stuck them to Phil Brown's answers from a separate interview. By the looks of it the plan was to make it appear as if the pair of us had been in conversation, which was, on paper, rather clever. The problem was, it made him look ridiculous, mainly because the video suggested that I had been taking the mickey out of him and was really rather cruel.

Now, I found the clip really offensive, especially as the radio station talkSPORT later used it on their website, which could have caused a real issue between Phil and me. Sky could also have kicked up a fuss had Phil seen it and complained. I have no idea if he did. It would have been terrible if he had caught sight of the video online and believed that either I or the *Soccer Saturday* team had been behind it, though I'm sure he wouldn't have fallen for the spoof. The biggest clue that it was a stitch-up came with every clip because the viewer could see that my tie had changed colour and style with every shot . . .

JEFF [RED TIE] 'A very good afternoon to you and welcome to this *Gillette Soccer Saturday*. Please welcome this afternoon . . . [BLUE TIE WITH GREY SPOTS] it's irritating, it's slightly nauseating . . . [BLACK TIE

WITH WHITE SPOTS] it's Phil Brown. How are you enjoying it so far?'

PHIL: 'So far this season it's been going OK. [CUE A ROUND OF LAUGHTER OFF CAMERA FROM YET ANOTHER EPISODE FROM *SOCCER SATURDAY*, BEFORE CUTTING TO A SHOT OF ME IN MY FAVOURITE BLUE TIE WITH GREY STRIPES] . . . We're just starting to dream.'

JEFF [NOW IN BURGUNDY TIE] 'Stop, please stop. Sorry Phil, let's start again. So you're starting to dream . . .'

PHIL: 'We're just concentrating on the next game, it's a massive match today.'

JEFF [BLUE AND WHITE TIE]: 'Make sure you win, that would be my advice.'

PHIL: 'Yes, that is important.'

JEFF [BLUE AND GREY TIE]: 'Brown, why do all my friends call you a loser?'

It was cheeky, it took liberties, but while it initially annoyed me that someone had taken a pop at Phil via *Soccer Saturday*, they had, at least, shown the world (well, talkSPORT) what a sartorially elegant chap I was. A man with taste and style; a man with a loyalty card at House of Fraser. And beware, ladies and gentlemen, I'm not afraid to use it.

Anyhow, I decided to make a stand against the jokers and set the record straight, so I signed up to Twitter and plunged into a strange world of hashtags and 'retweets'. And what a nightmare it was. At first, I admit, I was quite excited to be on there. I trembled with the thrill of working in a new medium as I typed my first tweet and pressed the send button. Suddenly I was out in the Internet ether:

@jeffstelling2: 'Look, this is the real me. I'm on here to stop the people pretending to be me.'

I sat back and then thought about what to say, and I have to admit, I couldn't think of anything. I'm not Kammy – a man with a contacts book that reads like a *Who's Who* of former professional legends. I'm not glamorous like Charlie or a gourmand like Matt. So what was I going to tweet?

'Having a cup of tea now #tea'

'About to mow the lawn #grass'

'I hate sprouts #xmasdinner'

I didn't want to tweet my opinions on the games that were going on during the festive period because I wanted to save my thoughts for *Soccer Saturday* and I really didn't want to communicate with my friends online, so I packed my laptop away and retired to my copy of the *Non-League Paper*.

When I logged on again the following morning, I had the shock of my life: my inbox was overflowing with emails, 44,000 of them, each one sent from my Twitter account. Every message said the same thing: '@joebloggs is now following you on Twitter.' As soon as I read and deleted the first message, email number

44,001 dropped into my virtual letterbox. This was quickly followed by numbers 44,002, 44,003 and 44,004. It was a night-mare. I retired to my drawing room to shut myself away from the world and fell into a fretful snooze where I dreamt that I had been pinned to the doormat of Stelling Towers. My house was besieged by a mob of junk mailers and they were forcing pamphlets through my letterbox – I was drowning in a sea of fast-food menus, minicab flyers and newsletters from the local Women's Institute. It was hellish (well, not the curry menus, just everything else).

When I woke, I decided enough was enough. Only 15 hours after logging on to Twitter, I was logging off, but not before I read a few of the more flattering tweets about *Soccer Saturday*. Michael Owen had even posted a comment on the show: 'Men talking about football on the telly, it's fantastic to watch.' My heart then skipped a beat when I saw that TV dish Christine Bleakley had made a comment about me.

'Jeff Stelling you're a legend,' she said. 'A master broadcaster.' I was all giddy with excitement until Mrs Jeff, somewhat cruelly, pointed out that her tweet coincided with me praising Frank Lampard to the hilt on *Soccer Saturday*. I clicked the cancel button and slammed the laptop shut.

The one thing I've learned throughout my years as a broadcaster is that one wrong word or misjudged sentence can be disastrous, especially if it's been aired or printed online. Whatever you've said is out there for ever. I've also learned to hold back on the emails late at night, especially if I've had a pint of Hoegaarden or three. That rant to a boss or colleague might seem like a good idea at kicking-out time, but it always feels bloody horrible the next morning, especially when accompanied with a sore head and the paranoia of a possible P45.

This brings me neatly on to the case of Garry Cook, the former CEO at Manchester City. As you may or may not remember, Cook resigned, rather unsurprisingly it has to be said, in 2011 following a high-profile email blunder that took place in the most insensitive manner. In the offending note, Cook was supposed to be emailing City's director of football and former Nike representative, Brian Marwood, regarding Nedum Onuoha, a fringe player at the club whose agent was his mum, Dr Anthonia Onuoha. Dr Anthonia had sent a mail to Cook explaining that though she had been ill, 'ravaged by cancer', she was able to continue to represent her son, at which point Cook chose to press send on a distasteful note, meant only for Marwood.

'Ravaged with it!!!' it read. 'I don't know how you sleep at night. You used to be such a nice man when I worked with you at Nike.'

The mail was accidentally sent back to Dr Anthonia. It was publicised and caused such a storm that Cook resigned, but not before he'd claimed that the message had been sent by somebody who had hacked into his account. The club conducted an invest- igation that concluded 'there were foundations to Dr Anthonia's allegations', but despite the off-colour content of his note, I did have some sympathy with the fact that he had accidentally sent a message to somebody it wasn't actually intended for. He'd had a private thought – a bad one, let's not forget that – and he only wanted to share it with one person, but his tasteless joke got out of control.

If that sounds awful, think of some of the grubbier comments you might have made with friends in the pub and ask yourself:

would you like the world and his wife to have heard that gag? Or even your mum or girlfriend, boyfriend or dad? Chances are, the answer would be a resounding no.

I'm aware that we're even guilty of it on *Soccer Saturday*. Of course, I'm not talking about anything nearly as offensive as the cruel jibe made by Garry Cook, but there have been times when a comment has been made by myself or one of the panellists that was meant only for the people in the studio. If those comments had been heard by other people, somebody, somewhere might have found it to be offensive. And that happens in every walk of life where private conversations take place.

Of course, there are moments when these slip-ups take place on air. Matt Le Tissier, for example, infamously made a comment off-air while a recorded interview with Blackpool keeper Matt Gilks was being run. It was so cheeky, I couldn't resist repeating it once we'd returned to the studio. Gilks had been explaining that the Blackpool players had been asked to wash their own training kit, which drew some sniggers from the panellists, Le Tiss in particular. I decided to name and shame him, out of my love and respect for the fairer sex, of course.

'Look, I don't want to be one to tell tales out of school,' I said, 'but when Matt Gilks said that they all have to wash their own kits, Matt Le Tissier said, "What? Hasn't he got a wife?"'

The studio fell about laughing, but Matt was mortified that I'd grassed him up. 'That's the last time I say anything off-air,' he said, before coughing up. 'I did say it, but I didn't mean it.'

At least he had the decency to try to keep it off-air. International Man of Communication, Paul Merson, has occasionally been less subtle. When assistant referee Sian Massey made a great offside call during the game between Liverpool and Swansea in November 2011, he described it thusly: 'What a decision from the woman linesman!'

Every day I thank the heavens that Merse hasn't got a Sky Sports email address.

WHAT A LOAD OF JEFFANORY!

Sometimes I've been amazed at the stories I've stumbled across while doing my research for *Soccer Saturday*, either from my drawing room in Stelling Towers or over a bucket of chicken wings in the Winchester Motorway Services, Northbound branch. The Beautiful Game never ceases to amaze me. And I'm not the only one. My old mate Neil Warnock has an apt way of surmising a weird or wonderful football event whenever he has been perplexed by a strange refereeing decision or unexpected player outburst. In many a post-match interview he has simply raised his eyebrows, shrugged his shoulders and sagely murmured, 'Well, that's football, in't it?'

Of course, these philosophical musings usually trail a volley of expletives not suitable for the younger readers here, but Neil has a point: sometimes football is stranger than fiction; football life imitates *Jeffanory* art. And no amount of head scratching or slow-motion analysis can rationalise the more absurd moments in our wonderful game of football . . .

REFEREE TURNS ON CHRISTMAS LIGHTS!

They say that Premiership refs should stay out of the limelight, that the man in black should cut an anonymous figure. Sadly, that hasn't been the case in recent times. In the modern game, some of the Premier League's officials have even carved out a career for themselves as local celebrities, most notably Martin Atkinson, who in 2011 was given the honour of turning on the Christmas lights in the village of Drighlington, West Yorkshire.

My goodness, what has the world come to if a referee is deemed famous enough to switch on the village Christmas lights! Most officials have trouble enough when it comes to punching the right digits on the board displaying the time added on to the end of a match. The control of a high-tech pyrotechnics display powerful enough to light a small town in the required festive manner would surely be beyond him. Nevertheless, the announcement whipped the people of Drighlington into a right frenzy.

'Drighlington will be lighting up for Christmas with the help of a very special guest,' reported the *Morley Observer & Advertiser*, somewhat over-excitedly. 'Martin Atkinson, 40, started his career as a schoolboy ref in Drighlington before progressing on to the highest level of his profession.'

Most of the village were probably scratching their head at that point, while murmuring, 'Why haven't we got someone more respectable, like maybe Jodie Marsh?' Luckily, the boys at the *Morley Observer & Advertiser* elaborated further on the career of this most prestigious of referees.

'He has officiated at some of the biggest grounds in Europe, including Milan's San Siro and realised his dream when he was given the [2011] Cup Final between Manchester City and Stoke City at Wembley. Martin's big responsibility tomorrow will be switching on the Christmas tree lights at 6.30pm at Drighlington crossroads. Drighlington Band will be playing carols and there will be seasonal refreshments in the scout hut afterwards.

'All the village is invited to go along and share in the festive fun.'

And to throw rotten veg and mince pies, presumably.

CRACKPOT ROMANIAN CHAIRMAN! CRACKPOT SWISS CHAIRMAN!

Nobody makes a crackpot football chairman quite like our friends in eastern Europe, and for a while the chaps at the *Observer* newspaper ran a very entertaining 'watch' on some of the more oddball executives and entrepreneurs ruling the game in the Continent's more far-flung corners in their 'Said & Done' column. Among them were Romanian football giants Steaua Bucharest, owned by oddball politician Gigi Becali. Ever since his arrival, the club has generated a hefty share of headlines, mainly due to the antics of their owner. It was once claimed that he'd attempted to 'incentivise' first-team players from Universitatea Cluj to the tune of a whopping €1.7m before a fixture against one of Steaua's main title rivals. Becali later told the press that the money was meant for sweets and chocolate bars, which seemed a reasonable explanation. But in May 2011 he repeated the trick, this time with Universitatea Craiova, though clearly Becali had suffered in the credit crunch before the game because the cash incentives per head were reduced to a slightly less exciting €5,000 per man; Gigi claimed his offers represented a legitimate sponsorship. Again, another reasonable explanation.

Becali wasn't afraid of standing up to his rivals, either. When Dinu Gheorghe, the president of neighbours Rapid Bucharest, mentioned Becali's previous career as a shepherd, he chose national telly as the perfect platform from which to air his replies.

'He is a filthy jerk,' he roared. 'A fat bum. I'll force this Gypsy back up his mother. I'm tired of him, all his irony and jokes. He forces me to lose control! He's way out of line.'

Thankfully, Becali had a heart. During an Easter speech at a press conference in 2011, he made several heartfelt apologies to a string of people offended by his motormouth. Among the recipients were gays, the club's fans and Jehovah's Witnesses.

'I'm sorry to all the religions, the cults, but I do have my views. Jehovah's Witnesses are on the way to perdition,' he said, metaphorical cap in hand, before remarking: 'That feels better, I feel reborn. And it'll make Satan crazy: he hates it when a soul gets cleaner. But I didn't just do this for me. I'm an inspiration to millions.'

I'm sure it was all done in a very humble manner.

Typically though, Becali later delivered a savage reminder to his team's general manager Mihai Stoica that he would not tolerate failure. When pressed on Stoica's role at the club and the pressure to succeed, Becali said, 'You really think he doesn't know what will happen to him, if we fail? God help him. Jihad will begin.'

Still, at least Becali didn't threaten any of his playing staff with physical harm. Across the Continent at Switzerland's Neuchâtel Xamax (a *Countdown* contestant's wet dream if ever I saw one), Bulat Chagaev (likewise) – a one-time associate of ex-Chechen 'warrior king' Ramzan Kadyrov (and again) – created his own reign of terror. A human resources nightmare, Chagaev embarked on a personal warpath between May and September of 2011, sacking four managers in as many months. Among the poor souls reaching for the P45s was Bernard Challandes, who managed to save the club from relegation in their last three games of his season in charge, before losing the Swiss Cup final to Sion. At half-time and with Neuchâtel Xamax trailing 2–0, it was claimed that Chagaev had burst into the team dressing room and yelled at his players.

'I'll kill you all!' he shouted.

His outburst clearly had no effect at all. Neuchâtel Xamax were unable to reverse the deficit and Challandes was given the boot shortly afterwards. It might come as a great surprise to learn that FIFA's head honcho, Sepp Blatter, was the club's honorary president. In January 2012 Neuchâtel Xamax had its Swiss Super League licence suspended after accusations were made that the club had falsified financial documents. Of course, these two facts are in no way related, I hasten to add.

SEXY FOOTBALL

Football can be a cruel game. One minute you're on the verge of breaking into football glory at Burnley, the next you're baring your torso to an audience of salivating ladies on an adult video phone chat app called SaucyTime. That might sound surreal, but it's exactly what happened to Danny Pitham, the one-time reserve team captain at Turf Moor who retired due to injury. Having quit the club in 2004, Pitham went on to play for a string of clubs before signing up to SaucyTime where he scooped up a tasty £1,000 a week by chatting to women on their iPad.

'It's a great site,' he told the *Clitheroe Times*. 'Anyone can call up to talk to me on video. A lot of the women just want to chat, but you do get the odd rude request, but it's a private call so it's up to them I suppose.'

THE TALE OF THE MISSING SHOE

As you can imagine, the research and writing of *Jeffanory* has uncovered some really rather fascinating tales of the unexpected. For example, while scanning the *Worcester News* at the start of the 2011/12 season, I learned that some controversy had been caused when Hereford United invested in a major clean-up of their Edgar Street ground. The club's makeover included the removal of a trainer that had dangled from the rafters of the Meadow End for nearly a decade. According to reports, the shoe had been booted up there during a televised FA Cup match between Hereford and Wigan Athletic in 2002 when fans began kicking a beach ball around the stands.

One chap, Richard Fensome, took a swing at the ball with his right peg and his inadequately laced £50 sneaker flew up in the air, so high in fact that it cleared Row Z and landed on a hook in the roof of the stand. Sympathetically, the Hereford faithful began taunting at him en masse: 'One shoe, you've only got one shoe.' To cement his misery further, Mr Fensome then had to cycle home to Belmont with only 50 per cent of the required footwear, though there was a silver lining to his rather grey cloud: he got tipsy, for free.

'Later that night, I went out in Hereford and was bought

drinks by people who recognised me off the telly coverage,' he said, rather proudly.

Once the shoe had been cut down in 2011 and Mr Fensome failed to claim it from the club, it was chucked in the bin, to some hoo-ha from the fans that congregated in the Meadow End on a regular basis. 'Where was the shoe?' they enquired. Debate 'raged' on Internet forums as to the final destination of the trainer; a newspaper reporter even 'descended' upon the club with a note-book, forcing United's vice-chairman into an explanation.

'We didn't realise it meant so much and would be so missed,' he said. 'It was never claimed by anyone. Nobody ever reported it missing – there was no Cinderella from the crowd who ever came to see if the trainer fitted.'

NEWS OF THE WORLD FOOTBALL SHOCKER!

The humorous legacy of Mr Fensome's trainer illustrates the lighter side of *Jeffanory*'s heavily researched journey, but for every dangling sneaker story, there have also been one or two darker discoveries to match. One of those involved AFC Wimbledon, the team who spiritually rose from the ashes of the Crazy Gang – the fearsome First Division Wimbledon team of the 1980s and '90s, and a side responsible for one of the greatest giant-killing acts of the 20th century when they defeated an all-conquering Liverpool XI in the 1988 FA Cup final. It's a well-known tale that their modern-day reincarnation began in a friendly against Sutton United in July 2002. But did you know that AFC Wimbledon's first ever goal came later that month against Bromley and was a 20-yard screamer scored by Glenn 'Trigger' Mulcaire?

Now if that name is ringing a bell or three at this particular moment it's because Mulcaire, a private investigator by trade, infamously hit the headlines in 2011 when it was revealed that the *News of the World* had been intercepting the voicemail messages of various celebrities. Mulcaire had previously been jailed for six months in 2007 for snooping on the likes of Prince William, Elle Macpherson and celeb publicist Max Clifford. Meanwhile, his lousy behaviour off the pitch was matched by some pretty unimpressive performances on it for AFC Wimbledon.

'He was long, lean and rangy,' said the club's chief executive Erik Samuelson. 'Never a physical or muscular player and with no great pace, but he had a good shot on him and a good eye for goal.'

Clearly, football's loss was tabloid journalism's unsavoury gain.

ASAMOAH GYAN

Cheese: so much to ponder. What's my favourite? Which one makes the best cheese on toast? These are the dilemmas I've often had to wrestle with as I've foraged through the Stelling larder, my glassy eyes staring at the Cheddars and Stiltons, in a manner not too dissimilar to David de Gea ogling the Krispy Kreme doughnuts and eating one without paying in his local branch of Tesco (unbelievably, that did happen). Thankfully, though, my relationship with this wonderful dairy product has never stretched to anything vaguely resembling a sexual experience, unlike Ghanaian striker Asamoah Gyan, who loved the stuff so much he even wrote a song about it.

Known equally back in his home country for his career as the pop star Baby Jet, Gyan is notorious for penning the song 'African Girls', complete with the lyric, 'African girls dey be/Them be sexy like cheese.' Now, anyone currently scratching their heads as to why cheese should be more arousing than, say, Christina Hendricks – a fine figure of a woman if ever I saw one – will be satisfied by Gyan's explanation to a journalist from the *Guardian* in 2011, where he explained that, well, the stuff just turns him on. 'When you go to the supermarket and you see the cheese designed in a triangle shape and you move it, it's sexy, something funny,' he said. Crikey, I thought. Do those Dairylea Triangles really ooze sex?

I guess I shouldn't be surprised that professional footballers have such an unusual relationship with food. Most of them spend their careers avoiding the good stuff like chips, pork scratchings and sausage rolls, so if a Premiership star finds an erotic quality in something that most of us would eat on a daily basis, like cheese or pork pies, well, that's probably because they're not allowed to stuff their faces like the rest of us.

Still, I have noticed that even the ex-pros are a little odd when it comes to their nutritional intake. A few years back we got some of the *Soccer Saturday* panellists together for a spoof take on *Come Dine With Me* and *MasterChef*, but the resulting footage really could have ended up on *Casualty*, such was the poor standard of their culinary expertise. The basic idea for the show was that the likes of Thommo, Kammy and Le Tiss would cook their signature dishes and present them to an expert panel of foodies: chefs Gino D'Acampo and Aldo Zilli, and myself. Both Gino and Aldo were on hand to offer some expert tips and advice to our 'chefs', but nothing could stop the panellists from creating some of the greatest cooking disasters known to man.

Thommo, for example, cooked the traditional Liverpool dish

'Scouse', but when it came out of the pan, it looked about as edible as a used jock-strap. It was disgusting.

'I've never been lost for words in the kitchen,' said Gino. 'Until now.'

I really felt for Aldo then because he didn't want to drink that day. As we were served dish after dish of slop in quite a convivial manner, it was clear that Aldo's resolve was unshakeable and he wasn't going to partake. But then came Thommo's 'Scouse'.

We all took one look at the plates of gloop and reached for our glasses of wine, even Aldo. Anything to save him from the vile taste of Thommo's 'cooking'.

THE MUPPET SHOW

Jens Lehmann, the former Arsenal goalie, has always been regarded as something of a liability. At set plays, he had a tendency to haul strikers to the ground in a fit of pique just because the very sight of them annoyed him. Then there were the infamous interviews in which Lehmann made a fair deal of trouble for himself by criticising his fellow goalkeepers, both at club and international level, where he regularly took a potshot at German number one Oliver Kahn.

'He takes himself far too seriously and thinks he is important,' said Lehmann. 'I don't like it when someone glorifies themselves.'

Talk about the pot calling the kettle black, but typically it was one such insult that sparked a legal row in 2010 when the retired Lehmann, by then a TV co-commentator, criticised the performance of Werder Bremen keeper Tim Wiese during the

Champions League group stage game against Tottenham. The following day, Wiese responded by firing off a few choice remarks of his own in a German newspaper, first by claiming that Lehmann should 'go on *The Muppet Show*' and later when he questioned his countryman's sanity.

'The man belongs on the couch,' he said. 'Perhaps that would help him. He should be committed – preferably locked up.'

Lehmann, obviously forgetting his own outbursts, decided that the comments were a violation of his personal rights and attempted to sue Wiese to the tune of €20,000. Unsurprisingly, the Munich court ruled against the claim, arguing that Wiese had not done anything untoward and the case, like most of Lehmann's goal kicks, was booted into touch.

TINO ASPRILLA'S PORN STAR WIFE AND OTHER TALES ...

For a short while, in the period known as Jeff BC (Before *Countdown*), I presented a show called *The Time of Our Lives* on Sky. It was cracking fun. Basically the programme revolved around three footballers from one team and the idea was that they would come in and talk about the best period of their footballing lives. Of course we would designate that period for them, but the lads would sit in the studio for a few hours and with the help of some good wine and fine cheeses, they would relive their glory years.

Through *The Time of Our Lives* I met some real legends, footballers that I wouldn't have dreamed of meeting as a kid watching the game. We managed to get three of the Lisbon Lions on the show, including the Celtic legend Billy McNeill.

Tottenham Hotspur heroes Bobby Smith, Cliff Jones and Terry Dyson came in to discuss the Bill Nicholson years. And Norman Hunter told some great tales from his Leeds United days about the rivalry with Chelsea. Apparently the two teams would set about one another for 90 minutes and when the final whistle blew, they would head to the players' bar for a few bevvies together.

The show got a really nice response from the fans and the papers were very positive about it. The *Guardian* wrote a lovely piece which said that 'it was good to see that Sky have finally acknowledged that football did not begin with the Premier League.'

We deliberately didn't show any footage on the programme because the premise of the show revolved around story-telling and player memories. I also thought that playing old clips would maybe detract from the anecdotes, and it was just great to hear the fantastic events and shenanigans that went on in the old days.

Among my favourite shows was the time when the Manchester City trio of Franny Lee, Mike Summerbee and Tommy Booth came in to see us. They told me that whenever City had an away game, the players would always go to the supporters' club afterwards for a few drinks. They also said that every year, the whole team would put on a Christmas panto for the supporters. Joe Corrigan once played Widow Twankey. Can you imagine City doing that now?

Another great show was when Steve Howey and John Beresford came in to the studio with David Ginola to discuss the exciting Newcastle team under Kevin Keegan in the 1990s. When Beresford and Howey arrived they came in, got miked up and looked across at David who was as immaculate as ever. They then scowled at me and said, 'Thanks a lot for bringing him in, we're going to look great sitting next to him. Like a right pair of ugly so-and-sos.'

They told me a great story about Colombian striker Tino Asprilla who was, by all accounts, the Mario Balotelli of the 1990s. He had a penchant for guns and was always hosting parties in his house. He even stripped naked for the cover of a Colombian magazine.

'Well, I'm a man with nothing to be ashamed of!' he told *FourFourTwo* when discussing the photo. 'They offered me the chance to be the first man to appear naked in a Colombian magazine – it seemed interesting . . . Luckily, the edition of the magazine sold out. It all started ages ago when my shorts fell off during a game – that started a myth, and now the myth has been revealed . . . [chuckles] I didn't think my sisters would forgive me, but they have!'

Anyway, according to the boys in the studio, the Newcastle team bus was pulling out of St James' Park for an away game one day and as it passed the hordes of waving fans, Asprilla walked down to the front seats where manager Kevin Keegan was sitting.

'Here, gaffer,' he said. 'Can you put this on?'

Kevin obliged thinking it was going to be a movie to entertain the troops or perhaps a compilation of great goals to inspire his players for the game ahead.

'Is it any good?'

'Of course it's good,' said Asprilla. 'It's one of my wife's films.'

Little did Kevin know that Mrs Asprilla was a porn star.

'Within seconds,' said Beresford, 'this really tasty girl comes on, stark naked and [the film] was full on. And I don't mean soft porn. The gaffer shouted, "Woah, get this off!" All the fans outside must have been wondering what the hell was going on.'

Possibly my favourite episode from the show featured Kenny Burns, Larry Lloyd and Peter Shilton, who came in to talk about Nottingham Forest's years under Brian Clough. They were a great bunch and Kenny told a cracking story about Cloughie's disciplinary measures.

'We came in at half-time during one game and we were a goal up,' he said. 'We'd played some football from the back and we got our goal when I rolled the ball across the penalty area to Larry and he kicked it upfield and we scored. Anyway, as we sat there in the dressing room, sucking on our oranges, Cloughie looked across at me and started wagging his finger. He snapped, "You know the rules young man: £50 will be docked from your wages. Passing it across the box is an immediate fine." Even though we'd scored as a result, I didn't dare argue with him. I knew I could never win.'

Shilts was equally entertaining. He told me a tale of how, before one of the European Cup finals, Forest had booked into a hotel without even planning where they were going to train before the big match. Can you imagine that happening now? It seemed unbelievable to me. Anyway, when they checked in, there was absolutely nowhere for them to have a practice session, so Shilts ended up on the grass bank of a roundabout with the goalkeeping coach. It was the only green area they could find. The pair of them ran through a series of training drills as scores of passing cars honked their horns, presumably at the balls that kept bouncing on to the road.

Ah, the good old days.

WORLD FOOTBALL'S GREATEST NAME BECOMES INVOLVED IN TRANSFER SAGA!

Given my former stint as the presenter of *Countdown* and my love of humorous word play, it seems fitting to mark the closing pages of *Jeffanory* with a pun. And they don't come any better than the tale of Belgian midfielder Mark De Man – a former Anderlecht player once coveted by Scottish team Kilmarnock. Can you think of a more suitably named player in world football?

Sadly, De Man opted to stay in Belgium to be closer to his family rather than move to the far flung corners of Scotland, and he signed with Third Division side Hasselt, though as one wag quipped on the Internet: 'Scottish football journalists were reported to be "disappointed" at the outcome but they looked forward to the potential signings of striker, Skor De Gaulle and goalkeeper Bloek De Schott.'

I have to say I was gutted too – the arrival of De Man would have ushered in a fresh season of puns. My joke pad in the drawing room of Stelling Towers would have been brimming with gags in next to no time. However, Belgium's gain is comedy's loss and instead, I'll have to content myself with stories featuring the likes of Paul Merson, Kammy and Emley's Mike Clark for side-splitting comedy. That and the fortunes of Madron FC. As a former TV pundit in the dim and distant past once said, 'Ah, football – it's a funny old game.'

He wasn't kidding . . .

JEFF'S BUMPER BOOK OF NEWSPAPER CUTTINGS
INCLUDES SCRAPS FROM THE FOLLOWING
PUBLICATIONS:

Introduction
Bradford Telegraph & Argus
Goalkeeper sent off as Eccleshill United game abandoned;
2 October 2011

Chapter 1
Sun
Six sent off in wrong colour underpants row;
27 September 2011

Chapter 2
Guardian
Intimate piercing leads to red card for Australian amateur team
captain;
23 June 2011

Metro
Japanese footballer receives fastest red card ever after just five
seconds;
11 May 2011

Guardian
The quickest sending-off of all time;
7 January 2009

Independent
Player sets record for fastest ever sending off;
29 December 2009

BBC News
Argentina prisoners train as football referees;
21 April 2011

Daily Mail
Jail for soccer player Joseph Rimmer who 'drove 4x4' on to pitch
at referee;
24 November 2010

Metro
Red-carded footballer Joseph Rimmer 'drove 4x4' at referee;
26 October 2010

Allvoices.com
Soccer-fan-throws-porridge-at-referee-after-match;
20 March 2011

Sun
Angry fan attacks ref with scooter;
23 August 2011

Metro
Montevideo Wanderers striker Diogo vents fury at linesman with
face slap;
24 August 2011

Guardian
Said & Done;
10 April 2011

Daily Mirror
Rod Stewart's football referee Don gets [*sic*] 50 years' service to the game;
10 November 2011

Daily Mail
Babak Rafati suicide attempt: German football referee saved by his assistants;
8 January 2012

Daily Mail
Assistants praised after saving life of German referee following suicide attempt;
21 November 2011

BBC Sport
Referee Babak Rafati seeks return after suicide attempt;
25 November 2011

Chapter 3
Scarborough Evening News
Dean Windass admits to suicide attempt;
16 January 2012

Chapter 4
Daily Record
Tolkien rubbish: Aberdeen ace Darren Mackie votes Lord Of The Rings his top book . . . then admits he's not read it;
7 November 2011

Chapter 6
Independent
Morrison labels Scharner 'Mr Moanivator' and 'a weirdo';
8 October 2010

Sun
Mick McCarthy shirty with Paul Scharner;
17 October 2011

Express
McCarthy angry over Scharner shirt;
17 October 2011

Chapter 7
Yorkshire Post
O'Driscoll is sacked by text as Rovers turn to Saunders;
24 September 2011

Daily Mail
'Anyone who doesn't like it can go to hell': Mohammed Al Fayed [*sic*] defends 7ft 6ins Michael Jackson statue at Craven Cottage;
4 April 2011

Daily Mail
It's off the wall! United star Ferdinand sticks the boot into Fulham's Jacko statue;
5 April 2011

Daily Telegraph
Manchester United Sir Alex Ferguson brands scrapping Premier League's promotion and relegation 'suicide';
18 October 2011

Chapter 8

Sun
Youngest footie boss Carolyn Still was an escort;
17 September 2011

Sun
Youngest footie boss is engaged . . . to the man who gave her the job two weeks ago;
27 September 2011

Metro
Brighton employ hawks to scare away pigeons from new stadium;
5 September 2011

Chapter 9

This is Staffordshire
Bolton fan has no regrets after leaving job in Oz to watch 5–0 defeat;
19 April 2011

Daily Mail
Aguero's number is up;
18 November 2011

BBC Sport
Fenerbahce only allowed to admit women and children;
21 September 2011

Hartlepool Mail
Poolie's Quaker mascot misery;
3 October 2011

Chapter 10
Metro
Manuel Neuer slapped with strict code of conduct from Bayern
Munich ultras;
20 July 2011

Daily Record
East Fife tell fans to stop slagging off the players . . . because it's
hurting their feelings;
3 March 2011

Chapter 12
Guardian
Middlesbrough rally round to help Gary Parkinson, one of their
own;
24 November 2011

Daily Mail
Macclesfield let him go, so he decided to knock on Fergie's
door . . . meet Max Lonsdale;
19 October 2011

Chapter 14
Daily Mail
Spurs defender Assou-Ekotto is a Smart guy;
22 January 2011

Chapter 15
Sun
A bonus to sink their teeth into;
3 December 2011

Sun
Redbridge set for Marbella after latest FA Cup heroics;
24 November 2011

Chapter 16
Daily Mail
Footballer ruled offside . . . for breaking wind as opponent took
penalty and missed;
6 April 2009

Daily Mirror
Football player gets booked for farting in the ref's face;
19 November 2009

Chapter 17
Sporting Life
Di Canio wants proud chihuahuas;
1 October 2011

Observer
Said & Done (Marius Sumudica);
10 April 2011

Chapter 18
FourFourTwo
Tracking down English football's first ever Brazilian;
9 March 2009

Sun
Kipper prank ruins Mario Balotelli's motor;
2 August 2011

Daily Telegraph
Chelsea's David Luiz convinced Chelsea can still win title;
13 January 2012

Chapter 19
ESPN
Jones reveals 'stupid' sock superstition;
18 November 2011

Guardian
The Sportblog: If you thought trainspotters were weird . . . try footballers;
22 October 2006

Daily Mail
Roberto Mancini interview by Martin Samuel;
5 January 2012

Guardian
Said & Done;
22 May 2011

Chapter 20
Daily Mail
X-rated Danny Gabbidon lets rip on Twitter before appearing to close account;
18 April 2011

www.sportsmemorabilia.com
Merson remembers

Metro
Rio Ferdinand defends Twitter posts after his vocabulary is labelled 'basic';
7 June 2011

Shields Gazette
Now Joey Barton's tweeting about politics;
21 July 2011

Guardian
Quote of the day: Joey Barton, The Fiver;
21 July 2011

Chapter 21
Metro
Shoe kicked onto Hereford stadium roof nine years ago is
retrieved, but disappears;
19 August 2011

BBC News
Glenn Mulcaire profile;
8 July 2011

INDEX

8 Out of 10 Cats 64

Abramovich, Roman 86, 170
Abu, Mohammed 177
AC Milan 40, 41
Adebayor, Emmanuel 176
AFC Emley 3–4
AFC GOP 197
AFC Wimbledon 175, 271–2
Aguero, Sergio 110, 111
Alcock, Paul 216
Aldershot Town 182
Al Fayed, Mohamed 82–4, 85
Allardyce, Sam 158–61, 162–4,
    165, 166, 167
Almere City 34
Andrews, Keith 112
Arnison, Paul 117
Arsenal 5, 15, 86, 88, 90, 170–1,
    183, 186, 216, 218, 254
Ashley, Mike 172, 173
Aspley House 197

Asprilla, Tino 277–8
Assou-Ekotto, Benoit 178–9
Aston Villa 86, 128, 175, 241,
    242, 243
Atkinson, Martin 266–7
Atlético Junior 217–19
Atlético Madrid 84
Ayre, Ian 171, 172, 173

Baddesley Park 12
Ba, Demba 29, 241
Bale, Gareth 89
Balotelli, Mario 31, 73, 177–8,
    226–8
Bangura, Al 155–7
Barnard, Darren 79
Barnsley 182
Barry, Gareth 239
Barton, Joey 254–5
Barton Town Old Boys 45
Bashley 26
Bath City 19–20, 21

Bayern Munich 125–6, 151, 223

Beagrie, Peter 244

Becali, Gigi 267–8

Beckham, David 79, 140, 175

Bellamy, Craig 195, 212

Benali, Francis 90, 91

Benitez, Rafa 131

Bennett, Tony 133

Benson, Adrian 4

Bent, Darren 40

Bentick, Janet 182–3

Beresford, John 276, 277–8

Best, George 46, 83, 243–4

Blackburn Rovers 44, 99–100, 101, 171

Blackpool 112–15, 141, 146, 156, 228–9, 268

Blatter, Sepp 269

Bleakley, Christine 261

Blunkett, David 156

Bolton Wanderers 29, 90, 107, 158–61, 162–3, 171

booing and whistling 122–4

Booth, Tommy 276

Botham, Sir Ian 101

Bould, Steve 138

Bournemouth 91

Bradford City 12, 42, 45, 182, 214–15

Brady, Karren 94

brainy footballers 52–3, 55

breaking wind on the pitch 197

Brechin City 149

Brevett, Rufus 83

Brighton & Hove Albion 91, 95, 156, 187, 190–1

Bristol City 43

Bromley 186, 271–2

Brownett, Joe 181–2

Brown, Phil 164, 166, 258–9

bungs in football 162, 163–7

Burnley 55, 56, 269

Burns, Kenny 278

Burns, Mickey 194

Burton Albion 24

Busby, Sir Matt 244

Butt, Nicky 140, 232–3

Caesar, Gus 15, 138

Cahill, Gary 29

Cambridge United 186

Capello, Fabio 152

Cape Verde 24

Carlisle, Clarke 52–3, 54–6

Carlsberg 101

Carragher, Jamie 130–1

Carson, Scott 226

Carvalho, Ricardo 26

Cavani, Edinson 169

Celebrity Mastermind 64

Chagaev, Bulat 269

Challandes, Bernard 269

Charlton Athletic 12

Chelsea 29, 131, 175, 231, 276

Cheltenham 190

Chesterfield 217

Chippenham Town 26

Chorlton Villa 196–7

Chris Moyles' Quiz Night 64–8

Christmas tree lights 266

Clark, Frank 194

Clark, Mike 3–4

Clarke, Leon 216–17

Clarke, Steve 237

Clough, Brian 125, 278

Cohen, George 83

Coldstream FC 124

Cole, Ashley 78

Cole, Cheryl 47, 137

Cole, Joe 215

Constantin, Marius 219–20

Cook, Garry 262

Cooper, Colin 147

Corbett, Ronnie 8

Corluka, Vedran 177

Corrigan, Joe 276

Cortese, Nicola 87, 88, 89, 90

Cottee, Tony 242

Countdown 49–53, 54–60, 61–3, 83, 211, 228–9

Coventry City 183

Craig, Thomas 108

Crawley Town 106

Crossley, Phil 109

Cross Park Farm Celtic 26–7

Crystal Palace 12

Cunningham, Conor 111–12

Cyril the Swan 218

D'Acampo, Gino 52, 59, 273, 274

dads' matches 205–6

Dagenham & Redbridge 43

Dalglish, Kenny 237

Darlington 43, 45, 117–18

Davis, Steve 59

Deadman, Darren 151

Dean, Mike 11–12, 29

Defoe, Jermain 158

De Man, Mark 279

Dennis, Les 51, 60

Dent, Susie 50, 58, 61, 62

Deportivo Pereira 218

Derby County 12, 97

Derbyshire, Victoria 166

de Souza, Alex 116

Diaby, Abou 100

Di Canio, Paolo 15, 214–17

Diouf, El Hadji 160

Dixon, Alesha 65, 66, 67, 68

Doncaster Rovers 81–2, 150

Dorchester Town 121, 122

Dowie, Iain 12, 15, 53, 139

Downing, Stewart 189

drinking 238–9, 243–5

Dumbarton 174

Dyson, Terry 276

Eadie, Damian 228, 229

Earls 12

East Fife 128–9

Eastleigh Juniors 12

Ebbsfleet United 182

Eccleshill United 3–4

Eccleston, Aaron 25

eco-friendly policies 97–9

email blunders 262–3

England friendlies 185

Eriksson, Sven Göran 46, 47,
     48, 185

Espindola, Fabian 79

Estonia 111–12

Evans, Jonny 195

Everton 140, 148, 240, 244, 251

excessive spending by clubs
     169–70

Exeter City 143–4

fans
   disgruntled 122–4, 125–8,
        131–2
   loyalty and/or fanaticism
        105–18
   mingling 190
   tribalism 189
   Twitter comments 251–3

Fans Reunited Day 187–9,
     190–1

Fenerbahce 116, 120

Fensome, Richard 270–1

Ferdinand, Rio 83, 252, 255–6

Ferguson, Alex 87, 151, 152–4

Fernandes, Tony 214

Fiennes, Sir Ranulph 101

fisticuffs 207–13, 219–20, 254

Fogarty, Carl 102

food 8, 97–101, 273–4

football chairmen 81–91,
     93–100, 125, 267–9

footballers
   earnings 174–6
   obsessive behaviours 235–7
   player incentives 183–4,
        267–8
   pranks 221–8, 233
   professional players as
        pundits 130–2
   spending 177–9

'foreign objects' on the pitch 24–5

Forest Green Rovers 96, 97–8, 155, 156–7

Forest Mere 157, 158–61

Foster, Levi 197

Fulham 82–4, 127, 128, 171, 175

Gabbidon, Danny 253

Gallagher, Dermot 16–17, 21, 142

Gallagher, Noel 47–8, 227

Gartside, Phil 164, 165

Gascoigne, Paul 223–4

Gattuso, Gennaro 41

Gaz Matan 34

Gerrard, Steven 33

Gervinho 254

Gheorghe, Dinu 268

Gibson, Darron 251–2

Gilks, Matt 263

Gillespie, Keith 26

Gill, Gary 147

Ginola, David 276, 277

Glazer, Malcolm 86

goal celebrations 77–9

Goals on Sunday 29–30

golfing breaks 134–7

golf tee 24

Graham, George 138

Gray, Andy 56

Greaves, Jimmy 101

Green, Russ 96

Groves, Perry 225

Guernsey FC 91–2

Gunnersaurus 218

Gyan, Asamoah 272–3

Hackett, Gary 184

Halsey, Mark 141–2

Hamann, Dietmar 223

Hamilton, Gary 147

Hangeland, Brede 84

Hanke, Mike 214

Harkness, David 32

Harrington 32

Hartlepool Sunday League 194–203

Hartlepool United 6, 27, 45, 68, 95–6, 105, 106, 107–9, 110, 113–14, 115, 122–3, 190, 191, 202

Hatton, Ricky 134

Havant & Waterlooville 121

Haynes, Johnny 83

Helder, Glenn 186

Hendricks, Christina 273

Henry, Thierry 216

Hereford United 144, 270–1

heroes and heroic tales 143–57
Hewer, Nick 62
Hilbrands, Matthias 196
Hislop, Steve 128
Hockaday, Dave 97
Hodcroft, Ken 95–6
Hodgson, Roy 84
Holloway, Dan 184
Hooper, Gary 144
Howey, Steve 276–7
Hughes, Mark 84
Hull City 12, 42, 71, 164
Humphreys, Ritchie 96
Hunter, Norman 276
Hunt, John 109–10
Hunt, Stephen 26, 74
Hutchings, Chris 70, 71

Ibe, Jordan 77–8
Ickenham Youth FC 204
Ilkeston FC 212–13
Illogan Reserves 203–4
injuries 26, 79–80
International Manchester
    196–7
Internet forums 126–7, 128,
    129, 253
Internet spoof 259–60
intimate piercing row 24–5
Ipswich Town 12

Jackson, Michael (statue at
    Craven Cottage) 82–3, 84
James, David 236, 237
Jensen, John 15
Jewell, Paul 12, 70
John, Elton 156
Jones, Cliff 275
Jones, Phil 235–6
Jordan, Joe 41

Kaboul, Younes 100
Kahn, Oliver 274
Kamara, Chris 2, 6, 12, 15,
    18–19, 44, 45, 59, 82, 116,
    133, 134, 137–8, 204
Kanda, Kazuaki 106–7
Kasabian 46–7
Keane, Robbie 213
Keegan, Kevin 84, 88, 90, 91,
    227, 277–8
Keys, Richard 56
Koumas, Jason 43
Kroenke, Stan 86

LA Galaxy 79
Lampard, Frank 53, 214, 215,
    261
Lawrence, Matthew 53
Laws, Brian 56
Leeds United 68, 115, 244, 276

Lee, Franny 276
Lee, Graeme 117
Lehman, Jens 274–5
Leicester 46
Lerner, Randy 86
Le Tissier, Matt 5, 9, 12, 21, 26, 48, 87–9, 91, 92, 126, 263
Limelight Syndrome 85
Lincoln City 181
Lineker, Gary 223
Liverpool 6, 12, 16, 86, 88, 90, 127, 128, 131–2, 134, 171, 173, 269, 271
Lloyd, Larry 278
loan system 176–7
Lonsdale FC 32
Lonsdale, Max 151
lower leagues and non-league sector 181–91
Luiz, David 29, 231–2
Luton Town 186
Lynam, Des 2, 56, 60

McAllister, Rory 149–50
McCarthy, Mick 68, 74, 75
Macclesfield Town 23–4
Macdonald, Malcolm 193
McGowan, Alistair 59
McGuinness, Wilf 244
McInally, Alan 12, 15, 136

Mackenzie, Neil 55
Mackie, Darren 53–4
McLintock, Frank 125
McMahon, Steve 112–14
McMenemy, Lawrie 90, 91
McNeill, Billy 275
Madron 203–4
Manchester City 47, 48, 50, 110, 111, 154, 169–70, 175, 176–7, 226–7, 263, 276–7
Manchester United 86–7, 88, 110, 111, 140, 151, 156, 171, 173, 229, 231, 232–3, 236, 239, 241, 244, 255
Mancini, Roberto 48, 237
Mansfield Town 94, 95, 212–13
Mansour, Sheikh 86, 170
Maradona, Diego 28
Marshall, Ian 161
Marsh, Rodney 3, 46, 221
Marwood, Brian 262
mascots 117–18, 217–19
Massey, Sian 264
Masukawa, Takahiro 26
match ball, kidnapping of 3–4
Meighan, Tom 46–7
Merson, Paul 5–6, 9, 12, 21, 46–7, 136, 137, 138, 154, 225, 238–43, 263–4

Middlesbrough 42, 43, 146, 147,
150

Miliband, Ed 254–5

Millwall 68, 101

Mirandinha 223–4

mismatched football boots
178

Moore, Bobby 82, 83

Moreno, Luis 218, 219

Morgan, Piers 229–30

Morrison, James 73

Mowbray, Tony 146, 147

Moyes, David 30

Moyles, Chris 64, 65, 68

Mulcaire, Glenn 271–2

Musgrove, Margaret 115

Nagoya Grampus 26

Nani 78

Nelson, Ryan 100

Neuchâtel Xamax 268–9

Neuer, Manuel 125–6, 130

Neville, Gary 96–7, 135, 140,
229–31, 232

Neville, Phil 140, 142, 230

Newbon, Gary 165

Newcastle United 29, 172, 173,
193, 194, 221–4, 241–2, 243,
254, 276, 277–8

Newport County 19–20, 21, 117

newspaper cuttings 2–3, 7–8,
281–90

Nicholas, Charlie 5, 11, 12, 15,
46, 48, 136, 137, 158, 245

Nicholson, Bill 276

Nicol, Steve 123

Non-League Day 185–7

Norwich City 50, 51

Nottingham Forest 278

Notts County 55

obsessive behaviours 235–7

OCD 236

O'Connor, Des 56

O'Driscoll, Sean 81–2

offensive comments 261–4

Old Hill Wanderers Reserves
25

Onuoha, Dr Anthonia 262

Onuoha, Nedum 262

Orlando Pirates 34

Oss 34

Owen, Dafydd Ryder 110–11

Owen, Michael 250, 261

owl (mascot) 217–19

Oxford City 184

Oxford United 42

Oxlade-Chamberlain, Alex
89–90

Palmer, Rob 37–9, 72, 75–6

Panorama 162, 163, 167

Pardew, Alan 29–30, 90–1

Parker, Scott 29

Parkinson, Gary 146–7

Parlour, Ray 238

Parrott, John 59

Parry, Alan 174

Pearce, Stuart 215

Pears, Stephen 147

Pedersen, Morten Gamst 100

Peterhead 149

Peterson, Shaun 117–18

pigeons and hawks 95

pitch invaders 32, 34, 119–22

Pitham, Danny 269–70

Platini, Michel 40

Platt, David 237

Plymouth Argyle 148–9, 156, 183, 187–9, 191

Poll, Graham 15, 16

porridge throwing 34

Portsmouth 44, 159

Poyet, Gus 91

pranks 221–9, 233

Pratt, Jimmy 26

pre-match rituals 236, 237

Premier League promotion and relegation, scrapping 86–7

Premier League TV rights 171–2

Preston North End 228–9

prison inmates as referees 27–8

Proctor, Mark 146, 147

pub leagues 207

Pulis, Tony 148, 221

Queens Park Rangers 139

Radford, John 94, 95

Rafati, Babak 35–6

Rapid Bucharest 34, 219–20, 268

Rea, Chris 47

Reading 26

Real Salt Lake 79

Redbridge 184

red cards, fastest 25–7

Redgrave, Sir Steve 101

Redknapp, Harry 38–42, 59, 214–15

Redknapp, Jamie 40

referees

    Argentinian prison inmates 27–8

    assistant referees 28–9, 30

    bad calls 29, 31, 77

    criticism and abuse of 31–4, 36, 142

fourth-official idea 30–1
Jeff Stelling's stint as a
    referee 12–22
post-match interviews 21
training 30
youth games 14, 32–3
Reid, Bunny 197
Reid, Peter 148–9, 166
Republic of Ireland 111–12, 216
Respect campaign 33, 230
Reus, Marco 214
Richards, Micah 158
Ricketts, Gary 213
Rigby, Manda 20
Riley, Rachel 51, 56, 61, 62, 63
Rimmer, Joseph 32
Ripley, Stuart 147
Roberts, Jason 130
Robinson, Paul 7
Robson, Bobby 83
Rochdale 141
Rodallega, Hugo 78
Rodriguez, Alejandro 28
Ronaldo, Cristiano 102, 153,
    158, 162, 236–7
Rooney, Wayne 33, 151–3, 154
Rosenthal, Jim 165
Ruutli, Tarmo 112
Ryan, John 81–2, 85

St Francis Rangers 12
St Joseph's 198
Saha, Louis 250
Salako, John 5
Salgado, Michel 100
Samuelson, Erik 272
Sansom, Kenny 238
Sarginson, Chris 77
SaucyTime phone chat app 269,
    270
Saunders, Dean 150
Savage, Robbie 130, 229
Scarborough Athletic 45
Scharner, Paul 69–70, 71–7
Schmeichel, Peter 232–3
Scholes, Paul 42
Scunthorpe United 106
Seaman, David 17
season tickets 96
semi-professional clubs 186
Sergeant, John 59
Shackleton, Len 85
Shakhtar Donetsk 116
Shankly, Bill 82
Sharp, Billy 150–1
Shearer, Alan 90
Sheerwater 92
Sheffield United 26
Sheffield Wednesday 12, 77,
    107–9, 216

Shilton, Peter 278

Skinner, Frank 65, 66, 67, 68

Smith, Alan 238, 239

Smith, Bobby 275

Smith, Delia 49–51

Soccer AM 108

Soccer Saturday 2, 4, 5–8

    Christmas Special 12–19,
        20–2, 53

    oddball cameo appearances
        72–3, 75–6

    panellists 5–6

       see also individual
          entries

    post-match analysis and
       interviews 21, 37–40, 2
       32

    rock star fans 46–8, 49

    team-bonding breaks 133–6,
       137–40

    what it is 5–8

Souness, Graeme 40

Southampton 87–91, 139, 216

Spikey, Dave 57–8

stadium name changes 172–4

Stam, Jaap 230, 233

Stansfield, Adam 143–6

Stansfield, Lisa 144

Steaua Bucharest 267–8

Stelling, Jeff

'bungs in football' incident
    162, 163–7

  and *Chris Moyles' Quiz*
     Night 64–8

  and *Countdown* 49–53,
     54–60, 61–3, 83, 228–9

  dads' match player 205–6

  fisticuffs 207–12

  Noel Gallagher on 48

  research 2–3, 7–8

  stint as a referee 12–22

  Sunday League player
    194–6, 198–202

  The Time of Our Lives
    presenter 275–6

  tweets 256–8, 259–61

Stelling Towers 1–2, 41–2

Stevenage 183, 184

Stewart, Don 34–5

Stewart, Rod 34, 35

Stilgoe, Richard 51

Still, Carolyn 94, 95

Stockport County 186

Stoke City 12, 45, 107, 171

Stourbridge 183–4

streakers 119, 120–1

Sturrock, Paul 109

Suarez, Luis 23

suicidal behaviour 35–6, 45–6

Summerbee, Mike 276

Sumudica, Marius 34, 219–20
Sunday League football 32, 194, 195, 197–202
superstitious behaviour 237
Super Sunday 105, 231
Sutton United 183, 271
Swansea 218, 269
swearing 27, 124–5
Swinburne University 25
Swindon Town 216–17

Talbot, Drew 109
Taunton East Reach Rovers 26–7
Taylor, Phil 101
Telford Junior League 202–3
Terry, John 33
Tevez, Carlos 4, 135
Thompson, Georgie 193
Thompson, John 213
Thompson, Phil 2, 6, 12, 47–8, 131, 134, 138, 194, 242–3, 273–4
ticket prices 90, 96, 122
The Time of Our Lives 275–6
Todd, Lee 26–7
toilets 182–3
Torquay United 7, 106–7, 189
Tottenham Hotspur 29, 38, 40, 88, 101, 171, 176, 274–5

trainer in the rafters 270
Treadwell, Ian 197
tribalism 189
Tudgay, Steve 164
Turf Moor 269
Turner, Chris 113
TV ads 100, 101–2
Twitter and tweets 83, 248–59, 259–61

under-14 knockout tournament 12–16, 17–19, 20–2, 53
underfunded clubs 181–91

Vanden Borre, Anthony 44
van der Vaart, Rafael 39, 250
Vassell, Darius 79–80
Vaughan, Richard 187
Veiga, Jose 24
Venables, Terry 101
Venky's Chicken 99–100
Vickers, Ashley 121–2
Villas-Boas, Andre 231
Vince, Dale 96–9
Vine, Tim 59

Wagstaff, Ian 107
Wakeling, Vic 165
Walcott, Theo 89
Walsall 5, 12, 174

INDEX

Warnock, Neil 265
Waters, Mark 204
Watford 156
Webb, Howard Melton 13, 23, 29
weird and wonderful moments 265–79
Wenger, Arsène 100
Werder Bremen 274
Werner, Tom 86
West Bromwich Albion 69, 73, 74, 75, 175, 226, 239
West Ham 94, 139, 214–15, 253
Westwood, Chris 109
Whelan, Dave 85
Whitstable Town 181–2
Wiese, Tim 274–5
Wigan Athletic 12, 38, 69, 70, 72, 73, 82, 85, 217, 270
Wilkins, Ray 74, 135–6
Winchester motorway services 7–8
Windass, Dean 42–4, 45–6, 59

Winterburn, Nigel 215
Winter, Jeff 15–16
Wise, Dennis 230
Wolverhampton Wanderers 74
women-and-children-only matches 116
Worthing 181
Wrexham 183
Wright-Phillips, Shaun 19
wrong colour underpants row 19–20
Wycombe Wanderers 77, 173–4

The X Factor 128, 153
The Xtra Factor 64

Yeovil Town 144
Yorke, Dwight 140
Young, Alan 121
youth games 12–16, 17–22, 32–3, 202–3, 204

Zilli, Aldo 273, 274

Tuffers' Cricket Tales

PHIL TUFNELL
WITH JUSTYN BARNES

A deliciously eccentric series of anecdotes, *Tuffers' Cricket Tales* was a *Sunday Times* bestseller in hardback.

Phil Tufnell, aka 'Tuffers', is the much-loved English cricketer from the 1990s who has now become one of this country's favourite broadcasters. Not cast from the same mould as other players of his generation, Tufnell became a cult figure for his unorthodox approach to the game . . . and to life in general. *Tuffers' Cricket Tales* is a collection of the great man's favourite cricket stories that will amuse and inform in equal measure. Tufnell's unmistakably distinctive voice, as heard to such good effect on *Test Match Special*, steers fans through dozens and dozens of terrifically entertaining and insightful anecdotes, garnered from his 25-year playing and broadcasting career.

He introduces a cast of genuinely colourful characters found in dressing-rooms and commentary boxes from around the world, and in the process offers a uniquely warm and quirky homage to his sport. A perfect Fathers' Day gift for all cricket fans.

Praise for *Tuffers' Cricket Tales*:

'Hilarious' *Daily Star Sunday*

'Amusing' *All Out Cricket*

To order, visit our website
www.headline.co.uk
or email orders@bookpoint.co.uk

NON-FICTION / MEMOIR 978 0 7553 6292 9

Miracle at Medinah:
Europe's Amazing Ryder Cup Comeback

OLIVER HOLT

Golf fans will not forge the 39th Ryder Cup in a hurry. Staged at the Medinah Country Club just outside of Chicago, the 2012 event has already gone down as the most remarkable competition in its 85-year history.

The American team had home advantage, and a golf course unapologetically set up to suit its own players. Supported by tens of thousands of loud and proud fans, the USA's star-studded line-up dominated the first two days and ended the Saturday with a seemingly unassailable 10–6 advantage. No way team had ever won the Ryder Cup from such an unpromising position.

Sunday was singles day, traditionally the forte of American teams. The situation looked bleak, especially when European team member and number 1 golfer in the world, Rory McIlroy, very nearly missed his tee-off time. Yet slowly but surely, the European team – who had top-loaded their line-up in one last throw of the dice – started to turn the scoreboard blue. With inspirational captain Jose Maria Olazabal stiring European blood with thoughts of the late Ryder Cup magician Seve Ballesteros (whose silhouette was emblazoned on the players' sweaters and bags), the tide turned and the previously dominant American players started to crumble in the face of the onslaught. Suddenly European players were holing miraculous putts to win holes out of the blue. Something very special was happening.

When German Martin Kaymer sank his putt on the eighteenth green to clinch the point that retrained the Ryder Cup, the most astonishing comeback in the event's long and distinguished history was complete. *Miracle at Medinah* is the compelling narrative of those amazing three days in Illinois, a fitting chronicle of an unbelievable sporting story.

To order, visit our website
www.headline.co.uk
or email orders@bookpoint.co.uk

NON-FICTION 978 0 7553 6481 7

Manchester City
Ruined My Life

COLIN SHINDLER

Colin Shindler first wrote of his deep love for Manchester City
in *Manchester United Ruined My Life*.

Now he tells the story of his sorrowful disenchantment with his home
town club as, on the instruction of its new foreign owners, it turns itself
remorselessly into a global brand.

From the nail-biting victory over Gillingham 1999 to the equally
dramatic winning of the Premier League in May 2012 Shindler
watches as his team becomes more successful yet, to his own
bewilderment, he feels increasingly alienated from the club.

This is the story of a frustrated romantic who finds in the glitz
and gamour of the current media-obsessed game a helter-skelter
of artificially fabricated excitement.

As he details how football courses through his veins, Shindler reveals
how it intersects with his own life, a life that has been marked by
family tragedy, and how he finally found personal redemption even
as his team lost its soul.

Praise for Colin Shindler:

'Evocative, funny-sad and warm-hearted' *The Times*

'His prose is never less than sharp, smart and easy on the eye' *The Guardian*

To order, visit our website
www.headline.co.uk
or email orders@bookpoint.co.uk

NON-FICTION / MEMOIR 978 0 7553 6360 5

My Liverpool Story

STEVEN GERRARD

Steven Gerrard is a genuine Liverpool legend.

Captain at the age of 23.

Two FA Cups.

Three League Cups.

One UEFA Cup.

And *that* Champions League win.

Gerrard embodies the spirit and passion of Liverpool football club like no other in the modern era.

From the raw but talented youngster who made the jump from the Melwood training ground and took to the famous Anfield turf at 18, to the talismanic skipper who has led his beloved club through thick and thin, this stunningly illustrated book, complete with exclusive new photographs, is the story of his fifteen momentous seasons at Liverpool FC.

Along with a foreword from Kenny Dalglish, this is Steven Gerrard's Liverpool story in his own words.

'Gerrard is so honest and sharp that the book is a joy'
Sunday Times

NON-FICTION / MEMOIR 978 0 7553 6394 0

Champions League Dreams
RAFA BENITEZ

This is a stimulating and deeply insightful football narrative by Rafa Benitez which focuses on the legendary manager's dramatic six Champions League campaigns with Liverpool.

Rafa expertly navigates fans through intriguing European adventures that embrace the triumph and despair of two Champions League finals, three semi-finals and five quarter-finals in what was a golden era for the Anfield club – an era that supporters felt gave them their pride back after years in the wilderness. What sets this book apart is the unique ways in which Rafa allows fans into his high-pressured world, the fascinating glimpses he offers of a top manager's thought processes and decision making during the cut and thrust of a high-octane European campaign.

Understand how a great manager prepares for, then executes, a master-plan for European success.

To order, visit our website
www.headline.co.uk
or email orders@bookpoint.co.uk

NON-FICTION / MEMOIR 978 0 7553 6364 3

The Didi Man:
My Love Affair with Liverpool
DIETMAR HAMANN

Dietmar "Didi" Hamann is a complete one-off. The foreigner with a Scouse accent. The German who now plays cricket for his local village team. The overseas footballer turned anglophile who fell deeply in love with the city of Liverpool, its people and its eponymous football club.

The classy midfielder had a long and distinguished playing career, but it was his seven seasons at Anfield that marked him out forever as a true Liverpool legend. His cult status was secured when he came off the bench at half-time during the 2005 Champions League final in Istanbul to inspire his team to a dramatic come-back and spectacular European glory.

The Didi Man is Hamann's warm, personal and highly entertaining story of his time on Merseyside at a football club which will always have a very special place in his heart.

'Trackie-splitting tales from Kaiser, the Mark I German Scouser. I'm chokka!" Jamie Carragher

'Before Didi came along, all we had in common with the Germans were dodgy moustaches and weird hair styles."
John Bishop

To order, visit our website
www.headline.co.uk
or email orders@bookpoint.co.uk

NON-FICTION / MEMOIR 978 0 7553 6281 3